P9-CRB-159

Writing to Learn
Mathematics and Science

Writing to Learn
Mathematics and Science

Edited by

Paul Connolly
Teresa Vilardi

TEACHERS
COLLEGE
PRESS

Teachers College, Columbia University
New York and London

Published by Teachers College Press, 1234 Amsterdam Avenue
New York, NY 10027

Library of Congress Cataloging-in-Publication Data

Writing to learn mathematics and science / edited by Paul Connolly,
Teresa Vilardi.
    p. cm.
  Bibliography: p.
  Includes index.
  ISBN 0-8077-2962-0
  1. English language — Rhetoric — Study and teaching.
2. Interdisciplinary approach in education. 3. Mathematics — Study
and teaching (Higher) 4. Science — Study and teaching (Higher)
5. Technical writing — Study and teaching (Higher) I. Connolly,
Paul H., 1942- . II. Vilardi, Teresa, 1943- .
PE1404.W75 1989   89-4478
808'.042'07 — dc20   CIP

ISBN 0-8077-2962-0

Printed on acid-free paper
Manufactured in the United States of America

96   95   94   93   92   91   90   89   8   7   6   5   4   3   2   1

Contents

Part III: Classroom Applications: What Works and How

Part IV: Programmatic Policies and Practices

Part V: The Context of Learning

Preface

This study of the role of language in learning is the second book from the Institute for Writing and Thinking, the first being *New Methods in College Writing Programs: Theories in Practice*, published by the Modern Language Association in 1986. In 1982 Bard College, led by President Leon Botstein, established the Institute as a professional research and development center for college, high school, and middle school teachers. The Institute built upon an intensive three-week Language and Thinking Workshop that Bard had developed for its own entering students in 1981.

Since that beginning, over 15,000 teachers have participated in Institute Workshops and conferences lasting from at least a day to a week and more, either within their own schools or on the campuses of Bard and Simon's Rock colleges. All Institute programs demonstrate interactive instruction in close reading, careful thinking, and thoughtful writing. All regard language not as a "basic skill" to be learned by handbook rules and handout exercises but as a liberal act in which individuals express themselves communally, construing and constructing our best knowledge of life.

Some of the essays in this book began as presentations at a conference on "The Role of Writing in Learning Mathematics and Science" held at Bard College in November 1987. That conference and the preparation of this book were supported by a grant from the ANL Foundation and we thank Agnese N. Lindley for her generous trust and support. Grants from the AT&T, Apple, Booth Ferris, Ford, Exxon, Hazen, Matsushita, Snow, Sprague, and Xerox foundations have further assisted the Institute's work, and we gratefully acknowledge this support.

We also want especially to thank Judi Smith, our administrative assistant in the Institute, for her invaluable contribution to all our work together, including the production of this book.

Finally, we thank our colleagues at the Institute for Writing and Thinking. All activities of the Institute are the fruit of the collective experience and generous collaboration of forty faculty associates, recruited nationally for their devotion to writing and the power it brings human beings to think and feel. We thank each of them for their work and friendship, and we dedicate this book to them.

Foreword
The Ordinary Experience of Writing

Fifty years have passed since John Dewey published his Kappa Delta Phi lectures entitled *Experience and Education*. Dewey argued for a strategy in education that could be regarded as the "intelligently directed development of the possibilities inherent in ordinary experience." He cautioned against blind support for pedagogical schemes merely because they carried the modifiers "new" or "progressive." He called on eager enthusiasts of the progressive movement to support "education pure and simple"; anything "worthy of the name education."

Despite Dewey's reasoned moderation, in the half century since 1938 we have witnessed the popularization, abuse (particularly in the 1960s), and vilification of the so-called progressive movement with which Dewey's name became closely linked. In recent years, especially the past fifteen, a radical disavowal of the Dewey tradition has become quite fashionable. In the place of progressive principles an appeal to traditionalism has succeeded, a "back-to-basics" effort designed to stress the provision of fixed bodies of knowledge. In the 1980s, as a result of the innumerable national reports on the poor quality of our schools, a stress on a specific canon of skills and knowledge — a required curriculum and a mandated set of standards — has become commonplace. The public seems convinced that what is at stake in the schools is exclusively the content of the subject matter that is taught and required of pupils.

This emphasis on curricular input derives in part from the implicit claim that American schools have declined in quality since the 1950s. The logic behind this view rests on a mythic and idealized picture of traditional schools two and three generations ago. These schools, the legend goes, were strictly centered on content. This popular, albeit false nostalgia has been fueled further by the notion that the extreme adoption of progressive pedagogical strategies, particularly during the 1960s, ruined the schools by devaluing subject matter content in favor of educational methods.

It is not at all clear that the historical record can substantiate the claim that there was an era during which the schools were actually better. Furthermore, this interpretation of the origins of the current educational crisis fails to acknowledge two crucial changes in American schools that have occurred since 1938 and certainly 1945. First, the demographic range of pupils has expanded so that the overwhelming majority of Americans now attend school through age 18, a circumstance that did not exist in any previous period of our history. The potential of democratization inherent in the unique American commitment to the common public school system has been realized only during the past thirty years. Second, the external culture in which children grow up — the realm of experience on which Dewey focused his attention — has changed in ways that directly influence the patterns of learning and retention in schools.

Since the distinguished contributors to this book attempt to take into account the real circumstances facing teachers in the late twentieth century, this volume can be considered part of a constructive reevaluation of current conventional wisdom about how to improve education. The authors shun a facile traditionalism and seek to develop useful strategies for the classroom that take into account demographic and cultural realities. Central to this book is a commitment to what Dewey termed "education with no qualifying adjectives prefixed"; to education that could be "a reality and not a name or a slogan." More important, however, is that what links this volume with Dewey is the intent to take language and writing as starting points, as elements of "ordinary experience" that can be used to enhance the teaching of science and mathematics. This book is therefore at once practical and progressive without sacrificing a rigorous concept of content to a deracinated definition of method.

Before considering the specific ideas contained in this volume, it is helpful to remember that the decisive school reform movements in this century all occurred in moments of national political crisis. The 1930s, for example, owing to the Great Depression, the rise of fascism, and the popularity of socialism, posed a challenge to the appeal and conceits of American democracy in theory and practice. Both John Dewey and Robert Maynard Hutchins, with quite contrasting approaches, recognized that by influencing the character of American education one could secure and strengthen an effective democratic vision of America against competing political and social ideologies. Likewise, the political crises of the 1960s — the demand for racial equality, the conflict between generations, and the domestic unrest surrounding the Vietnam War — were mirrored in contemporary movements to change American education. The initiatives of Ivan Illich, John Holt, and Jonathan Kozol represented efforts to render the schools — and ultimately American society — more tolerant, fair, free, and supportive of egalitarianism.

The educational reform movement of the 1980s (to which this book seeks to make a contribution), in turn, has reflected more than a decade of profound political malaise about America. We have come to doubt America's potential as an effective economic competitor in an international economy marked by high worker productivity and dependency on technology; as an effective military power and force for freedom and justice in the world; and as a nation sufficiently unified on essential matters of belief so as to be more than an amalgam of warring interest groups and factions. The struggle over the schools has consequently become one over competing claims about our common heritage; over notions of patriotism and, most significantly, over whether the demand for equity in our schools (and, by implication, also in society) can be actually reconciled with the demand that our schools produce a level of educational excellence that is both competitive and subject to objective measurement.

Unfortunately, the dominant response in the 1980s has been to emphasize school reform that focuses on curricular content within a debate that continues to accept the untenable but alluring distinction between method and content. No serious scholar or scientist should defend any educational strategy that seeks to extract a methodology by placing detail and specialized knowledge at a distance. However, in order to rectify a supposed overemphasis on process in the 1960s — a supposed legacy of the progressives of the 1930s — the major effort on the state and local level has been to strengthen, uncritically, teacher training in key subject areas, raise standards through testing, and increase subject matter requirements for high school graduation. This has been particularly true for science and mathematics, since these are areas in which American performance has been deemed uncompetitive in comparison with Japan and the Soviet Union. Furthermore, the shortage of qualified teachers is greatest in these subject areas. This particular concern for science and mathematics accurately reflects widespread recognition of the fact that the level and complexity of essential literacy in science and mathematics that society will need during the next 50 years will be higher than at any time in the past.

This volume addresses the three decisive challenges facing American schools that the school reform debate of the 1980s has overlooked. First, it offers strategies that take into account the altered cultural environment. Second, it provides approaches that can be applied to the full range of the population in the schools. Third, by integrating a sophisticated understanding of modern mathematics and science, it circumvents the simplistic and trivializing dichotomy between method and content.

In the first instance, the claim that common ordinary language, through the use of writing, is crucial to the effective teaching of science and mathematics rehabilitates a valid and central premise of Dewey's emphasis on cultivating experience as the motivating factor behind learning in the school. No doubt, notwithstanding a passing reference to Hogben's *Mathematics for the Million* in 1938, Dewey's confidence that one can easily inspire a young person to learn science and mathematics by easy reference to daily life was too facile. This underestimation of the difficulty appears even more striking from the perspective of the 1980s. In general, the progressive tradition has always had an easier time with the subject areas outside of modern science and mathematics, even though historically and philosophically, owing to the success of empiricism, positivism, and experimentalism, the pedagogical implication of Dewey's ideas ought to have been most applicable in science and mathematics.

The use of ordinary language in the teaching of science and mathematics enables the teacher to connect what otherwise might seem an arcane and distinct set of languages, thought processes, insights, facts, and understandings to *experience*, in the everyday sense that Dewey realized could constitute the basis for motivating learning, memory, and long-term comprehension. Ordinary language, particularly in its notated forms—writing—must be construed as part of everyday experience. Even at low levels of general literacy, the complex cognitive and epistemological processes imbedded in everyday speech (as opposed to tacit experience) and action constitute a sufficient link to understanding mathematics and science. The act of writing in the process of learning these subject areas is essential to developing curiosity and comprehension in the learner.

The conception of writing as an experiential precondition and instrument in the learning of science and mathematics enables teachers to confront several contemporary commonplace dilemmas encountered in teaching science and mathematics. The young person in the 1980s has become—unfortunately—accustomed, without any glimmer of understanding, to depending on gadgets and technology. This daily dependency is not only deep, it is as effective and painless as it is passive. It remains untroubled by ignorance. We all use, directly or indirectly, cars, telephones, computers, airplanes, satellite communications, lasers, CAT scans, diagnostics, calculators, pharmaceuticals, foods, energy, and entertainment devices for essential and leisure activities without the remotest unease at our own powerlessness in commanding the various technologies, their theoretical underpinnings, or practical potentialities. The paradox facing both pupil and teacher in the 1980s is that the more we rely on science and mathematics, the more distant and irrelevant the motivation to understand seems to have become.

The answer to this dilemma rests in part on the fact that the science and mathematics on which modern progress depends is not simply derivable from daily life and experience. Therefore, the bridge between the technical and specialized worlds of modern mathematics and science and daily life and experience must be constructed out of ordinary language. Writing must become the instrument for translating the seemingly foreign and unrelated but indispensable worlds of science and mathematics into comprehensible and relevant matters. Ordinary language can also reach beyond the utilitarian, by opening up the beauty of science and mathematics.

Precisely because the civilization of the late twentieth century and the twenty-first century will remain tied, in terms of daily life and global politics, to science and mathematics, it is imperative that a high order of understanding and skills in these areas be attained in our schools. If we have a citizenry unable to understand the issues of probability, to approximate, to manipulate large quantities of data, or to analyze statistical reasoning, then the profound and decisive premise of Dewey's ideas — facilitating, through education, the enlightened political participation by all citizens in our democracy — will be fatally undermined. The answer, as the authors represented in this volume realize, does not rest merely with loading the classroom with more facts and technical subject matter, but with finding pedagogical strategies that enable pupils to ask appropriate questions and to actively find their answers.

Breaking the daunting barriers of complexity and specialization requires clarity and simplicity in the process of teaching. After all, the triumphant breakthroughs of modern science and mathematics, from relativity theory to the foundations of molecular genetics, have shared the virtues of elegance, economy, clarity, and simplicity, no matter how counterintuitive the discoveries may have been. Why then should mathematics and science be taught in our schools as laden with, and characterized by, the obscure, the complex, the incomprehensible, and the difficult? Here again, one solution lies in the active use of the epistemologically sophisticated linguistic capacities of all learners — their command of ordinary language.

The approach developed in this book also provides a strategy to combat the unfortunate image given science and mathematics to young people, in and out of our schools. It is the common perception that these are arenas reserved for the specially gifted, that speed of learning is equivalent to ability. These prejudices only further the idea that knowing about science and mathematics is peripheral and irrelevant, for most of us, to living the good life as either private person or citizen. The use of ordinary language also helps combat the popularization of the scientist and mathematician as an abnormal type, a member of an elite in possession of a secret tongue. This view, fueled by popular culture in films and television, heightens the natural predisposition to fear what one does not understand. Fear and mistrust towards scientists and mathematicians among nonscientists abound in our culture, along with a concomitant ambivalent sense of awe and mystery. The greater use of writing (a skill possessed, in the ideal circumstance, by all teachers) may also enable teachers with more limited backgrounds in science and mathematics to teach these subject areas more effectively and less apprehensively, particularly on the elementary school level.

The 1980s have witnessed the growth of a disturbing anti-intellectualism directed towards modern science. Politicians have successfully exploited this sentiment to try to limit the freedom of research, to confuse legitimate issues of ethics and public policy with unreasonable spectres of an elite community conspiring to control life and destroy traditional values. Ironically, the only way to preserve freedom and resolve the need for legitimate political oversight on the uses (not the pursuit itself) to which modern science and mathematics might be put is a proper education for all citizens, the attainment of a level of literacy that liberates science from superstitious fear and improper censorship and directs it to contribute to human progress.

The emphasis on writing in the teaching of science and mathematics can empower classroom teachers to reach all sectors of the pupil population. The use of ordinary language can help break the cultural barriers that have prevented minorities and women from achieving well in proportionate numbers in these fields. By encouraging motivation and understanding through a method that connects the subject matter to the pupil's initial frames of reference, the pedagogical strategies outlined in this volume can help rectify the distorted selection process within the school system through which a minority, mostly white males, emerges as sufficiently trained to consider careers in science and mathematics. In this way, the guiding principle redeems Dewey's approach in a fashion that takes into account the actual population in our schools.

This volume is not an example of pedagogical trivialization through a mere emphasis on process. Rather, it represents the necessary use of ordinary language to teach science and mathematics in all their subtlety, complexity, and richness. The gain will be society's, for a larger number and wider range of scientists and mathematicians may emerge from our schools. And our country needs not only a citizenry better educated in science and mathematics, but more scientists and mathematicians at all levels of employment.

In the late twentieth century, two powerful factors complicate any effort to deepen the motivation among future generations to love and learn mathematics and science. First, despite the traditional rhetoric that links knowledge with power, most citizens and their children display, explicitly and implicitly, a high level of pessimism and doubt their ability to exercise, as individuals, effective influence in our democracy. Political passivity remains a serious danger (if not a trend), which in turn reduces the motivation to learn and study in school over the span of the twelve years of compulsory education. The use of writing and ordinary language and the development of novel pedagogical strategies to teach science and mathematics are all ways not only of demonstrating what can be learned, but also of indicating where, why, and how legitimate intervention in those aspects of public life connected to science and mathematics can be achieved. This effort to improve the effectiveness of our classrooms in science and mathematics is crucial if the presumed link between education and democracy is to be realized by future generations.

Second, no discussion of the problem of teaching mathematics and science can overlook the extent to which citizens in America and Europe and their children recognize, if even tacitly, that in modern history progress in science and mathematics have not automatically been correlative with progress in ethics and politics. Perhaps these expectations (characteristic of the late eighteenth century) should never have been encouraged since science and mathematics, and their practitioners, have not been responsible for the abuse of science and technology. For example, the scientists who developed the atomic bomb were among the first to argue against its use in 1945. But the fact remains that we live in an age in which the modern instruments of warfare can destroy, for the first time in human history, all life and render the earth uninhabitable. Furthermore, the genocide practiced in modern history, particularly by technically civilized and modernized societies, has utilized brutal instruments made possible by advances in science and technology.

Only through a serious effort at education in science and mathematics can generations who grow up with these two historical legacies recognize that radical evil and the impulse to destruction do not derive from science, mathematics, or even the inventions of technology. They derive from the active and passive behavior of citizens. The exercise of political power (or failure to do so) is that which permits barbarism cloaked in modernity to flourish. To ensure that the progress of knowledge is made to serve humane ends — the amelioration of suffering, the elimination of disease, the creation of universal well-being and comfort, and the facilitation of communication and cooperation among differing peoples — widespread knowledge is needed. Suppressing the progress of science and mathematics or relegating its pursuit and appreciation to a minority of individuals detached and separate from the rest of the citizenry are unacceptable alternatives.

In 1938, John Dewey sought to provide, in summary form, an approach to education that he believed would enable future Americans to assume reasoned responsibility for their nation in the name of freedom and democracy. This book, although not a tract of educational philosophy, is dedicated to the same task. It offers practical advice to teachers. Like Dewey, the authors begin not with idealized outcomes, but with the experiential foundations shared by all learners. Because it combines a profound faith in the possibilities of education with genuine substantive expertise and the willingness to develop new pedagogical strategies, it is proudly in the center of the progressive tradition.

However, despite its practical and modest scope, this book seeks to serve the immodest, highest, and noblest ends of education: the empowerment of a new generation to command the insights and tools of the modern mind. This book is dedicated to the hope that at a crucial moment in the history of American education teachers will be successful in broadening the understanding of science and mathematics sufficiently to enable citizens to serve universal freedom, peace, and justice in a pluralistic world.

Leon Botstein
President
Bard College

Writing to Learn
Mathematics and Science

CHAPTER 1

Writing and the Ecology of Learning

Paul Connolly

In the middle of *How to Solve It* (1945), George Polya's classic essay
on mathematical problem-solving, there is a very short section on writing,
entitled "Rules of Style." In its entirety, it states:

> The first rule of style is to have something to say. The second rule of style is to
> control yourself when, by chance, you have two things to say; say first one,
> then the other, not both at the same time. (p. 172)

Immediately following are "Rules of Teaching" that are only slightly longer. They begin:

> The first rule of teaching is to know what you are supposed to teach. The
> second rule of teaching is to know a little more than what you are supposed to
> teach. (pp. 172–173)

These are compelling rules for teachers and writers. Know your subject. Have something to say. Why question such advice, delivered with
economy and precision? But on closer inspection neither precept speaks to
the messy *process* of learning nor to the even murkier process of thinking
through written language. Polya's rules imply that teaching is an efficient
transmission of information from master to novice, dependent for its success mainly on the teacher's mastery of the subject and the student's capacity to listen. Writing is even more simply "having something to say" and not
stuttering over a plethora of ideas. The aphoristic bite of this advice is in its
suggestion that "style" follows from thought; if one has something firm in
mind, words follow clearly.

Polya's "Rules of Style" and "Rules of Teaching" remind us, nonetheless, by their precept and example, of the force of fine writing and informed lecturing. In those areas of life where there is strong social agreement — where what is "real" seems self-evident, and what is "true" is a
stable source of confidence and consensus — the refined expression of com-

1

mon understanding is a credal act, a declaration of faith. Deeply established "knowledge," a community's shared sense of how it experiences life, deserves fine exposition and finished lectures.

Where life is more uncertain, however, and the contingent character of knowledge is felt, words seek not to report rules thought to be "discoverable in nature" but to constitute the very rules that create a society's basic sense of nature. Throughout the interstices of knowledge, where the net of what is real and true is continually being ripped and rewoven, understanding is a trial of essays written in probative, exploratory language.

School serves two valuable and quite different functions. It exists to share conventional knowledge—to indoctrinate new members into the operative beliefs of a community: its scientific, social scientific, humanistic, and artistic body of learning. But it exists also to initiate passive participants in the common life into active observers who understand what knowledge is and how it is made, and can participate in its production.

Much of the language used in school serves primarily the first function; it conveys and confirms a community's basic creed: its history, science, literature, sense of its own economy, psychology, and the like. An instructor gives formal lectures that organize information into systematic knowledge. Students write formal papers that aim to recite accurately what is known. Used this way, writing is particularly helpful in preserving a precise exposition of what is known. It does not, however, strongly extend or enhance a personal understanding of received doctrine.

The truth of Polya's "Rules of Style" applies to how we *present* knowledge once we have it, not to how we acquire understanding in the first place. Polya's rules are rules for editing and transmitting established knowledge, rather than for acquiring initial understanding. Transmitting information is an art. But how is it, we must still ask, that we ever find something to say in the first place, much less have two things to say in sequence?

WHAT IS WRITING TO LEARN?

At first, the "Writing Across the Curriculum" (WAC) movement seemed, and seems still to some, to be primarily a way of improving exposition of knowledge. The practice of writing regularly in all classes, using the forms and conventions of various "communities of discourse"— scientific, social scientific, as well as literary—promised to clarify meaning and reinforce memory. More recently, the phrase "Writing to Learn" has replaced "Writing Across the Curriculum," however, because it suggests the powerful role language plays in the production, as well as the presentation, of knowledge. "Writing to Learn" is less about *formal* uses of writing to display memory and test mastery than it is about *informal* writing; about language that is forming meaning; about writing that is done regularly in and out of class to help students acquire a personal ownership of ideas conveyed in lectures and textbooks.

In school, students are expected to have something to say at the drop of a teacher's assignment, and preferably something approximating what the teacher or textbook said first. But "a writer," as poet William Stafford has written (1982), "is not so much someone who has something to say as he is someone who has found a process that will bring about new things he would not have thought of if he had not started to say them."

A math student or a chemistry major, furthermore, is not so much someone who knows the answers as she is someone who has a successful way of addressing questions and working on problems. Having rules for writing — or algorithms for computing or manuals for experimenting — is only good enough to perform school exercises. Just as students need a composing process that helps them find something to say, they need problem-solving procedures in mathematics, such as Polya sought to provide in his book. Learning involves manipulating, not just memorizing, inert information. It involves hearing what the teacher of math or science knows; but it also involves "making sense" for oneself: producing, applying, and extending knowledge in the way a mathematician or scientist does.

Not too long ago, virtually all writing teachers taught by exhortation, propounding E. B. White's "elements of style" or other rules for good writing; feeling little obligation to write themselves; expecting conscientious students to apply the rule while "thinking for themselves." There was no intervention by most teachers in the act of composing, which occurred outside the classroom. Training consisted of talk about writing and examination of finished writing in anthologies. It did not require either teacher or student to do any actual writing. Elsewhere in school, writing served principally to display and test knowledge, defined as information acquired from teacher and textbook. But in what is now widely described as a "process approach" to teaching writing, the classroom is less a lecture hall for an Authority than it is an intricate ecological system where organisms interact with one another and their environment. What learning occurs within that system depends less on the teacher's knowledge than on the climate for thinking and on whether the environment encourages experimentation, tolerates mistakes, and respects differences, in the service of the whole community's need to know. In a "process" classroom, teacher and student are mutually responsible for the habits of writing that develop, the composing processes that become "second nature." The teacher moves physically from the front to the middle of the room, as learning that had been data-based now becomes task-oriented. Learning becomes more demanding of teacher and student than it was in the didactic mode, and what Theodore Sizer (1984) called "Horace's Compromise" — Don't ask too much of me and I won't hassle you! — becomes less possible.

Writing teachers have begun to acknowledge that students do not learn from an assignment/product/rating course that merely sets a task, collects its product, and evaluates same without further practical training in the writer's craft. A new generation of composition teachers, less exclusively preoccupied with the literary canon than their elders, has read (or read of) John Dewey's *How We Think* (1933); psychologist Lev Vygotsky's *Thought and Language* (1962); philosophers of language J. L. Austin's *How to Do Things with Words* (1975) and John Searle on the performative character of all "speech acts" (1969); social historians Eric Havelock (1963) and Walter Ong (1982) on orality and literacy; and "social constructivists" such as Thomas Kuhn in science (1962), Clifford Geertz in anthropology (1983), Jerome Bruner in psychology (1986), and Richard Rorty in philosophy (1969) on the pragmatic nature of knowledge as what Rorty calls "socially justified belief." It is not possible or necessary to recount the theory and history of this "new rhetoric" here, but the significant central strands in its thinking are two: first, that knowledge is socially constructed within a community, not discovered raw in nature by individual intellects; and second, that the agents of construction are the symbol systems through which people "make meaning" — musical, mathematical, graphic, kinetic, but most important, verbal. It is in the "natural" language of speech and writing that we conduct for all other symbol systems the "metadiscourse" that helps us to teach one another what each of us would otherwise have to relearn by personal experience. While musicians may speak to one another through their notes or mathematicians may spring to a blackboard to talk in numbers, natural language remains the most important mediator of concepts we do not yet fully hold. It negotiates all the necessary integrations between the experiences we have stored in our personal stories and the more abstract lessons that are filed in a culture's various systems of thought.

WRITING TO LEARN SCIENCE AND MATHEMATICS

"Writing to learn" in science or mathematics classes is most basically about developing students' conceptual understanding of these subjects by developing their capacity to use the languages of these fields fluently. Traditional pedagogy has often assumed something different: that using the language of a field fluently depends on prior conceptual understanding. The writing-to-learn movement seeks to share with colleagues in other fields what the "new rhetoricians" are learning from a process approach to written language instruction. "If there is one thing we have learned about concepts in recent decades," Richard Rorty (1982) writes, "it is that to have a concept is to be able to use a word, that to have a mastery of concepts is to be able to use a language, and that languages are created rather than discovered" (p. 222). The writing-to-learn movement is fundamentally about using words to acquire concepts.

Initially, advocates of "writing across the curriculum" argued that more writing would make better writers and claimed that experience in the "discourse conventions" of the lab report or the case study, as well as of the literary paper, would improve students' writing in various fields. Such views are not untrue, and they have influenced many teachers of freshman composition to have their students read and write something other than literary essays in their courses. But more important than whether writing across the curriculum will improve students' *writing* by increased fluency and versatility is whether using writing to learn will improve students' *learning*. Writing to learn is not, most importantly, about "grammar across the curriculum" nor about "making spelling count" in the biology paper. It is not a program to reinforce standard English usage in all classes. Nor is it about "formatting across the curriculum": mastering the formal conventions of scientific, social scientific, or business writing. It is about the value of writing "to enable the discovery of knowledge," as Knoblauch and Brannon (1983) have written:

> Presumably what any classroom seeks to nurture is intellectual conversation, leading to enhanced powers of discernment. Since writing enables both learning and conversation, manifesting and enlarging the capacity to discover connections, it should be a resource that all teachers in all disciplines can rely on to achieve their purposes. (p. 473)

Most of the essays in this book are by teachers of mathematics and science interested in using "natural" written language, as well as mathematical symbol systems, as an integral part of their teaching. This is an unusual feature of this book; more often "composition theorists" address their colleagues in other disciplines about "writing across the curriculum" — with a credibility inversely proportionate to their fervor. But many mathematicians and scientists are as eager to address the passivity of students and their dependence on rote learning as are literature or writing teachers. They too are dismayed that in our high-tech, information-overloaded culture, education is often a spectator sport, in an arena of frontal lecturing. They would like students to assume ownership of their education, even if this entails (as it must) a redistribution of authority in the classroom that makes the student and her work the principal text in the classroom. They know that being able to perform operations without being able to explain those operations to oneself or others is at best an ignorant skill.

Finally, scientists and teachers alike recognize that many students are frustrated at their inability to articulate even what it is they don't understand, until curiosity and confidence are vanquished by the imperviousness of the languages of math and science to their own circumstances and problems. Such understand all too well why Lynn Arthur Steen (1987), setting an agenda for the future of mathematics education, has written that

> The chief objective of school mathematics should be to build student confidence. Retaining natural curiosity, promoting confidence in clear reasoning, and building favorable attitudes are far more important than specific techniques for solving school book problems. (p. 302)

These are, in fact, three of the things that informal classroom writing can do best: retain natural curiosity; promote confidence in reason's ability to construct order by trial and error, even in problematic circumstances; and overcome the anxiety that occurs when education stresses answers, not options, and product, not process.

There is a profound difference between the preliminary use of language to serve thinking and the ultimate display of thought that we call exposition or argument. The essays that follow focus primarily on informal uses of writing to learn. Informal writing is done independently of, or at least prior to, any formal writing assignments in a course. It is unconstrained by a need to appear correctly in public. It is not yet deliberately arranging, asserting, or arguing. It is still reflecting and questioning. Such probative, generative thinking may not always be read by a teacher. Generally, it is not graded. Parts of it may be heard in class, but as a means of collaborative learning, not of individual testing. Its basic purpose is to help students become independent, active learners by creating for themselves the language essential to their personal understanding.

Though informal, however, such writing still serves to develop

1. *Abilities* to define, classify, or summarize; to imagine hypotheses and trace inferences; to recognize and evaluate patterns; to establish procedures and analyze problems
2. *Methods* of close, reactive reading; of recording data; of organizing and structuring; of formulating theories; and, most important, of recognizing and regulating method itself

3. *Knowledge* of central concepts in a course; of the broad aims and methods of a discipline; of one's own writing, thinking, and learning
4. *Attitudes* toward learning, knowing, oneself, one's work; toward mistakes and errors; toward the knowledge and opinions of others
5. *Collaborative learning* by encouraging open exploration within a community of inquiry, rather than isolated competition; promoting connected, not separated, teaching; developing active listening; and locating the motivation for learning neither in the relevance of the subject nor in the performance of the teacher but in the interpersonal dynamic of the learning community itself
6. *In summary, general capacities for learning* including the ability to question, to wonder, to think for oneself while working with others

Writing in Science Education

In science education, the issue is more remembering than recognizing the importance of written language. So-called "double-entry" or "dialectical" notebooks now advocated by many writing teachers to train students to observe closely while noting their own reflections and reactions are derived directly from the field notes and lab books of science. Indeed, the whole notion of maintaining throughout a course a "learning log," in which one enters classroom notes and summaries of readings, as well as other types of original thinking, is indebted to the empiricist's habit of collecting information and conjectures; suspending premature closure; and committing oneself to formal argument only when all evidence is collected and all explanations have been entertained.

The uses of writing in science courses are self-evident. It is the essential tool of recording, reporting, generalizing, theorizing—provided, of course, that a positivistic notion of "fact" has not made right answers more important than inquiry into problems. In that case, the significant feature of an experiment becomes reporting the correct results, not observing and wondering about what happens. The important feature of education becomes saying the right words, not learning how to use one's own words. In such circumstances the "language" of science remains for many students a set of foreign words, dead as Latin, to be memorized from a book. It is not the constructive speech of a vital culture. Students then regard "definition" as a chain of words that bonds one to "truth" and "reality"; if one link is forgotten, the whole chain of understanding is broken. They have no sense of words as spider webs that catch meaning in their sticky strands; no experience of words as an approximate schematic of conceptual understanding; no notion that meaning is recomposed in each new personal performance on the public instrument of language.

What "informal" writing to learn, as opposed to the longer, finished "research paper," restores to science education is the contingent quality of the scientific process. Scientists speak to one another in at least two basic, but quite dissimilar, interpretive repertoires or linguistic registers, according to the research of G. Nigel Gilbert and Michael Mulkay (1984). In formal publication, where scientists would like it to seem that their actions and beliefs correspond faithfully to the innate truths of an impersonal, natural world, they rely most heavily on an "empiricist repertoire":

> The guiding principle . . . appears to be that speakers depict their actions and beliefs as a neutral medium through which empirical phenomena make themselves evident. The stylistic, grammatical and lexical resources of the empiricist repertoire . . . are consistently depicting participants' professional action and scientific views as inevitable, given the realities of the natural world under study. (p. 56)

In informal talk, on the other hand, scientists use a "contingent repertoire":

> Its guiding principle is in direct opposition to that of the empiricist repertoire in that it enables speakers to depict professional actions and beliefs as being significantly influenced by variable factors outside the realm of empirical . . . phenomena. When this repertoire is employed, scientists' actions are no longer depicted as generic responses to the realities of the natural world, but as the activities and judgements of specific individuals acting on . . . their personal inclinations and particular social positions. (p. 57)

In the lectures they attend, the textbooks they study, the scientific articles they read, students often hear only the "empiricist repertoire" used to exhibit and lend authority to the products of scientific processes. Understandably, this strengthens their tendency to memorize and mimic such language, not only to participate in its authority but also to obey its tacit claim that it contains exactly all the knowledge there is on a particular subject. The rest, its formal precision implies, is either misstatement or misunderstanding. To hear a "contingent repertoire" (more commonly spoken in a small seminar or experiential laboratory than in a large formal lecture) and to feel invited to speak in this register oneself is to feel welcomed into the scientific community.

Every "community of discourse," not just the community of biochemists or astrophysicists but also the community of Marxist historians and of Keynesian economists, has these same two repertoires or linguistic registers, one to bolster the best possible public claim that can be made to having constructed new knowledge; and the other to deconstruct and reconstitute knowledge that is in the process of being remade. Allowing more oral, colloquial, contingent speech and more informal, tentative writing into the classroom allows students to think for themselves — however imprecisely and haltingly at first — as opposed to only knowing secondhand what others have thought before them. If the latter is all a student gets from a class, in any field, the end is less than a complete education.

Writing in Mathematics Education

The case of mathematics is significantly different from that of science when it comes to using writing. Mathematicians and their students regularly do more writing, in truth, than is done in many composition courses. But the "writing" is in mathematical, not verbal, symbols. Given that mathematics has its own symbol system, through which practitioners can think and express themselves, it is not immediately apparent why a second, "natural" written language is helpful to learning or how, exactly, it might serve a class in learning mathematics.

What, after all, makes learning difficult in school, particularly mathematics? One possible set of answers is ineptitude, genetics, "the way you're wired." But another possible answer is the way the classroom's wired, and whether the teacher's plugged into the students. A better question than what makes mathematics hard, however, is "Who is better at it?" or "In what circumstances is *everyone* better at learning math?"

Not being a part of learning, remaining an outsider unable even to ask "intelligent" questions, certainly makes any learning difficult. Any student succeeds better where the language available to engage and construct knowledge is plentiful and variable. Teachers are also beginning to recognize that when students do not write or think well, one possible explanation is that there has been too little opportunity to write or think at all. When math classes, like writing classes, are focused on rote performance of academic exercises, there is equally little opportunity to think.

Language, oral or written, is an expressive instrument through which we communicate what we have previously thought. It is also the reflective instrument through which we think, alone or with others, about what we are doing. Our natural language, operating as the "metadiscourse" of all our other symbol systems, from math through money, from dance to drawing, enables us to distance ourselves from, for example, our own mathematical problem solving, and reflect on our procedure, thereby making knowledge of it.

Oral language is invaluable for collaborative reflection and the social evolution of thought among individuals. But written language, because its very slowness makes it more deliberately self-conscious, enhances our sense of details and choices. Within the classroom, written language is more useful than oral, too, if *all* students are to think, not just a dominant few; if all are to rehearse their own understanding in their own terms; if all are to be heard: only by themselves at first, perhaps, but it is by ourselves that we mainly practice our personal performance of social understanding, not in front of teachers.

And how exactly can writing serve learning in the math class? In broad summary, there are many types of, and occasions for, informal writing:

1. *Freewriting* at the beginning of a class, to become present and centered, eliminating the distractions we bring to class.

2. *Focused freewriting* to cast a net of inquiry, initiating exploration of a term, issue, question, or problem.

3. *Attitudinal writing* to discover attitudes that affect aptitudes for learning by asking students: What expectation or experience do you bring to this reading? What difficulties did you have with the last assignment? What is most difficult for you at this point in the course? What do we need to do differently?

4. *Reflective, probative writing* to initiate or to conclude a class discussion or, mid-class, to refocus a discussion that is confused or lacks energy.

5. *"Metacognitive" process writing* to observe how one reads, takes an exam, works on a problem, writes a paper, thinks about an issue. Writing that records one's own learning behavior, allowing one to become more autonomous and less reliant on the information and authority of teachers or texts.

6. *Explaining errors* on a test or homework—a particular type of "process writing" that helps students and teachers recognize where things went wrong and why.

7. *Questioning* while doing homework or at the end of class (yet another type of "process writing"), enabling students and teachers to recognize doubts, reservations, confusions, and uncertainties.

8. *Summarizing* what was said in a class or reading.

9. *Defining*—substituting personal definitions, however imprecise, for memorization of textbook terms.

10. *Creating problems*—defining problems and issues of one's own, as alternative to answering others' questions.

11. *Writing to read*—through double-entry notebooks, reporting what an author says and, in a facing column, responding to it. Such dialectical

notebooks integrate attitudinal writing; questioning; summarizing; and process writing.
12. *Learning logs, microthemes, paired problem solving*, and so forth.

Barbara Rose's chapter, which follows, and many of the other essays in this collection are specific in their descriptions of what individual teachers have done, and why. Another example here, however, can be illustrative. Helen J. Schwartz (1984) has invented a very useful computer software program for hypothesis testing that can be modified to support writing a literary analysis or figuring out word problems. Students can work at a computer on an integrated tutorial/network that allows them both to write independently and to converse with classmates about math problems. A series of "prompts" invites students

1. To restate the problem, exactly and in paraphrase, taking conceptual ownership through defining
2. To summarize the data, what is given and what is not yet visible but needs to be known
3. To estimate an answer, in speculative, probative language
4. To plan a solution, in hypothetical language that looks for useful laws, formulas, and equations but also formulates a way of using them
5. To recognize attitudinal problems — expectations, difficulties, blocks — that may interfere with effective problem solving
6. To join with other students, talking about ways to understand and approach problems

Written language becomes, in such a case, an invaluable heuristic of learning. It develops students' abilities (to read, define, hypothesize), inculcates methods (of problem solving), increases knowledge (particularly, metacognitive awareness), recognizes attitudes, and promotes collaboration.

THE ORGANIZATION OF THIS BOOK

Used as an instrument of learning, not just as a way of publicly demonstrating and validating what has been learned, writing helps students to appreciate that knowledge is socially constructed and negotiated within a community's field of language. As students recognize that knowledge is culturally constructed, not somehow "discovered" in nature, their view of themselves and of their teachers matures. Authority for learning and knowing is shared within the class, not reserved exclusively for the teacher. "Connected teaching" is more important than isolated, competitive schooling (Belenky, Clinchy, Goldberger, & Tarule, 1986). The motivation for learning is located in the social dynamic of the classroom, not in the performance of the teacher nor in the relevance of the subject. Using writing to learn does not just add a facet to teaching, another hard edge to the diamond of education; it radically alters the ecology of learning by engaging students in a system where they need not, like Virginia Woolf's Mr. Ramsey, "perish each alone."

The hope of the contributors to this book is that our essays make a persuasive case that one of the ways we construct our worlds is with language, particularly language that explains to ourselves how and why we regard the world in a certain way, as opposed to language that repeats a dogmatic, canonical formula in the superstitious belief that words capture "reality itself." It is what writing to learn is about—learning—and it is encouraging for the state of education generally that in the exchange of ideas on this subject of the "two cultures," mathematicians and scientists on the one hand and writers and literature teachers on the other, seek to learn from one another.

Following Leon Botstein's Foreword, the twenty-three chapters in this book are organized into two prefatory essays—this introduction and Barbara Rose's bibliographic essay—and then six parts. Essays in the first three parts identify broad problems and possibilities in using writing to learn, and then turn at once to classroom applications: what works and why. Essays in the next two parts move from classroom practice to departmental programs and look at the role of writing in the greater ecology of learning. In Part VI, the final two essays offer a concluding overview and response to the rest of the book.

It is not immediately self-evident to mathematicians or scientists why they should embrace "writing to learn," particularly when it seems to steal precious time from an already overcrowded syllabus. The three chapters in Part I, by Marcia Birkin, Sheila Tobias, and Alan Marwine, acknowledge that these are very valid concerns, yet go on to show how writing can enhance learning.

In Part II, the next three essays by Russel Kenyon, William Berlinghoff, and David White and Katie Dunn all examine the value of writing in problem solving, both in the mathematics classroom and among a collegial faculty. Each of these essays, like most in this book, provides fully detailed accounts of how exactly writing assignments have been designed and used.

At the center of this book, each of the six authors in Part III provides a fully elaborated account of how writing is a principal mode of learning in courses in biology (Kathryn Martin), in core courses in general science

(David Layzer), in mathematics electives (Sandra Keith), in developmental or remedial math courses (Richard Lesnak; and José López and Arthur Powell), and within teacher-education courses in science (Mary Bahns). Part IV moves from accounts of what is happening in individual classrooms to three descriptions of programmatic changes at institutions that have developed writing requirements and courses in mathematics and science. Joanne Snow, William Mullin, and George Gopen and David Smith describe developments in their institutions' implementation of writing across the curriculum.

Part V moves to larger issues still, as each of the four authors — Erika Duncan, Anneli Lax, Hassler Whitney, and Dale Worsley — looks at writing in the broad context of learning, and argues, sometimes passionately, for educational change that allows and supports fuller active participation by students (and teachers) in their own development.

In Part VI, two scholars were invited to see this collection whole and to write a "meta-essay" attending to any larger issues that may unify individual perspectives. The two essayists are Vera John-Steiner — author of *Notebooks of the Mind: Explorations of Thinking* (University of New Mexico Press, 1985) and co-editor of Lev Vygotsky's essays, *Mind in Society: The Development of Higher Psychological Processes* (Harvard University Press, 1978) — and Reuben Hersh, co-author of *The Mathematical Experience* (Boston: Birkhauser, 1980).

Despite a number of recurrent themes that run through this book, the authors certainly do not always agree. Readers should not be surprised to find various expressions of uncertainty, disagreement, or puzzlement in these essays. The greatest value of current speculation about the relation of language to learning in mathematics and science is probably that deep, hard questions are being asked. Here, as in the classroom, the search to formulate new questions is at least as valuable as the clear exposition of full answers.

REFERENCES

Austin, J. L. (1975). *How to do things with words*. Cambridge, MA: Harvard University Press.

Belenky, M. F., Clinchy, B. M., Goldberger, N. R., & Tarule, J. M. (1986). *Women's ways of knowing: The development of self, voice, and mind*. New York: Basic Books.

Bruner, J. (1986). *Actual minds, possible worlds*. Cambridge, MA: Harvard University Press.

Dewey, J. (1933). *How we think*. Boston: D. C. Heath.

Geertz, C. (1983). *Local knowledge: Further essays in interpretive anthropology.* New York: Basic Books.

Gilbert, G. N., & Mulkay, M. (1984). *Opening Pandora's box: A sociological analysis of scientists' discourse.* Cambridge: Cambridge University Press.

Havelock, E. (1963). *Preface to Plato.* Cambridge, MA: Belknap Press.

John-Steiner, V. (1985). *Notebooks of the mind: Explorations of thinking.* Albuquerque, NM: University of New Mexico Press.

Knoblauch, C. H., & Brannon, L. (1983). Writing as Learning Through the Curriculum. *College English, 45,* 5.

Kuhn, T. (1962). *The structure of scientific revolutions.* Chicago, IL: University of Chicago Press.

Ong, W. (1982). *Orality and literacy: The technologizing of the word.* London: Methuen.

Polya, G. (1945). *How to solve it.* Princeton, NJ: Princeton University Press.

Rorty, R. (1969). *Philosophy and the mirror of nature.* Princeton, NJ: Princeton University Press.

Rorty, R. (1982). *Consequences of pragmatism.* Minneapolis: University of Minnesota Press.

Schwartz, H. J. (1984). SEEN: A tutorial and user network for hypothesis testing. In W. Wresch (Ed.), *The computer in composition instruction: A writer's tool* (pp. 47–62). Urbana, IL: National Council of Teachers of English.

Searle, J. (1969). *Speech acts: An essay in the philosophy of language.* Cambridge: Cambridge University Press.

Sizer, T. (1984). *Horace's compromise: The dilemma of the American high school.* Boston: Houghton Mifflin.

Stafford, W. (1982). *Writing the Australian crawl.* Ann Arbor, MI: University of Michigan Press.

Steen, L. A. (1987, July). Mathematics education: A predictor of scientific competitiveness. *Science,* pp. 251–252.

Vygotsky, L. (1962). *Thought and language.* Cambridge, MA: MIT Press.

Vygotsky, L. (1978). *Mind in society: The development of higher psychological processes* (Michael Cole et al., Eds.). Cambridge, MA: Harvard University Press.

CHAPTER 2

Writing and Mathematics: Theory and Practice

Barbara Rose

Mathematics teachers recognize that students have only a very limited understanding of the nature of mathematics. From the student's perspective, mathematics is a subject in which answers are right or wrong and the teacher is the authority whose responsibility it is to pass on a mystical "bag of mathematical tricks" to the next generation. "Doing mathematics," then, consists of memorizing rules and plugging new numbers into old formulas. Because of the highly symbolic nature of mathematics, students try to slide through courses by externally manipulating the symbols without constructing meaning of their own.

Changing deeply rooted beliefs about teaching and learning mathematics involves transforming the classroom into a place where students may experience mathematics as a creative activity, particularly through written language. What follows is a review of recent publications that describe efforts to use writing in teaching mathematics and to consider the impact of writing activities on the mathematics classroom.

WRITING THEORY

In recent years, the emphasis in the teaching of writing has been away from formal correctness and finished product and towards process, context, and meaning. Those identified with new methods of teaching writing, sometimes called the New Rhetoricians, understand writing as a recursive, rather than a linear, process. Unlike the more traditional view, which defined writing as a product, newer theories of composition understand writing as a unique learning strategy in which process is at least as important as product.

Among the most influential theorists of the relationship of language to learning is James Britton, author of numerous essays and studies on how

15

children and adults manipulate language to make meaning and shape their worlds. Avoiding the more traditional approach to understanding and classifying types of written language, Britton examines the functional uses of language, making a crucial distinction between participant and spectator (Britton, Burgess, Martin, McLeod, & Rosen, 1975). According to Britton, when we use language, we are either participating actively in the world to get things done, that is, using language instrumentally, or we are reflecting on the meaning and significance of our activities, when, as spectators, we use language to tell our stories. From these two functions of written language Britton derives his classification of written language into transactional and expressive.

Transactional writing, for Britton, allows us to act as participants in the world. It is the language we use to inform, persuade, or instruct and is directed towards an audience. In transactional writing our focus is on the final product. On the other hand, expressive writing is "thinking aloud on paper." It is writing intended for the writer's own use, or at least for the reader familiar with the "context" in which it was written. Britton believes that expressive writing is the language closest to primal thought; that is, it is the messy, exploratory writing closest to the self, from which we construct a finished product. In this scheme, expressive writing—preliminary, exploratory writing—may be said to precede transactional writing, but it also serves a separate function which makes it independent from transactional writing. Expressive writing records present feelings as well as our thoughts about a problem, issue, or text. It is the writing most often associated with diaries or journals.

The distinction between expressive and transactional provides a useful framework within which to consider recent contributions to our understanding of the writing process. Janet Emig, for example, extends Britton's ideas of expressive writing to all writing in several of her essays, particularly in "Writing as a Mode of Learning" (1977). For Emig, writing is uniquely integrative, functioning as an important mode of learning involving hand, eye, and brain. In addition, writing requires a "deliberate structuring of meaning" (p. 215) and provides a unique form of reinforcement and feedback.

Precisely because of its value as a heuristic, expressive writing has attracted the attention of theorists concerned with the use of writing to learn. Unfortunately, expressive writing is often lacking in the teaching of writing at the secondary level. In studying over 2,000 students in 65 British secondary schools, Britton found that 84 percent of school writing is transactional, 7 percent poetic, and less than 4 percent expressive.

There is evidence of new interest in expressive writing in the literature, where teachers are increasingly using expressive writing to encourage independent learning. In *Writing Without Teachers* (1973) and *Writing With Power* (1981), Peter Elbow advocates freewriting, a form of expressive writing, as the easiest way to get words on paper. According to Elbow, freewriting allows the writer to separate editing and revising from generating; to clear the mind by emptying thoughts and feelings on paper; and to bring a surface and immediate coherence to writing.

WRITING AND MATHEMATICS

Despite the apparent disparity between the fields of writing and mathematics, a review of recent literature and conferences reveals a growing interest in the relationship of writing to teaching mathematics. Teachers are discovering that writing activities are flexible in addressing a variety of needs, depending on such variables as class size and instructional purpose.

Transactional writing seems to be the type most frequently assigned in the mathematics classroom. This is public writing, meant to be read by an audience, usually the teacher. Students use this kind of writing—in summaries, reports, projects, essays, and notetaking—to develop clear expression of their mathematical understanding. Writing down mathematical concepts, processes, and applications in order to inform, explain, or report invites students to record their understanding through written language, a process that also improves fluency.

The forms of expressive writing most often used in mathematics classrooms are freewriting and journal writing. Students use freewriting to generate thoughts about mathematical concepts and processes and to record, in journals, their problems, questions, and feelings. The emphasis is on thoughtful meaning rather than on grammatical correctness. "Journal writing" is usually used to describe a category of expressive writing that is done both in and out of the classroom, and can be either personal or academic, focused or unstructured, shared or private. Alternatively called logs, notebooks, diaries, and thinkbooks, journals involve the writer in making new knowledge by making connections between new information and what is already known.

Transactional Writing Activities

Barbara King (1982) describes six writing tasks that serve the transactional function: summaries, questions, explanations, definitions, reports, and word problems. Others report the use of term papers, stories, projects, essay questions, books, notetaking, and dialogues.

Summaries. When teachers ask students to summarize information, they invite students to focus on the material, select the parts they feel are pertinent, and restate them in their own words. Whether students rewrite a page or paragraph of the text or summarize a class session, whether it is done in journals or submitted to the teacher to be read and returned, summaries make the material more personal and facilitate retention of the concepts (King, 1982; Johnson, 1983).

Questions. King (1982) proposes that when students formulate and write questions, they focus on what they do not understand. This often reduces anxiety, as students are able to transfer their confusion onto paper, which subsequently may lead to resolution or provide a reminder to ask the teacher.

Questions can be utilized in several ways. At the beginning of a class, teachers can collect questions students encountered during their homework and respond during class or write back to the student later. Also, students can respond to each other's questions during class discussion, in small groups, or in writing.

Explanations. Teachers can ask students to write mathematical explanations for various purposes, including how they solved a particular problem and how to avoid or explain errors (Ackerman, 1987; King, 1982; McMillen, 1986; Schmidt, 1985). For example, students can profit from writing explanations of errors to avoid when solving a particular type of problem. Whether students list items to be careful of in simplifying products and quotients of rational expressions, or classify statements as true or false with a rationale, they participate in an exercise that moves them towards understanding.

Writing explanations of mathematical concepts and procedures encourages precision in verbal expression, engages all students in simultaneous participation, and makes available the written word for both student and teacher to review.

Definitions. When students use their own words to write out mathematical definitions, they are forced to think about the meaning of the concept and generally remember it better.

Reports. Formal reports help relay the message to students that writing is important in every field and that mathematics is more than solving equations. Suggested topics for math reports include problem-solving reports, biographies of famous mathematicians, research on math anxiety, new developments in computer technology, careers in mathematics

(King, 1982), calculus papers (Mett, 1987), and book reports (Johnson, 1983; Schmidt, 1985). Most teachers grade formal reports for both content and quality, and many give feedback at several stages.

Word Problems. Students can either rewrite story problems they don't understand, helping them see the key words and relationships (Johnson, 1983), or they can be invited to construct their own word problems.

Hodgin (1987) gives her elementary students a picture or cartoon and asks them to construct a problem from the picture, give it to a friend to read, rewrite it if necessary, and then copy it neatly on a sheet of paper for the class bulletin board.

Others ask students to demonstrate their understanding of mathematical concepts by writing word problems of their own (Kennedy, 1985; King, 1982; Stempien & Borasi, 1985). Variations range from students supplying their own data to incorporating data provided by the teacher.

When students write their own problems, they often choose situations from their own experience and thus see how mathematics applies to their own lives, giving them more confidence to read and solve word problems from the textbook. In addition, writing word problems demands clear, specific, and complete instructions, which requires good understanding of the mathematical concept underlying the problem. This activity also provides a break in the monotony of traditional mathematical tasks.

When students are asked to go one step further and share their problems with the class, the gaps and omissions become apparent and students can demand immediate clarification from each other. They are exposed to a wide variety of similar problems and feel they are making a valuable contribution to the class. This activity increases the verbalization and communication among students about mathematics.

Term Papers. Term papers, like reports, are an opportunity for students to practice writing skills while investigating mathematical issues that are not generally covered in the traditional mathematics curriculum. In addition, students are encouraged to do research to think creatively. A variety of topics can be suggested, such as the use of mathematics in relation to another discipline, a practical job-related application of mathematics (Lipman, 1981), a biography (Johnson, 1983), or a particular mathematical question (Burton, 1985).

Projects. Abel (1987) requires that students interview a mathematician by doing enough research to generate ten intelligent and interesting questions. Other projects require that students choose a mathematical process and write a radio ad for it, choose a career they want to explore and write questions they would need to have answered about that career, or write mathematical bumper sticker slogans or license plate captions.

Essays. Essays generally fall into two classifications. One involves the frequent practice of requiring students to write essays on tests, such as "What does it mean to 'solve' an equation?" Not surprisingly, students often balk at this practice, for most would rather plug numbers into equations than formulate an articulate response in writing about a mathematical concept. The test essay takes the teacher more time to correct, but gives valuable feedback about the students' understanding of the material and can more adequately test the higher levels of thinking.

Essays are also assigned to investigate nonstandard contexts and ways of doing mathematics. For example, students are asked to respond in writing to mathematical problems set in social and political contexts (Frankenstein, 1986), or concerning the relation between pairs of mathematical statements, such as "probability and event" Geeslin, 1977).

Stempien and Borasi (1985) propose that students can enrich their understanding of mathematics if asked to write essays on "meta-concepts" like definitions and proofs in mathematics. They report that when graduate students in a mathematics education class were asked to write a short essay on "What characterizes a mathematical definition?", the task stimulated a series of interesting activities concerning definitions. Likewise, Goldberg (1983) has students respond to statements such as Bertrand Russell's "Mathematics may be defined as the subject in which we never know what we are talking about nor whether what we are saying is true."

Another intriguing type of essay is the "microtheme"—short essays typed on one side of a 5″×8″ notecard (Abel, 1987). Assignments focus on different cognitive problems: summary microthemes require no interjection of a personal point of view; a thesis-supported microtheme requires taking and supporting a position by using empirical evidence, syllogistic reasoning, or appeal to appropriate authority; a data-provided microtheme requires students to draw conclusions from data and discover a meaningful way to describe their findings; the quandry-posing microtheme asks students to solve mathematical puzzles and teach their solution to an imaginary learner who does not comprehend the concept.

Books. Harriet Montague (1973) gave her students in grades 10–12 the opportunity to author a book on matrix algebra. After first drafts, peer and teacher review, and final drafts with an abundance of group cooperation, Montague reports that the project was extremely successful, with value to all participants. The benefits to the students were numerous:

students learned more information when they located their own reference sources; peer discussion and criticism were stimulating; an appreciation of the complexity and difficulty of the communication process developed; the final expository product was exemplary; and the pride of accomplishment was rewarding to the entire class.

The teacher, likewise, benefited from the production of the book, by finding release from traditional classroom activity, being prodded to engage in fresh and serious study of the subject matter, and gaining a glimpse into the individual personalities of the students.

Notetaking. When students take notes, either from a class presentation or from the textbook, students are active participants rather than daydreaming in class or reading without comprehension. In addition, they tend to retain the information longer since they engage in multirepresentational learning and they have a written record for latter referral. Other variations are possible, including the method used by students in a "Mathematical Thinking" class at New York University, who take turns writing class notes and distributing them to the entire class. Then students do cut-and-paste jobs individually, add their own comments and observations, and eventually produce their own private textbook (McMillen, 1986).

Dialogues. Dialogues can report on problem-solving activities or examine philosophical or epistemological issues in mathematics. Stempien and Borasi (1985) recommend dialogues for several reasons. First, the presence of different characters makes it natural to discuss different points of view and analyze paradoxes. This could be particularly helpful for students who view mathematics as a precise and rigorous discipline. Second, dialogues are an easy and natural form of writing, which may encourage the writing process.

These transactional writing activities cover a wide range of tasks. Some of those reported as transactional can easily fall into the fuzzy overlap between transactional and expressive writing. When students write summaries, for instance, they can serve either function. If the intention of the writing is to inform the teacher of what the student knows, then the summary qualifies as transactional. If, however, summaries are written by students for themselves, to come to know and understand the material through the very act of writing, then the summary can be considered expressive writing.

The distinction between transactional and expressive writing is often blurred, but both can serve useful purposes for the learning of mathematics. Britton maintains that expressive writing often becomes transactional as it develops into public writing. Certainly the "product" of expressive writing is valuable for later reference.

Expressive Writing Activities

An emphasis on the process of writing and thinking finds an audience among mathematics teachers who want to explore the potential of "writing to learn" in the classroom through expressive writing—personal and exploratory writing intended to make the thinking process explicit. What kinds of assignments, then, might qualify as expressive writing?

Freewriting. Freewriting is thinking aloud on paper, writing down whatever comes to mind. Most freewriting is short, uncensored, ungraded, done in class for 3–7 minutes, and concerned strictly with content and ideas, not mechanics. It can either be focused or unfocused and occur during different parts of class, depending on the purpose and context. Whatever the configuration, it affords an excellent opportunity to engage all students simultaneously in an active learning experience.

At the beginning of class, students may be asked to write for five minutes on topics such as, What still bothers me about solving quadratic equations? What was my biggest problem on the homework? How do I feel about the test I took yesterday? They may also be asked to summarize the unit just completed or to freewrite on the unit just starting. This helps show the students what they already know about the upcoming topic.

When students end a class with a short freewrite, they can respond to questions such as, What was the main idea of today's lesson? What is the muddiest issue in this unit on solving linear equations? What is the process of related rates? What questions do I have from this lesson?

Freewriting during the middle of class can refocus students on the material or be used to express frustrations or ask questions. Used before an exam, freewriting can clear students' minds and focus their thoughts (McMillen, 1986) or be used creatively at any point during class to respond to questions such as, How is learning mathematics like learning to ride a bicycle? (Burton, 1985).

Freewriting is also used by Burton (1985) in mathematics education classes before, during, or after a lecture to give students a chance to generate ideas and relationships that can be explored, reshaped, or reread for later oral or written treatment. Freewriting also helps students become more specific about areas that are causing problems.

In Mett's (1987) calculus classes, students often freewrite whenever a particularly important topic needs more attention. For example, students in a business calculus class might freewrite about the difference between average and instantaneous velocity to prepare them for further discussion.

In a class of hearing-impaired students in their first year of an engineering technology program, Sachs (1987) asked his students to freewrite about the following questions: How will the content of Unit B help you in your major? What did you like best about Unit B? What did you like least about Unit B? How did you like the written materials of Unit B? How did you like the teaching of Unit B? He found the students' writing enlightening, as they focused on their problems and frustrations and offered suggestions for eliminating them. In addition, Sachs received valuable insight about both the students and the course.

Countryman (1987) labels her form of freewriting as "process writing," describing it as a means to examine how and why one acts or did act in a situation, e.g., before and after reading an assignment, taking an exam, examining a problem, writing a paper, or thinking about an issue. She claims that process writing encourages both anticipating and observing one's learning behavior to become more active and less reliant on the information and authority of teachers and texts. Suggested process-writing tasks include writing about how to attack a word problem before solving it; exploring errors on a test or homework, thereby indicating where students went wrong; listing questions from homework or a class session, thus allowing students to locate areas of confusion or focus on the reading or class lesson; writing personal mathematical definitions, so as to develop conceptional understanding; and creating word problems to help students define problems of their own.

Notice again that these activities can be used as either transactional, expressive, or both, even by the same student in a single activity.

Letters. Letter writing has several advantages over other writing tasks: students are familiar with writing letters, like to have an audience for their writing, and feel comfortable including both affective and cognitive thoughts. King (1982) asks students to write to a friend or peer, telling how they feel about mathematics, discussing how to solve problems, or giving advice on how to get better grades in math.

Towards the end of the school year, Schmidt (1985) asks his junior high students to write to an imaginary cousin who is coming to junior high, about what she or he needs to know to get along in the class. Through writing, Schmidt's students realize that their feelings and concerns about school have an audience and value, and they subsequently give advice that shows they accept responsibility for their own learning.

Another audience for student letters is the teacher. At various times during a course, students can be asked to write a "Dear Teacher" letter to convey to the teacher what's going on with them in the course. This gives students an opportunity to reflect on their performance, identify study patterns, and take additional responsibility for their own learning. In addition, the teacher gains insight into students' attitudes, areas of concern, and feedback about the course and teaching.

Kennedy (1985) requires his middle school students to write him letters during the last ten minutes of class, including (1) what they understand (with examples) about the work in class, (2) what they don't understand (with examples), and (3) what they're wondering about (specific questions). He claims students can admit ignorance on things they'd never confess in class. As Kennedy reads the letters at night, he claims he learns more about his students than in two or three class periods of observation, and then prepares his next day's class to respond to the content of the letters.

Admit Slips.   Schmidt (1985) uses "admit slips" with his junior high students, having them write their thoughts on a slip of paper and fold it once, following the constraints of nothing nasty, nothing personal, and guaranteed anonymity. Schmidt then shuffles them and reads them to the class, claiming the slips give students a chance to tell how they like it at school, to express mathematical anxiety, to share their academic successes and problems, and to stop and consider what they have and can still learn.

Autobiographical Writing.   This form of writing is a comfortable way to initiate writing, since it gives students a chance to write about something with which they're familiar. Whether written as a narrative about previous experience or in response to structured questions provided by the teacher, both students and teachers benefit. Students realize that the writing process is a vehicle by which they can recognize feelings and experiences and that the written product can become a record for referral and reflection. The writing is also a source of data for teachers about students and their experiences with and conceptions about mathematics.

Students can be asked to write a biographical narrative with the following instructions: "Write about any mathematical experiences you have had. The narratives should be told as stories, with as much detail and description as possible. Include your thoughts, reactions, and feelings about the entire experience." Or, students can be asked to write completions to and elaborations on sentences such as, My most positive experience with math was _____. My background in math is _____. I liked math until _____. Math makes me feel _____. If I were a math teacher, I'd _____.

Journals. Journal writing can be expressive, transactional, or a combination of both, with a broad range of possibilities to accommodate individual classroom and teacher needs. The following variations illustrate only a few of the possibilities.

Students can write to different *audiences*, for journals can be purely private or can be a dialogue with others, usually the teacher. Private journals are used as a therapeutic tool, and students can indeed profit from using the journal to think for themselves on paper, explore new ideas, solve difficult problems, express feelings, diagnose errors, and consider alternative solutions. Yet students report that they find journals more beneficial when using them as a dialogue with the teacher. The functions remain the same, but the added benefit of teacher as reader and responder adds an incentive to write the journal consistently. When students write and teachers read and write back, there is a unique relationship established between each student and the teacher. Students eagerly anticipate the teacher's answers to their questions or comments on their entries. Students and teachers find something to talk about and the classroom becomes more cooperative and humanized as each see the other in a new and personalized light.

Journals serve a *function and purpose* somewhere between diaries (personal thoughts and experiences) and class notebooks (impersonal facts, usually other people's ideas) (Fulwiler, 1980). Like diaries, they are written in the first person about ideas important to the writer; like class notebooks, they focus on academic subjects, narrowly or broadly. Unlike a diary that may be a record of daily trivia, however, journals are deliberate exercises in expanding the awareness of what is happening, personally and academically. By nature, they are interdisciplinary and developmental.

Journals can assume different *structures*, from highly focused entries, usually in response to a teacher-assigned topic or question, or to unstructured entries where the students determine the content. An interesting combination uses the left-side pages of a spiral-bound notebook for in-class writing in response to teacher-generated topics or questions and the right-side pages as unstructured out-of-class entries. A list of topics can be provided for students to use when they are stuck for lack of content.

The *content* of the journals can vary, including summaries of class/text, explanations or questions about the material being covered, description of mathematical processes, the solution to a problem, or feelings about class, mathematics, the teacher, or course. Some teachers use daily logs to review the day's events and record feelings and questions about the class and topic (Mett, 1987; Shaw, 1983). Each Monday at the University of Akron, students in the basic mathematics program turn in their journals composed of a graph showing the number of homework hours, a record of all grades earned during the week, and at least one paragraph concerning the students' math experiences during the week (Vukovich, 1985).

In dialogue journals between teacher and student, the teacher can give content suggestions to the student based on individual needs. The "double-entry journal" is another variation, where students write summaries of what they read on one page in their notebook and record comments and reactions on the facing page (McMillen, 1986).

Journal entries before tests allow students to write about how they feel about taking the test and how they prepared for it. After the test, but before the test is handed back, it is useful to write about how they felt about the test, how well they anticipated what was on the test, what concepts they didn't know, and what they could have done differently to prepare for the test. After the test is handed back, students can profit from considering a couple of specific errors by reconstructing their thinking for that problem, recording their new thinking about it, and stating any confusion or questions that still remain from the unit.

The *format* needs to be appropriate to the particular class and teacher needs. Some teachers ask students to write only in class (Burton, 1985; Countryman, 1987; Nahrgang & Petersen, 1986; Powell, 1986) and others, entirely on the students' own time. Some use loose pages that the teacher keeps in a folder and others prefer a bound book. All have their advantages and drawbacks.

One of the greatest concerns to mathematics teachers about journals are the *procedural* questions. Again, various approaches are possible, depending on context and need. The journals can be collected or not, collected randomly or routinely, collected frequently or infrequently, responded to or not responded to, and graded or not graded. The combination of factors producing the greatest success for me is to collect the journals randomly, every couple of weeks, reading and responding back in a day, and giving credit for keeping up with frequency and volume of writing (Rose, 1988). For teachers who have many students in multiple classes, the collection of the journals can be staggered and only short responses need be given. Students appreciate the fact that teachers respond individually more than to the volume of that response.

Teachers report a variety of benefits as students write journals:

- When students are stuck on a problem and write out their thought processes, they see their errors and often solve the problem (King, 1982).
- Journal writing slows the thinking process, which gives students a chance to arrive at their own solutions as well as to understand their thought processes (McMillen, 1986).

- Teachers benefit as they receive feedback on lessons and become aware of when students are reached by certain activities (Powell, 1986).
- Students *make* notes, not *take* notes, and produce interpretive comments and personal reminders (Kennedy, 1985).
- As the teacher writes back to the students, students realize the teacher hears and cares (Watson, 1980).
- Students gain the opportunity to formulate, organize, internalize, and evaluate concepts; answer self-generated questions; and generate a record of their thinking (Nahrgang & Petersen, 1986).

CONCLUSION

Despite growing interest in using writing to learn mathematics, there is also resistance, both on the part of students and faculty. Some professors resist writing assignments both because of the anticipated time to read and grade the work and because they feel untrained as a composition teacher. Students are also reticent about writing, since most were never required to write in previous mathematics courses.

For writing to be effective, several ingredients seem desirable:

- Professors should participate in the writing assignments and share their own writing with the class (McMillen, 1986).
- Students need help and encouragement at the beginning of this new adventure of writing in math and need to receive regular feedback from the teacher (Countryman, 1987).
- The teacher needs to establish an atmosphere of trust if students are going to risk the exploratory and personal aspects of writing to learn (Kennedy, 1985).

Writing in the mathematics classroom allows students to proceed at their own rate, using their own experiences and language; increases writing fluency; combats passivity; facilitates personal engagement in learning; provides the teacher with a unique diagnostic tool; keeps a record of students' individual travel through their mathematical experiences; and promotes a caring and cooperative atmosphere through writing interaction. Also, as students write expressively to learn mathematics, their writing becomes the transactional record or expression of that process of acquisition. When students and teachers become the writers and readers of their own mathematical stories, they regard mathematics and each other in new ways.

REFERENCES

In addition to works cited in the text, this list contains references about writing in mathematics and in other contexts in order to provide a range of writing theory and practice that may be applicable to mathematics instruction.

Abel, J. P. (1987). *Using writing to teach mathematics.* Paper presented at the annual meeting of the National Council of Teachers of Mathematics, Anaheim, CA.

Ackerman, A. (1987). *Writing across the curriculum: Hints for the math classroom.* Paper presented at the annual meeting of the National Council of Teachers of Mathematics, Anaheim, CA.

Bell, E. S., & Bell, R. N. (1985). Writing and mathematical problem solving: Arguments in favor of synthesis. *School Science and Mathematics, 85,* 210–221.

Britton, J. B., Burgess, T., Martin, N., McLeod, A., & Rosen, H. (1975). *The development of writing abilities (11–18).* London: Macmillan Education Ltd.

Burton, G. M. (1985). Writing as a way of knowing in a mathematics education class. *Arithmetic Teacher, 33,* 40–45.

Cloud, G. (1981). The student journal: Improving basic skills. *Clearing House, 54,* 248–250.

Countryman, J. (1987). *Writing to learn mathematics: Some examples and strategies.* Paper presented at the annual meeting of the National Council of Teachers of Mathematics, Anaheim, CA.

Elbow, P. (1973). *Writing without teachers.* New York: Oxford University Press.

Elbow, P. (1981). *Writing with power.* New York: Oxford University Press.

Emig, J. (1977). Writing as a mode of learning. *College Composition and Communication, 28,* 122–127.

Evans, C. S. (1984). Writing to learn in math. *Language Arts, 61,* 828–835.

Frankenstein, M. (1986, October). *Critical teaching and mathematics.* Paper presented at the Mathematics Conference, Indiana University, Indiana, PA.

Fulwiler, T. (1980). Journals across the disciplines. *English Journal, 69,* 14–19.

Fulwiler, T. (1982). The personal connection: Journal writing across the curriculum. In A. Young & T. Fulwiler (Eds.), *Language connection: Writing and reading across the curriculum* (pp. 15–31). Urbana, IL: National Council of Teachers of English.

Gambrell, L. B. (1985). Dialogue journals: Reading-writing interaction. *The Reading Teacher, 38,* 512–515.

Geeslin, W. E. (1977). Using writing about mathematics as a teaching technique. *The Mathematics Teacher, 70,* 112–115.

Goldberg, D. (1983). Integrating writing into the mathematics curriculum. *Two-Year College Mathematics Journal, 14,* 421–424.

Goodkin, V. (1982). *The intellectual consequences of writing: Writing as a tool for learning.* Unpublished doctoral dissertation, Rutgers University.

Harris, R. J. (1981). *The use of student journals in teaching psychology.* Paper presented at the annual meeting of the Rocky Mountain Psychological Association, Denver, CO.

Hirsch, L. R., & King, B. (1983). *The relative effectiveness of writing assignments in an elementary algebra course for college students.* Paper presented at the annual meeting of the American Educational Research Association, Montreal, Quebec, Canada.

Hodgin, K. W. (1987). *Teaching mathematics through a writing experience approach.* Paper presented at the annual meeting of the National Council of Teachers of Mathematics, Anaheim, CA.

Johnson, M. L. (1983). Writing in mathematics classes: A valuable tool for learning. *Mathematics Teacher, 76,* 117–119.

Juell, P. The course journal. In A. R. Gere (Ed.), *Roots in the sawdust* (pp. 187–201). Urbana, IL: National Council of Teachers of English.

Kennedy, B. (1985). Writing letters to learn math. *Learning, 13,* 58–61.

King, B. (1982). Using writing in the mathematics class: Theory and practice. In C. W. Griffin (Ed.), *New directions for teaching and learning: Teaching writing in all disciplines* (pp. 39–44). San Francisco: Jossey-Bass.

Leahy, R. (1985). The power of the student journal. *College Teaching, 33,* 108–112.

Lipman, M. R. (1981). Mathematics term paper! *Mathematics Teacher, 74,* 453–454.

McMillen, L. (1986). Science and math professors are assigning writing drills to focus students' thinking. *Chronicle of Higher Education, 22,* 19–21.

Mayher, J. S., Lester, N. B., & Pradl, G. M. (1983). *Learning to write/writing to learn.* Upper Montclair, NJ: Boynton/Cook Publishers.

Mett, C. L. (1987). Writing as a learning device in calculus. *Mathematics Teacher, 80,* 534–537.

Montague, H. (1973). Let your students write a book. *Mathematics Teacher, 66,* 548–550.

Nahrgang, C., & Petersen, B. T. (1986). Using writing to learn. *Mathematics Teacher, 79,* 461–465.

Oaks, A. B. (1987). *Effects of the interaction of conception of mathematics and affective constructs on college students in remedial mathematics.* Unpublished doctoral dissertation, University of Rochester.

Pallmann, M. (1982). Verbal language processes in support of learning mathematics. *Mathematics in College,* 49–55.

Platt, M. D. (1975). Writing journals in courses. *College English, 37,* 408–411.

Powell, A. B. (1986). Working with "underprepared" mathematics students. In M. Driscoll & J. Confrey (Eds.), *Teaching mathematics* (pp. 181–192). Portsmouth, New Hampshire: Heinemann.

Reece, S. C. (1980). *The journal keeps the person in the process.* Paper presented at the annual meeting of the Conference on College Composition and Communication, Washington, DC (ERIC Document Reproduction Service No. ED 193 665).

Rose, B. (1988). *Using expressive writing to support the learning of mathematics.* Unpublished doctoral dissertation, University of Rochester.

Sachs, M. C. (1987). *Writing in the mathematics curriculum: Back to basics or something different?* Paper presented at the Ninth Conference on Curriculum Theory and Practice, Dayton, Ohio.

Schmidt, D. (1985). Writing in math class. In A. R. Gere (Ed.), *Roots in the sawdust* (pp. 104–116). Urbana, IL: National Council of Teachers of English.

Selfe, C., & Arbabi, F. (1986). Writing to learn: Engineering student journals. In A. Young & T. Fulwiler (Eds.), *Writing across the disciplines* (pp. 184–191). Upper Montclair, NJ: Boynton/Cook Publishers.

Selfe, C. L., Petersen, B. T., & Nahrgang, C. L. (1986). Journal writing in mathematics. In A. Young & T. Fulwiler (Eds.), *Writing across the disciplines* (pp. 192–207). Upper Montclair, NJ: Boynton/Cook Publishers.

Shaw, J. G. (1983). Mathematics students have a right to write. *Arithmetic Teacher, 30,* 16–18.

Snodgrass, S. E. (1985). Writing as a tool for teaching social psychology. *Teaching of Psychology, 12,* 91–94.

Staton, J. (1983). Dialogue journals: A new tool for teaching communication. *ERIC/CLL News Bulletin, 6,* 1–2.

Stempien, M., & Borasi, R. (1985). Students' writing in mathematics: Some ideas and experiences. *For the Learning of Mathematics, 5,* 14–17.

Vukovich, D. (1985). Ideas in practice: Integrating math and writing through the math journal. *Journal of Developmental Education, 9,* 19–20.

Watson, M. (1980). Writing has a place in a mathematics class. *Mathematics Teacher, 73,* 518–520.

Wisconsin Writing Project. (1983). *A guide to journal writing.* Madison, WI: University of Wisconsin – Madison, School of Education.

Wotring, A. M. (1980). *Writing to think about high school chemistry.* Unpublished master's thesis, George Mason University.

Yinger, R. J., & Clark, C. M. (1981). *Reflective journal writing: Theory and practice.* (ERIC Document Reproduction Service No. ED 208 411)

Yinger, R. (1985). Journal writing as a learning tool. *Volta Review, 87,* 21–33.

Part I

DEFINING PROBLEMS, SEEING POSSIBILITIES

Writing is not salvific. It does not heal all that is lame in learning nor resurrect what is dead. This needs to be said first, so that what *can* be claimed for the role of writing in learning may be honestly appreciated.

In these first three essays, Marcia Birken, Sheila Tobias, and Alan Marwine all begin with caveats: writing exercises are no more valuable than any other form of teaching, says Birken, "unless they allow the student to explore, think, test, take risks, and learn through the process." Tobias warns any writing missionaries who would convert the unbelievers that most mathematics teachers did not gain their own expertise through writing. A way of teaching presumes a way of knowing, adds Marwine, and we must reexamine, as Socrates did, what we believe knowledge is, not simply plug in new teaching gimmicks.

Still, all three speak from experience of the power of writing to alter learning: of its ability to establish interest; to aid conceptual understanding; to improve problem solving; and to integrate present learning with past knowledge, making the connections that transcend rote schooling. Tobias is the first in this volume to emphasize particularly the value of meta-cognitive writing and thinking; Marwine introduces a recurrent distinction throughout the book between using writing for a formal display of knowledge and using it as an informal medium of learning itself; and Birkin speaks to the value of "natural" language in overcoming "the mystique and privacy of mathematical symbolism."

These three essayists all know the problems of "writing to learn," yet each testifies to the value of informal writing (as well as formal writing to display knowledge) in helping students to become mathematicians.

CHAPTER 3

Using Writing to Assist Learning in College Mathematics Classes

Marcia Birken

Seven years ago, when I began to experiment with writing in my mathematics classes at Rochester Institute of Technology, it was difficult to find any literature to support my endeavors. A few articles appeared in journals (Geeslin, 1977) but, although the "writing across the curriculum" movement was growing, mathematics was virtually unaffected. Proponents of using writing to assist learning, primarily members of English departments, either accepted the claims of those mathematicians who insisted their field could not lend itself to writing assignments or felt it was not worth trying to convert those set against using writing. My own colleagues in mathematics and statistics who knew I used writing in college math classes, although occasionally sympathetic to what I was trying to accomplish, predominantly felt I was creating a monster that would make more work for the teacher with little reward for either student or faculty. At best, colleagues congratulated me for my persistence but warned me not to expect them to follow.

I began using writing assignments not to develop students' understanding, but merely as an offshoot of a project in small group learning. I had become discouraged with the traditional lecture format for introductory calculus classes because of the passivity of students. I tried a project utilizing small groups where technical reports were merely an attempt to give each group member some accountability for grading. Seven years later I now only occasionally use small groups, but every mathematics class I teach provides multiple opportunities for students to write.

QUESTIONS ABOUT WRITING IN MATH

Today, attitudes towards writing in the sciences are quite different. Journals, even college mathematics journals, are filled with articles about writing in mathematics and science curricula (Azzolino & Roth, 1987; Goldberg, 1983; Johnson, 1983; King, 1982; Labiance & Reeves, 1985; Nahrgang & Petersen, 1986; Williamson & McAndrew, 1987). Conferences are held featuring, even highlighting, sessions on mathematics and writing. But skeptics question, with justification, whether writing is just the latest fad; whether it will have a measurable effect on mathematical learning; and, if it does have an effect, whether we can incorporate "writing to learn mathematics" into the mainstream of the American mathematics curriculum. Each of these questions deserves careful consideration.

Is Writing in Math a Fad?

Although I am a firm believer in using different types of writing exercises and assignments to help students clarify, analyze, and synthesize mathematics, I think we sometimes unfairly imply that writing is the panacea for all the ills of our curriculum or of our students. With deep conviction and fervor we lecture on the benefits of writing until it has been raised to almost a "cult" status among mathematics professors who employ it actively in class. It is difficult not to see writing as "The Answer" for all students and all teachers when we see such positive results in our own classes, but writing by itself is not a cure-all. Writing exercises are no more beneficial than tests unless they allow the student to explore, think, test, take risks, and learn through the process. Is writing a fad? The answer is yes, for those who blindly imitate another's assignments without tailoring them to their own curricula and students. And again the answer is yes for those who are forced by a higher level administration to implement writing assignments of any type without being asked for input.

There are many effective ways to teach college mathematics, there are many outstanding mathematics professors who will never utilize writing, and there are many college students who will master the intricacies of theoretical mathematical understanding without writing about them in English prose. After all, none of the brilliant faculty under whom I studied ever heard of "writing to learn" when they were students. It is important not to legislate teaching style, nor to take one concept and hold of it expectations that can never be met. With these caveats in mind, I will state affirmatively that I think writing is not a fad; its impact on mathematics can be strong, but it does not have to be universally applied, and it should not be forced.

Furthermore, the impact I most hope for from learning about mathematics through written language is that the mystique and privacy of mathematical symbolism can be opened up to a wider student audience. This should be the goal of our educational system, but there has always been a segment of the mathematical community that holds that those who understand mathematics should be part of the "closed group" and those who fall by the wayside in college math classes didn't belong there in the first place. The concept of "the mathematical elite," those privileged few who hold the knowledge, and hence the power, in the mathematics classroom, drives many students from pursuing further mathematical study, even when they have enjoyed a course. It is difficult to want to engage in learning when one cannot communicate in the same sophisticated mathematical language that others have adopted as their private language. Adding English, a common language for communication, to the mathematics class has the possibility of allowing more students to enter the dialogue and find success in mathematical thinking.

How Can Effectiveness Be Measured?

The second question of the skeptic—how do we measure the effect writing has on learning mathematics—is for me the most crucial question, and one that has been ignored for too long. Along with most of my colleagues at conferences, when questioned about statistical proof of the effectiveness of what I do, I take comfort in the fact that at least I am trying to improve the quality of learning in the classroom, but I respond with answers like "there is no time," "there is no support to set up a study," or "yes, I think someone should be publishing research data in journals mathematicians read." Although I am confident that my students learn more about mathematics when they write and my students confirm repeatedly, both formally through questionnaires and informally in discussion, that they have a much deeper level of understanding of the concepts in a course and the connections between these concepts and between related courses when they write, it is time to set up research studies and publish the results.

More effort has to be put into formalizing our talk of success if we expect others to be willing to put time, resources, and effort into improving mathematics classes through writing. Granted, some of the success our students find through writing may be difficult to measure, since depth of understanding and facility with symbolic language is not easily discerned through standard testing procedures, but more grant proposals and research dollars must be focused on studies that will provide data both to teachers who are skeptical of trying something new and to administrators who grant promotions, raises, and professional development leaves.

The faculty teaching remedial math courses and employing "writing to learn" in community and public colleges have a head start in publishing in this area, since they are often forced to be accountable to state legislators and taxpayers when budgets are set. Many of them have the statistics to back up claims of success, and some journal articles are surfacing that show this research. But more kinds of research, across a wider student base, must be done and the results published in "mainstream" mathematical journals if we expect to attract the attention of the broad spectrum of mathematics faculty.

How Can Writing Be Incorporated?

The final question of how to implement writing to learn in the mathematics curriculum is the easiest one to answer since there is no single correct response. The variety of writing that students can do in mathematics courses is astounding, and each type has benefits. I agree with Paul Connolly who stated in his opening remarks at a 1987 Conference on Writing to Learn Mathematics and Science that informal writing must be used to allow students to explore their mathematical understanding and gain ownership of knowledge. Yet informal writing does not provide the only framework within which to do this. A variety of opportunities for language-based learning will make writing, both in class and outside, appealing to students and faculty.

To clarify the difference between informal and formal writing I would like to refer to the three categories proposed by James Britton, an early advocate of writing across the curriculum, who suggests that writing can be divided according to purpose (Britton, Burgess, Martin, McLeod, & Rosen, 1975):

POETIC WRITING

This is language used as art, not constrained by any particular rules of usage. Examples might be fiction, poetry, song and drama, and the writings of James Joyce and e. e. cummings can be cited as exhibits. The features of poetic writing include varied forms and imaginative and often unconventional styles. (p. 161)

EXPRESSIVE WRITING

The purpose of this writing is for the writer to explore what he or she thinks, feels or knows. Examples would be journals, diaries, first drafts, and letters to friends where the writer is revealing his or her own thought process. It is informal, often characterized by first person pronouns and is close to speech. It is a written expression of the internal thinking process. (p. 90)

TRANSACTIONAL WRITING

The purpose of transactional writing is to communicate to an audience, to inform, persuade or instruct them. Examples would be reports, proposals, memos, term papers and essay exams and the features of this type of writing include clear, audience based, conventional prose. (p. 160)

I have used various types of expressive and transactional writing assignments in my math classes at Rochester Institute of Technology (RIT) to spark interest in the subject, to show students how math will be used after they graduate from college, and to aid students in synthesizing, analyzing, and understanding mathematical concepts. I have come to believe that transactional writing, also referred to by some as formal writing (to distinguish it from expressive or informal writing) is another mode in which the writer can explore, think through, and learn. In fact, I have found *both* transactional and expressive assignments to be effective vehicles for encouraging student learning.

PURPOSES OF WRITING IN MATH

RIT is a highly technical four-year, private university where students in almost all majors take math courses. Many majors have required sequences of seven or eight math courses. Mathematics is taught here, in general, in a traditional lecture format, with many students beginning a four-quarter calculus sequence when they arrive as freshmen. Students are usually goal-oriented and think of themselves as fairly good technicians, often disdaining the required liberal arts courses they must take. In the mathematics classroom these students minimize risk-taking, exploration, and self-revelation on paper, particularly revelation about misunderstanding or lack of understanding. On the other hand, when students understand that a formal technical report is due at the end of the quarter, it is much easier to get them writing in a variety of expressive or informal modes from the beginning. Drafts of their technical reports provide an effective mechanism, furthermore, for gaining deeper understanding and engaging in dialogue with the professor.

I began working at RIT eleven years ago in the Learning Development Center where my major responsibilities included working in a math lab, developing curricula for students unable to handle traditional mathematics classes, and teaching as an adjunct to the mathematics department, so I have broad experience with students who struggle to understand mathematics. Two years ago I accepted a full-time faculty position in the Mathematics Department of the College of Science and now teach higher level courses. It has been fascinating for me to discover that students in Calculus IV struggle in the same way students in Remedial Algebra do; the only difference is the outward appearance of mathematical sophistication. When I ask students to relate extrema problems in three dimensions back to problems studied in Calculus I in two dimensions, I am met with the same blank faces that I saw in Remedial Algebra when I asked students to relate algebraic fractions back to adding simple fractions. Students see topics in mathematics as unrelated steps rather than as building blocks of knowledge. Little opportunity exists in the fast pace of college courses for professors to reflect on past learning, to tie together concepts, or more importantly, to ask students to make these connections on their own. This is where I see the greatest and most lasting value for writing in mathematics classes.

But writing can serve other purposes as well. I've tried various techniques to motivate students in class, such as the aforementioned small-group work, extra-credit projects, and oral presentations, but I have always come back to writing assignments as the most successful way to involve students in the concepts they are studying. Writing can revive the bored students and provide a less threatening activity for the student who is math-anxious or has a lower skill level. For the strong math student, writing is a chance to show creativity. Informal writing allows for reflection and analysis of a day's lecture, as well as an opportunity to vent frustrations and explore where understanding broke down.

The higher level math student who runs into his or her first mathematical stumbling block needs the same type of assistance that a weak or remedial student needs: a personalized method of understanding the topic. If my explanation is unclear, then the student needs to internalize the concept and construct his or her own attempt at explanation. Writing about the blockage, about the problem, or just writing in prose about the professor's steps to solution can aid in bringing about some clarity.

Transactional writing may require students to use mathematical knowledge in an applied setting and to analyze answers and make decisions. The answer often matters less than the problem-solving strategy or the analysis of the situation. The same type of logical order is needed to work through a problem from statement to solution as is needed to construct a well-organized essay. Some features of essay writing include focusing a paragraph with a topic sentence, progressing through multiple paragraphs in a coherent thought pattern, and closing an essay with a summary statement. This parallels the formal process of a mathematical argument. Doing both simultaneously seems to reinforce the problem-solving process.

In some of the projects I assign, students must communicate with one another or with me in order to complete the assignment. Sometimes a group or the entire class is charged to come to consensus on the answer to a problem before beginning to write about what they have learned, what they have done, or how they differed in approach. Thus, writing about mathematics can allow students to begin to engage in discourses about mathematics in the same way professors do in a colloquium setting.

TYPES OF WRITING IN MATH

The types of writing my students may encounter in a quarter include some or all of the following:

- Short, in-class writings, usually expressive or informal
- Homework problems to interpret or analyze, or homework assignments calling for reflection on a concept
- Essay questions on tests and departmental final exams
- Formal (transactional) technical reports

Not every course will have the same number of assignments, nor will multiple sections of the same course necessarily even have the same type of assignments. I do not grade informal writing, but I always respond to it. Here is where I learn the most about my students, and it is crucial that students feel their opinions, queries, or confusions are worthy of the professor's time and consideration. I do grade formal writing, in particular essay questions and technical reports. While essay questions are usually graded for mathematical content over grammatical structure, the formal, transactional technical report is graded in three areas: mathematics, English, and analysis.

In-Class Writings

To start students writing early in the quarter I usually select a problem that the class solves in groups. Armed with *the answer*, each student writes a short paragraph explaining to his or her roommate how to solve this problem. (See Assignment 1 in the Appendix for an example.) Students exchange papers, comment on them, and have a few minutes to rewrite. I collect the papers and add my comments or suggestions, and sometimes make immediate referrals to the Writing Lab on campus if a student cannot put two connected thoughts together.

Another in-class writing task, which I call the "logical order question," is presented in a generic version applicable to any level of mathematics as in Assignment 2 in the Appendix. Here the student works with two sheets of paper on which are posed the same problem at the top. On sheet 1 the student writes mathematical steps to solution, while on sheet 2 she writes English sentences or phrases that correspond to the mathematical steps. Pairs of students (who have different problems of the same type to solve) then exchange English pages and on a third piece of paper must follow their partner's English and convert sentences and phrases back to mathematical steps. At the end, partners compare answers and usually discover that the translation became garbled from the sender to the receiver. Rarely do answers agree, and it is the responsibility of the pair to decide where communication broke down.

Homework Assignments

Assignment 3 in the Appendix is a three-part reflective homework assignment I recently gave in which students in a matrix algebra class were struggling to come to their own understanding of the purpose and structure of mathematical proof, using an induction proof as an illustration. First, students had to come up with their own independent ideas about the purpose of proof, comment on their feelings about doing formal proof, as well as comment about how they saw mathematicians using formal proof. In the second part they outlined in prose an induction proof for their problem, and in the third part they used a "split page" with a formal induction proof in mathematical symbols on one side and English phrases and sentences to explain their steps on the other side. Each part of this assignment was handed in separately, and the students received comments and feedback from me before proceeding to the next part.

Essay Questions

Essay questions on exams are simple to construct, but not so simple to grade. Should the student be graded on grammar, spelling, and sentence structure or merely on the mathematical content? What about the essay that is so poorly written that you are unsure of what the student is trying to say? What about the student who refuses to write prose and attempts to answer the question in mathematical symbolism? Despite these problems, I continue to include one essay question on almost all of my exams. Assignment 4 in the Appendix includes a classic Calculus II question: Explain how the Fundamental Theorem of Calculus relates the indefinite and the definite integrals. Before the exam I usually give the students two or three possible examples of questions that could appear.

Formal Technical Reports

Assignments 5A, B, and C in the Appendix illustrate the formal technical report. I wish I had the time and strength to give this assignment to every class, but it does require class time for adequate preparation and a great deal of "teacher-time" if students do extensive rewriting in the draft stage. This transactional writing task not only requires the student to think through a problem from the beginning to end, draw conclusions, interpret mathematical answers, and construct a logical, well-ordered explanation, but also allows the students to reflect on their mathematical thinking, revise their thinking after consultation with peers or the professor, and experiment and play with mathematics as they might in later careers.

I spend at least half of one class period explaining to students the principles of technical writing (Houp & Pearsall, 1980; Lannon, 1982):

- The purpose of technical writing is to convey a single meaning without ambiguity.
- Clarity takes precedence over being interesting.
- The main task is to get the facts down in a logical order.
- The emphasis is on brevity, precision, consistency, audience, and style.
- The sentence structure is short and succinct.

I tell the students to expect to rewrite. I suggest they use the Writing Lab for assistance, if needed, and I give written guidelines and reminders with an assignment. Students respond so positively about what they have learned in mathematics from doing this type of writing that I feel it confirms placing transactional writing within the category of "writing to learn."

CONCLUSIONS

In trying to summarize the benefits my students have derived from writing in mathematics classes, I reflect on the many students who have told me they never before thought about what they did or why they did it while problem solving. Since writing requires the ability to communicate (even if only to oneself) a process or an idea, most students comment that they have a deeper understanding, further clarity, and better retention of concepts after writing. Writing allows students to explore the constructs of a foreign language (mathematics) using a language in which most are fluent.

Fortunately, the benefits of having my students learn mathematics through writing have been as many and positive for me as for my students.

I've learned a great deal about students' mathematical misconceptions, and I can usually pinpoint exactly where their thinking went wrong and help to redirect it. I find writing generates an enthusiasm in the classroom and changes students from passive learners to active thinker-participants. Most important, writing allows students to engage deeply in the content of a course in a way that tests and quizzes simply cannot, while providing a new forum in which to engage in discussion about their mathematical thinking, perception of the course, and interest in the subject.

APPENDIX

Assignment 1. In-Class Assignment

A rope is tied tightly around the equator of the earth. A second rope is tied around the earth in a circle one foot in the air above the first rope. Assuming that the earth is spherical and that you could rise directly into space above the North Pole, your "bird's eye" view of the situation appears below. How much longer is the second rope than the first rope?

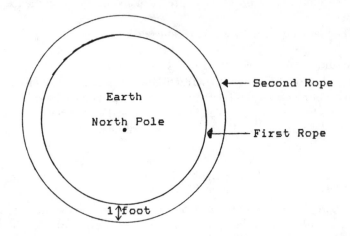

Write a one-paragraph explanation to your roommate of how to solve this problem. Remember, your roommate is most concerned with the process of solution, not with a numerical answer.

Assignment 2. Logical Order Question

[This assignment consists of two worksheets; the following six shapes are reproduced on the upper half of both sheets.]

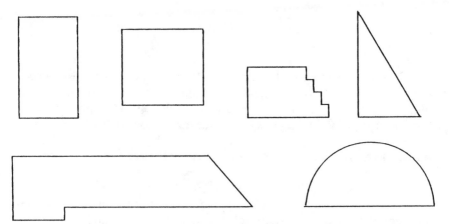

Instructions for Sheet 1. On this sheet of paper construct a geometric design using the six shapes given above. You must use all of the shapes, without repeating any shape, and keep their relative scale. You may turn, translate, rotate, reflect, or otherwise move the given shapes in any manner you feel satisfies your artistic desires.

Instructions for Sheet 2. On this sheet of paper write down, in English, the steps that are necessary to create your design. No drawing should take place on this sheet of paper — only instructions given in English sentences. Be explicit enough that someone else can follow your instructions and recreate your artistic masterpiece.

Assignment 3. Matrix Algebra Formal Proof

Part 1. The following is one example of a mathematical statement:

$$(A^T)^T = A$$

Using any mathematical statement from Chapter one or two of our textbook, write one to two paragraphs that explain the difference between giving an example of your mathematical statement and proving your mathematical statement. Include how you would feel about formally proving the statement, why you think proof is required on the syllabus, and why you think mathematicians think proof is important.

Part 2. Using the problem below write a paragraph (in English, not mathematics) that explains what would be involved in an induction proof for this problem. Also, outline the three steps to the induction proof using English sentences or phrases.

Problem: Use mathematical induction to prove that if A is an $(n+1)\times$ $(n+1)$ matrix with two identical rows, then $\det(A)=0$.

Part 3.   Solve the problem in Part 2 using a "split page" to do your induction proof. On the lefthand side of the paper write out the mathematical steps to the proof. On the righthand side keep a running commentary (in prose) of your thoughts and/or feelings as you write out the proof.

Assignment 4. Essay Question on Calculus II Test

We have just finished studying the Fundamental Theorem of Calculus. Write one to two paragraphs explaining why this theorem is so named and how it links the indefinite integral (antiderivative) and the definite integral.

Assignment 5. Technical Reports

Problem 1.   Your company, Hi-Tek Security Systems, has been selected to provide a fencing system for a triangular-shaped office park bordered on one side by route 490 and on the other side by the barge canal. The canal and highway are at right angles to each other, as shown in the picture above. In order to secure the park, the fence running along the third side (hypoteneuse) of the right triangle must connect to already existing fencing along the full length of the highway and the canal. Additionally, the fencing must go through the guard's station at point P, which is located 9 miles east and 3 miles north of the intersection of the highway and the canal.

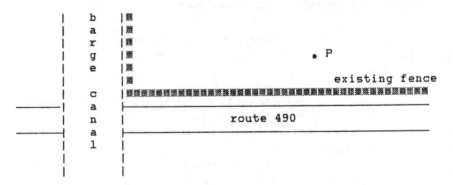

1. What is the smallest area (measured in square miles) that can be enclosed by such a fence?
2. What is the largest area that can be enclosed?

Write a two- to five-page technical report that clearly states the problem you are trying to solve, describes the method of solution, and analyzes the solution in order to answer the two questions above. You will be graded in three areas, mathematics, English, and analysis. You may work with anyone in the class (including the instructor) to solve the problem mathematically, but you are to have no mathematical help from outside sources.

Problem 2. During the construction of a barn and silo our company decided to use a scale model to aid in making decisions about the dimensions of the structures. The scale model is constructed from a piece of cardboard 4″ by 36″ that simulates the amount of wood available for the sides of the barn and silo.

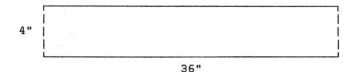

The piece of cardboard must be cut as follows:

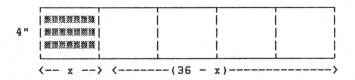

The shaded portion is rolled into a cylinder without top or bottom to simulate the silo, while the unshaded portion is to be folded along the equally spaced dotted lines to make a box without top or bottom to simulate the barn.

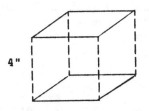

x = circumference of circle which forms bottom of cylinder

36 − x = perimeter of square which forms bottom of box

Find where the cardboard should be cut so that the total volume enclosed by the barn and silo is maximized.

Write a two- to five-page technical report that clearly states the problem you are trying to solve, describes the method of solution, and analyzes the solution in order to completely answer the question above. You will be graded in three areas: mathematics, English, and analysis.

Problem 3. A powerhouse is located on one bank of a straight river that is one mile wide. A mill is located on the other side of the river, ten miles downstream from a point P which is exactly opposite the powerhouse.

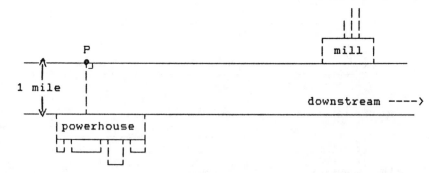

The cost of underwater cable is $5 per foot, while the cost of land cable is $3 per foot. Find a route for laying cable from the powerhouse to the mill that minimizes cable costs by finding how far downstream from point P the overland cable should begin.

Write a two- to five-page technical report that gives an explanation of the assigned project and provides a mathematical solution. Be clear about what each variable stands for and how you determine equation(s). Explain all major steps in the mathematical solution, but avoid a blow-by-blow account of each line. Use illustrative diagrams as necessary. Keep in mind that your audience is unfamiliar with the assigned project, but does have an understanding of calculus.

As a final part of your report, consider the following:

1. A second mill is located five miles downstream from point P.
2. A third mill is located one-half mile downstream from point P.

Assuming that cable costs remain the same, find routes for laying cable to both the second and third mills so that cable costs are minimized. Again, minimize the costs by finding how far downstream from point P to begin the overland cable. Discuss any similarities and differences in the cable routes for the three mills. Explain what role point P plays in choosing a cable route.

REFERENCES

Azzolino, A., & Roth, R. (1987, Fall/Winter). Questionbooks: Using writing to learn mathematics. *AMATYC Review*:9.

Britton, J., Burgess, T., Martin, N., Mcleod, A., & Rosen, H. (1975). *The development of writing abilities (11-18)*. London: Macmillan.

Geeslin, W. E. (1977). Using writing about mathematics as a teaching technique. *Mathematics Teacher, 70*(2), 112-115.

Goldberg, D. (1983). Integrating writing into the mathematics curriculum. *Two-Year College Mathematics Journal, 14*(5), 421-424.

Houp, K. W., & Pearsall, T. E. (1980). *Reporting technical information* (4th ed.). Beverly Hills, CA: Glencoe Press.

Johnson, M. L. (1983). Writing in the mathematics classes: A valuable tool of learning. *Mathematics Teacher, 76*(2), 117-119.

King, B. (1982, December). Using writing in the mathematics class: theory and practice. In C. W. Griffin (Ed.), *New directions for teaching and learning: Teaching writing in all disciplines* (p. 12). San Francisco: Jossey-Bass.

Labiance, D., & Reeves, W. (1985). Writing across the curriculum: the science segment—a heretical perspective. *Journal of Chemical Education, 62*, 400-402.

Lannon, J. M. (1982). *Technical writing* (2nd ed.). Boston: Little, Brown.

Nahrgang, C., & Petersen, B. (1986). Using writing to learn mathematics. *Mathematics Teacher, 79*(6), 461-465.

Williamson, M., & McAndrew, D. (1987). Writing in college developmental mathematics. *Research & Teaching in Developmental Education, 3*(1), 14-21.

CHAPTER 4

Writing to Learn
Science and Mathematics

Sheila Tobias

Though writing to learn science and mathematics may appear to be
an obvious innovation, our task is likely to be a most difficult one. We must
persuade a group of teachers who themselves did not learn science and
mathematics this way, that writing to learn is not only useful but essential
for a certain type of student. From the scientists' point of view, there
already *is* an equivalent to writing to learn in science and mathematics.
That equivalent is problem-sets. Practitioners will surely argue that problem solving causes students to come to grips with their incomplete understanding in an active and self-stimulating fashion. What more could writing offer?

Indeed, when science instructors write on the chalkboard at the beginning of the semester the old truism: "I see and I forget. I hear and I
remember. I do and I understand," by *do* they mean doing problems and
doing experiments. When writing instructors think *do*, we imagine the
student constructing a personalized understanding of the subject by means
of the written or spoken phrase.

I have long been aware of the contrast between a scientist's view of
writing and my own. Clear, precise statements, closely reasoned argument, unambiguous and very often felicitous use of language are much
admired and sought after among scientists. But writing, to *them*, is a kind
of aftermath of thought or work; not the means to understanding. In one
of my more whimsical moments as a visitor to a mathematics teachers'
convention, I once suggested that since one source of students' alienation is
how the subject is evaluated, it might be wise for mathematics teachers to
alter not just their pedagogy but their grading system. My proposal was
that they offer one-third credit for a right answer, one-third (elastic) credit
for finding a variety of ways to get to that answer, and one-third credit for
an essay, perhaps only one paragraph in length, in which the student

48

would be asked to reflect on "what makes this problem mathematically interesting."

While educators committed to writing to learn readily see the value of such an approach, the math–science people I talked to were appalled to realize that in my system a student could get a right answer and still *fail*.

WRITING STYLES IN SCIENCE AND MATH

Just as writing is unlikely to be seen as a way to learn science and math, reading has a different pedagogical use in science as well. Even a cursory examination of math and science textbooks reveals that these books are not meant to be *read* as we understand the act of reading. Authors of math or science texts follow rules of rhetoric uniquely their own. As I write elsewhere (Tobias, 1987), clarity in books on other subjects is achieved through repetition, using different words to restate a single idea, slowing the pace, using a spiral kind of organization that keeps coming back to the same idea at different levels, using topic and summary sentences to nail down what the paragraph contains, and always foreshadowing the point to be made later on. In math and science texts, we find, instead, pages of information with virtually no repetition, no varying of pace, few topic and concluding sentences, as few words as possible, written with the expectation that the reader will not proceed to the next sentence or point without having thoroughly mastered the one at hand. It is not that the author wants to keep the reader in the dark. It is rather that in mathematical writing clarification is achieved by constructing very precise sentences without any extra words.

This writing style is by design. Mathematics and science teachers expect students to read slowly and with a pencil, constructing their understanding as they go along. They are not supposed to attend to, certainly not to be distracted by, context, connotation, or any other aspects of spoken language. Spoken language, rather, is a temporary scaffolding to be discarded in favor of symbolic language as soon as the new code is mastered.

Thus, to the extent that writing is perceived to be a *substitute* for either problem solving or mastering the code, I believe science and mathematics instructors will resist writing to learn.

TECHNIQUES FOR USING WRITING TO LEARN

Still, there is a case to be made for writing to learn mathematics and science. My own relation to writing to learn began with a study of mathematics anxiety and avoidance in the 1970s. It appeared to me (and others) that failure to succeed at "quantitative studies" — mathematics by another name — had become a most serious barrier to the educational and occupational mobility of women and minority students. At the time I began my research, people who did not do well in mathematics (or science) were considered simply "dumb in math." My program found differences in learning styles, attitudes, and confidence levels instead (Tobias, 1976, 1978; Tobias & Weissbrod, 1980). By teaching students to pay attention to their past experiences with mathematics, to the random thoughts that intrude upon their concentration, and to their errors, we were able to move them from a paralyzing fear of mathematics back into the mathematics classroom.

Our experiential findings confirmed in part the "misconceptions" literature, which indicates that students bring with them models of the universe that, because they are so deep-seated and comfortably familiar, remain entrenched even after new information and new conceptual models have been learned (Kilpatrick, 1987).

All of this suggested that getting students to *write* about their feelings and their misconceptions would relieve their anxiety and help them unlearn models and techniques that were no longer useful to them. Eventually, they could approach the new with confidence. That, you might think, would constitute a very strong case for employing writing to learn in science and mathematics. My research, however, is only suggestive, and our techniques, which are described below, may only have worked because our math-anxious and math-avoidant clients were already predisposed to verbal expression.

The Comfort/Noncomfort Zones

Since my work in "mathematics anxiety" initially began in an effort to identify the reasons that otherwise intelligent and school-successful students had a task-specific disability in mathematics (Tobias, 1976), my colleagues and I were dealing with students who had at least one area — a "comfort zone" — in which they studied efficiently and well. It was our task to dissuade them of the prevailing view, and one that they had internalized; namely, that they were "dumb in math" (or science) congenitally. We wanted to get them to think of their problem as partially self-imposed. Many techniques were invented to help students deal with their math anxiety, but all of them had in common some kind of self-monitoring. We urged students to watch themselves doing mathematics and to contrast their learning style with study habits they employed in their "comfort zones." Math, we had them hypothesize, was but a "noncomfort zone" for them and needed to be treated as such.

One technique involved nothing more complicated than keeping a journal of the time, the circumstances, and the kind of stress they experienced in doing mathematics in contrast to, say, writing a paper (which most of these students did very well and with pleasure). Following is an example of how one student expressed her contrasting feelings:

> When I have a paper to write, I clear my desk, sharpen my pencils, give the children pizza money and tell them not to come home before 10 P.M. I *allow* myself actually to enjoy the work. When I have math homework to do, I find myself sharing the kitchen table with one of my children, doing calculations on bits of paper, losing track of my thought process and of my confidence.

And here are the comfort/noncomfort zone notes from another:

> I never give up on a "problem" in the life of my child just because a beginning strategy doesn't work. I have lots of alternate approaches to try. But doing math, I tend to quit when the going gets rough, even if that happens right away.

After doing the comfort/noncomfort zone exercise, students would return to their math-anxiety discussion group with real insights into how they were disserving themselves in handling mathematics (and science). By comparing strategies in the two zones, they would eventually devise new ways of working. This entailed noticing, as mentioned above, that a mathematics or science text needs to be approached differently; also, that they set higher standards for themselves in their noncomfort zone than elsewhere. Getting a pretty decent first draft in three hours at the writing table would give them a feeling of accomplishment. "Making a little headway" in math in the same amount of time would not. Reviewing, revising, and learning to be critical of their own thinking was the essence of math-anxiety reduction once students had been motivated to try mathematics again.

The Divided-Page Exercise

Another device, more focused on the learning task, we called "the divided-page exercise," by means of which students learned through journal writing to "tune in" to their feelings, their negative self-statements, and their confusions. Similar benefits from having mathematics students hand in their journals instead of exams have been reported by Selfe et al. (1986). Our goal was to get them to make better use of their teachers by becoming more precise in posing questions. But we were also concerned that they slowly become independent of their teachers as well.

In their journals, the lefthand side of the page was reserved for "thinking out loud," including (never excluding) what might seem irrelevant to the teacher. They used the righthand side of the page for straightforward laying out of problems, sketches, and calculations. While initially the students' divided-pages were filled with emotional detritus, they soon began to focus rather on posing and answering two kinds of questions of themselves: (1) What is making this problem difficult for me? (2) What could *I* do to make it easier for myself?

To illustrate, a student was given the following problem: A car goes 20,000 miles on a long trip, rotating its five tires (including the spare) regularly and frequently. How many miles will any one tire have driven on the road?

His comments on the left-hand side of the page: as he worked on solving the problem were as follows:

> I assume there is a formula for solving this problem, but I have forgotten (if I ever knew) what it is.
> I am being confused by the word "rotate." Simply by driving, we cause our tires to turn or "rotate" on the road. But "rotate" means something else in this problem. I had better concentrate on that.
> I wonder how many miles each tire will have gone while in the trunk? Is this a useful approach? Let me try.

Indeed, while not exactly orthodox, trying to find the number of miles any one tire will have traveled in the trunk of the car is a productive approach. Twenty thousand miles, divided by five tires, equals four thousand miles per tire in the trunk. Subtracting four thousand miles from the total of twenty thousand miles driven, yields the correct answer: each tire, rotated into the four on-road positions during the trip will have traveled in total sixteen thousand miles.

Peer Perspectives

By 1981 I had come to realize how useful the perspective of any outsider might be to the problems of math and science pedagogy. Turning to the physical sciences I decided to invite groups of highly educated, confident newcomers to science, namely professors in the humanities, the arts, social science, and even law, to attend artificially constructed learning experiences in physics, mathematics, and chemistry (Tobias, 1985, 1986, and 1988; also Tobias & Hake, 1988). Again, the divided-page format was employed to encourage these "peers," as I called them (since in every way except newness to the fields, they were peers of their instructors), to note in as much detail as possible what were the barriers to learning that were getting in their way. From their notes, they wrote long narratives incorporating their on-site observations. Their narratives were wide-ranging. They touched on the instructor's use of language, ambiguities in demonstrations, confounding of abstract and concrete examples, the uses of mathematics in science, and so on.

A biologist wrote after a session on waves in elastic media:

> I had difficulty picturing the presumably familiar phenomena that were used to illustrate more abstract concepts, such as oscillating springs. I could follow what was being described, but I could not grasp what was actually happening in what was being described. It was like seeing without any faculty of intelligent perception.

A philosopher commented on a lecture on relativity:

> I think the problem of definitions is particularly important for physics. One starts out being aware that "ordinary" words will have special meanings and the meanings of some words may be quite different from what they are in other uses. When [Professor] Mel Shochet started talking about "static measurement," I was a bit nervous. Did he mean measuring something that is still and not moving? Or some special kind of measuring called "static?" I didn't know then and still don't know.

A theologian was confused by not knowing what to *look for* in the demonstrations. He wrote after the sessions:

> One question the demonstrations did not answer for me was the relation of formulas to experiment. Sometimes it seemed that the initial and "crucial" experiments led to the discovery of theory. At other times, one felt that the experiment merely illustrated a known formula, which is really quite different. The old positivist distinction between the logic of discovery and the logic of justification came to mind. The questions I kept jotting down were: how are the formulas derived? Do the experiments *reveal* them? Do they *confirm* them? Or do they *illustrate* them to subsequent generations? Or, all three?

The comments made by peers suggest other uses for these outside observers: as critics of textbooks, as writers of supplementary materials, as learner-advocates.

Minute Papers about Muddiest Points

Writing to learn science and mathematics may have another progenitor in an educational innovation having to do with increasing student feedback to college teachers. As reported by K. Patricia Cross (1987) in an unpublished paper, a physics professor at the University of California employs what he calls "minute papers." Four or five times a semester, Cross reports, the instructor stops class one minute early to ask students to write the answers to two questions: What is the most significant thing you learned today? What question is uppermost in your mind at the conclusion of this class session? The professor says this simple feedback device guides him as to how well students are understanding and whether there are important questions left unanswered.

Fred Mosteller, professor of statistics at Harvard, has devised a modification of this feedback device. At the end of some self-contained unit in his introductory course, he asks students to write a few sentences on the "muddiest point" in the material just covered. On the basis of this information, Mosteller provides a handout for his next session or reworks his next set of lectures. Both techniques require writing full sentences and even paragraphs. Both result in some amount of self-monitoring, analysis, and assessment through expression.

CONCLUSIONS

None of these experiments is systematic. Nor are the designs sufficiently controlled so that we who do them can bring any more than anecdotal evidence to bear on the subjects we observe. However, *writing* as a means of self-exploration in mathematics and science learning does seem to achieve two important goals: It provides classroom-based specific feedback, and it gives students opportunity to and experience in identifying and trying to unravel their own misconceptions.

REFERENCES

Cross, K. P. (1987, April 20). *Using assessment to improve instruction*. The deGarmo Lecture for the Society of Professors of Education, presented at the AERA annual meeting, Washington, DC.

Kilpatrick, J. (1987, Summer). Inquiry in the mathematics classroom. *Academic Connections*, pp. 1–5. (See also the bibliography on the "misconceptions literature" appended to the article.)

Selfe, C. L., Petersen, B. T., & Nahrgang, C. L. (1986). Journal writing in mathematics. In A. Young & T. Fulwiler (Eds.), *Writing across the disciplines: Research and practice* (pp. 192–207). Upper Montclair, NJ: Boynton/Cook.

Tobias, S. (1976, September). Math anxiety: Why is a smart girl like you counting on your fingers? *Ms. Magazine*, pp. 56–62.

Tobias, S. (1978). *Overcoming math anxiety.* New York: W. W. Norton.

Tobias, S. (1985, June). Math anxiety and physics: The problem of teaching "difficult" subjects. *Physics Today,* pp. 61–66.

Tobias, S. (1986, March/April). Peer perspectives on teaching. *Change,* pp. 36–41.

Tobias, S. (1987). *Succeed with math: Every student's guide to conquering math anxiety.* New York: The College Board.

Tobias, S. (1988, February). Peer perspectives on physics. *The Physics Teacher,* pp. 77–80.

Tobias, S., & Hake, R. R. (1988). Professors as physics students: What can they teach us? *American Journal of Physics, 56*(9), 786–794.

Tobias, S., & Weissbrod, C. (1980). Anxiety and mathematics: an update. *Harvard Educational Review, 50*(1), 63–70.

CHAPTER 5

Reflections on the Uses
of Informal Writing

Alan Marwine

Since 1985, the Bard Institute for Writing and Thinking has offered
workshops for teachers of science and mathematics that permit us to explore the ways in which writing might facilitate learning in those disciplines. My own exploration of the uses of writing began when teaching
weeklong Language and Thinking workshops for entering freshmen at
Simon's Rock of Bard College, and it continued when teaching the three-
week Language and Thinking workshops for entering freshmen at Bard
College. During those workshops, I was forced to confront many unfamiliar texts from all disciplines, and I discovered that writing facilitated my
understanding and deepened my appreciation for them. I observed similar
positive effects for the students and also observed the growth of an environment where collaboration and sharing were the rule rather than the exception. Although we may not often take the time to ground what we do in
theory, let me begin with my own theory as it has grown out of my
experiences as a workshop leader and classroom teacher, because such a
theory may help explain why particular techniques attract me, and may
help you decide whether to adopt any particular exercise.

KNOWLEDGE AS RECOLLECTION

Ever since I first read Plato's dialogue *Meno* (1977), I have found
myself drawn to a theory of knowing revealed by Socrates just as he is
about to embark on a very famous lesson in geometry. Socrates tells Meno
that learning is a process whereby one is reminded of what one already
knows (p. 303). In order to "prove" that doctrine to Meno, Socrates pro-
ceeds to question Meno's slave boy about the problem of doubling the size
of a square. Two preconditions are required for such a proof: that the slave

boy have no prior instruction in geometry, and that he speak Greek. Socrates asks the following question: What is the length of a line which, when squared, would produce a square double the size of the one drawn in the sand? Through careful questioning, during which he makes several mistakes, the boy comes to see that the square can be doubled by taking a length equal to the diagonal of the original square. Moreover, he is certain that he has discovered the right answer by himself because the questions have been artfully arranged by Socrates to take advantage of his mistakes. Though the slave boy could never have embarked alone on such an adventure, he is quite certain of the answer when he finds it. Having performed this demonstration many times on unsuspecting friends who also knew no geometry, the patterns of responses, including the mistakes and the outcome, are quite identical to those in the dialogue. My friends are convinced that they know the correct answer, and they experience some pleasure at having discovered it themselves.

It is certainly true that such an understanding does not exhaust the interesting problems of the diagonal and though Socrates admits that the "proof" is not yet secure through lack of practice he also claims as follows:

> If he were repeatedly asked these same questions in a variety of forms, you know he will have in the end as exact an understanding of them as anyone. Without anyone having taught him, and only through questions put to him, he will understand, recovering the knowledge out of himself. (p. 319)

While there are undoubtedly many important aspects of this claim worth exploring, the first might involve disputing the assertion that the slave boy has not been *taught* by this method of questioning.

"Of course," one might say, "the boy never knew the answer, but he has been taught it nonetheless. The *method* was strange, and time-consuming, but it is only a different method. Teaching is a matter of imparting facts, information, and interpretations, and the facts in this case were simply the questions that Socrates (who of course was already in possession of the answer) asked of the slave boy. The clear advantage that Socrates possessed was that he was able to alter his questions to suit the slave boy's mistakes and *guide* him to the discovery of the correct answer. The slave boy certainly never knew the answer, if only because he had never thought to put such questions to himself."

Perhaps this is a fair, if brief, rebuttal. If so, we may have noted a difference in tone between the words "impart" and "guide" that could be considered further. As lecturers, we certainly "impart" and from experience that enables us to anticipate the problems students have with the subject matter, we also, in our lectures, try to "guide." If Socrates has any advantage as a guide, it is in his sure knowledge of the position of the slave boy because he uses the boy's mistakes as his own guide to formulating the next question. In Plato's *Phaedrus* (1982) Socrates makes clear the importance of such knowledge to the teacher:

> He must understand the nature of the soul, must find out the class of speech adapted to each nature, and must arrange and adorn his discourse accordingly . . . either for the purposes of instruction or of persuasion. (p. 571)

Yet there may be more to Socrates' claim that "knowledge is recollection" than has met the eye so far. Teaching does involve communicating facts, procedures, and interpretations by one who "knows" to those who do not. When we discover, usually on examinations, that the communication, which should have been clearly understood (because it had been clearly presented in lecture or in the textbook) has been garbled beyond recognition, we wonder what went wrong. Most of us become more inventive. We artfully anticipate the problems, usually on the basis of experience rather than theory, and we arrange our communications to circumvent the most likely misunderstandings. Often we are still not as successful as we would wish to be because, since we are not perfect mind readers, we can never fully anticipate or appreciate the diversity of minds in any classroom. But it could also be argued, as does Socrates, that no teacher really imparts information directly into even the mind of the most willing student.

Peter Elbow (1973), in his book *Writing Without Teachers*, was concerned about why students cannot write, not about why they were having difficulty learning mathematics or science. However, since all teaching and all learning involves communication not of facts, but of facts that *mean* something, all learning must involve meaning. Elbow, without referring to Socrates directly, affirmed something about Plato's theory that all knowledge is recollection when he wrote the following:

> When people speak or write successfully with each other, it looks as though there is a transfer of meaning: the speaker puts the meaning *into the words* and the listener *takes it out* at the other end. If you look at it from the larger perspective this account is fair: the listener ends up knowing what the speaker wanted him to know and ends up knowing something he never knew before, and so it must be that the words put this knowledge into his head. But it is important also to take a closer perspective and realize that, strictly speaking, words cannot *contain* meaning. Only people have meaning. Words can only have meaning *attributed to them by people*. The listener can never get any meaning out of a word that he didn't put in. Language can only consist of a set of directions for building meanings *out of one's own head*. Though the listener's knowledge seems new, it is also not new: the meaning may be

thought of as *structures* he never had in his head before, but *he* had to build these new structures out of ingredients *he* already had. The speaker's words were a set of directions for assembling this already-present material. (p. 151)

This is what we are doing when we provide definitions. We are expecting one word to stand for a set of instructions for making meaning. And this is not always a simple process, because these instructions have to engage other rules already present. This is why we often try out different formulations, and why multiple examples and pictures and diagrams are so useful to us. The already-present rules differ drastically between students in the same class. As teachers, we are constantly searching for the right words that will engage the rules for making meaning out of what we say. That such rules are there we all assume, because our students have not, after all, come to us directly from the womb. Yet, prior to our first conversations with them, we have no control over those rules, and we often find ourselves lamenting our own lack of understanding of the rules they *do* possess when we are trying to construct a definition. It is required of any successful communication, whether by lecturing or reading a text, that the speaker or author be as certain as possible of the rules that are already there and that will determine the understanding or misunderstanding that results.

PURPOSES OF INFORMAL WRITING

Socrates could monitor the progress of the slave boy at each step. He only had one student to work with. We probably use tests and quizzes or discussion to check on the quality of the communication with our students. I would maintain that having students engage in various forms of *informal, ungraded* writing exercises is a valuable addition not only to check on the quality of the communication but also to provide ways of immediately enhancing that quality for both teacher and student.

Reading what students write permits insights into their own views on the material—views which may be quite divergent from our own, but which, when articulated, provide us with avenues of communication unknown to the "method of anticipation." We can become even more inventive because we actually get to hear *what* they are thinking and *how* they are thinking it.

As they share their writing with their peers, students begin to take one another seriously as partners in a common enterprise. Finally, they even begin to include us as partners. Most important, perhaps, they gain the confidence to find their own meanings and to discover their own answers.

They begin to ask questions and seek answers themselves without always turning to us for the answer. They begin to discover, to make conscious, the rules by which they are making meaning. They begin to see how their own minds are approaching a problem. They, too, get to hear *what* they are thinking and *how* they are thinking it.

Two questions remain central to a discussion of the uses of writing in *any* discipline:

1. Can a teacher use writing to enhance an understanding of the relationships students are developing with the material so that he or she can be a better "guide"?
2. Can writing enhance the quality of that relationship?

Numerous pragmatic questions are also relevant to teachers in any discipline. They include the following:

- What kind of writing exercises should be used?
- When are they assigned?
- How should a teacher respond to them?
- Does a teacher have to sacrifice content to find the time for such exercises?
- How does a teacher deal with large classes and short periods?
- Will students write?

Such theoretical and practical questions are of special concern to science and mathematics teachers. Scientific writing is a very highly organized and specialized form of writing, suited for the dissemination of results. Mathematics has its own symbol systems which, in their highest forms of expression, both pure and applied, permit the communication of ideas and understandings in ways that defy precise verbalization. Werner Heisenberg (1974), who was keenly aware of the importance of both linguistic and mathematical symbolization, wrote the following:

> The tension between the demand for complete clarity and the inevitable inadequacy of existing concepts has been especially marked in modern science. In atomic physics we make use of a highly developed mathematical language that satisfies all the requirements in regard to clarity and precision. At the same time we recognize that we cannot describe atomic phenomena without ambiguity in any ordinary language. . . . It would be premature, however, to insist that we should avoid the difficulty by confining ourselves to the use of mathematical language. (p. 119)

This must be especially true for the beginning student of science or of mathematics. It should not simply be enough to memorize vocabulary or tricks for solving equations (though we cannot do without such memorization). Memorization without understanding is certainly not enough for those students who are having the most difficulty with the material.

Informal writing exercises *do* permit teachers to become better guides, and even if they *only* encouraged students to identify their own problem areas, such exercises would enhance the quality of the student's understanding of the material. I submit that writing will do even more, but let us rest content with these as goals and reasons for incorporating writing into our classes.

It is important to keep in mind that we are not teaching writing by attempting to correct grammar and spelling and organization. Nor is it being suggested that to ignore these important aspects of written communication is to undermine the good efforts of our colleagues in English departments. The distinction must be made between writing meant to be tentative, exploratory, and open to drastic modification, and writing meant to be polished and "final."

IMPLEMENTING INFORMAL WRITING

Establishing Expectations for Writing

All informal writing in a course can be done in a single spiral notebook. I have found it useful if students do not keep separate notebooks or in any way separate their class lecture notes from the writing exercises because it is most helpful to me to see both. Rather, they should simply date each entry. It is essential, however, that they write only on one side of the page, because I will need the space to respond to them, and they will have space to respond to me or to their earlier entries.

All of this writing is what I term "informal writing" because I wish to distinguish the journal from more formal assignments like lab reports, tests, and term papers, where I am always critical of both form and content. For "informal writing" I establish the following guidelines:

1. It will never receive a grade.
2. I will not correct, nor do I care about, spelling or grammar, but I will insist that I be able to read and understand what is being written.
3. I do not punish errors of understanding.
4. I will often pose questions to which I hope students will respond.
5. My questions do not mean that I disagree with what is being said, but they are meant to stimulate further thought.

6. I *may* answer questions which the student poses.
7. All of my comments are meant to aid, assist, and extend a student's observations.

My goal is to establish a written dialogue between myself and the student, and the rewards for the student must come, as they did for Meno's slave boy, from engaging in the experience itself. As the term progresses, and I sense that I will be heard, I can become more directive in my responses regarding error.

Many students hate to write because they have never had much success with it. Most of the feedback they've ever received has been negative. We do not characteristically praise good work, but we regularly condemn poor work. Students rarely read our comments carefully, and few profit from them. Telling students that they have nothing to fear and everything to gain by keeping a journal is not enough because there is no reason that they should believe you. Telling students that you will read and respond to what they write but will not grade it is not enough because many students equate being graded with being taken seriously, desiring to work only when they can receive a grade. Yet attaching a grade places an emphasis on performance that is out of place since performance will be tested in so many other ways. This is not the time to make it difficult for students to be honest about their problems with the material. The experience of writing affords the only cure, and modeling what you want during the initial class sessions is crucial. These experiences build trust and give everyone something to work with.

One can always begin a course, and a journal, by asking students to write in response to questions like the following:

- What are your expectations for the course?
- What do you hope to learn?
- What do you want to accomplish?
- Why have you enrolled in the course?
- What are your first thoughts on statistics or geology or mathematics?
- What are your first thoughts on [geology] teachers?

Answers to such questions, especially when students share their answers with one another in small groups, often provide opportunities for discussion that contribute to a trusting atmosphere and work toward building a learning community. In addition, you can also write your own responses during the class and share them with students. Writing along with students and sharing what is written are critical aspects of community building.

Emphasizing Collaborative Learning

Let me model a journal-based lesson that most readers would probably never teach. If I were beginning a course in Euclid's geometry (based on a direct translation of Euclid), I would first ask a few of the aforementioned questions. When it came time for content, but prior to the students' having done any reading, I would begin by asking them to write definitions for the following terms: point, line, straight line, and surface.

This exercise works for any subject matter when you can be reasonably sure that few, if any, of the students know the answers, and when the terms have everyday usage, or where prior knowledge can be misleading or at best different. In order to alleviate their anxiety at having to respond before a large group (assuming a class size of 20 or so), I would establish groups of three to five students, have them share their definitions with one another, and have them reach a consensus on a "best definition" for each term. I would then ask a member from each group to share the group's definition. If any discussion erupted, I would monitor it for relevance and permit it to continue for as long as it seemed profitable to do so.

Students will write definitions very different from Euclid's, so it would be useful to have them write a few words about such differences. I might therefore want the students to read Euclid's definitions and react in writing to them: Any reaction will do. I would have them share what they had written while still in groups, and then provide an opportunity for general discussion and questions before moving on to the next task or definitions.

Before the end of class, I would ask students to respond in writing to the following question: What stands out for you about the class you have just been through? We could share some responses or begin the next class with them.

What, in fact, has been accomplished so far? There is probably less than one full page of writing from each student. We have addressed the first four substantive definitions in Euclid, and we have practiced collaboration in small groups. As the teacher, I have heard the students' voices as they puzzled through some initially perplexing definitions, and I have learned what stood out for them.

How long does this really take? I think it could be accomplished in one 50-minute period with a group of cooperative students, but it could certainly take more time than that. Anyone who uses writing in the classroom will have to confront the limits of time by establishing deadlines for each portion of an assignment. For example, one might spend no more than one minute writing on each definition; 10 minutes in small groups to share; five more minutes to reach consensus; five minutes to report to the whole. That is about 25 minutes of task time allotted to the first portion without any discussion of the results. During the remaining time, I would have to decide how to manage the reports and any discussion, and decide whether or not enough time remained to begin responding to another set of definitions or if such work should be done out of class (in the journal). I would want to allow time for a "What stood out for you?" question at the end of class. If such a pace seems too hectic, slow it down. It is most important to remember that, for a time, all writing and sharing go into the "community building" portion of the agenda. Efficiency increases as students become more comfortable with the method.

I generally try to introduce the collaborative method using situations where no one knows the answer, or where there might always be an element of doubt about the correctness of an answer. Of course, the method of sharing opinions and evaluating them in an effort to reach consensus will work when there are right answers to be had. It does not work well when the right answers are always discovered by the same students and the rest sit back to await that student's pronouncement.

Responding to Texts

From the beginning, I encourage students to "respond to text" in their journal entries. I supply them with the guidelines provided in Fig. 5.1. Most students equate writing in response to a text with taking notes or outlining the text, so it does not surprise me that they begin responding to texts in their journals by attempting an outline. Indeed, I suspect that many have difficulty beginning responses to text because they think I want them to take notes, and they hate to do that. On the other hand, one of my students in an upper-level course repeatedly, despite many appeals to respond, produced such good outlines of the textbook that I would not have needed my own copy. One day, after reading five pages of her notes, I read the following comment: "I've got to quit! I've been doing this for over two hours and I don't know one thing that I've been writing!" I wish I could say that such a revelation marked the end of the outlining stage, but it did not. It did, at least, confirm my suspicion that students often *appear* to know something because they have the structure mastered, while in fact, they understand little of what goes into that structure.

Dialectical or double-entry notebooks are designed to encourage more

Figure 5.1   Response journal guidelines

- You should think of writing in your journal as a regular accompaniment to your reading.
- Think of your journal as a place where you use *writing as a tool for learning.* It should serve as a means for discovering, probing, speculating, questioning, inventing, reacting, connecting, believing, and doubting, etc.
- Other useful responses: Connections between the present text and other things you have read; character analyses; reflections on the overall structure of a work; comprehensive thematic issues; connections between ideas in the reading and personal experience; paper topics. In every one of these cases, however, I think you will learn more from your writing by focusing as much as possible on specifics.
- Think of the journal as the place where you can carry on a dialogue with the texts you're reading, and with me. You needn't feel that you have to put your book down every five minutes and write in your journal. If something you're reading provokes you strongly, then go ahead and write; but you can also make notes in the margins, or underline, as long as you come back later and *write responses* to those portions of the text.
- To a large extent, try to respond to specific words, lines, passages, images, ideas in your reading. Try to avoid vague responses: e.g., "I really understood (did not understand) what the author said in this section": or "I just don't understand the definition." Don't *merely* summarize "plot" or outline arguments. You may want to do that to help you get your bearings, but then *respond* to your synopsis. Justify your reactions to ideas and arguments as fully as possible.
- Review your response journal entries *frequently* so that you can begin to respond to your own responses and to get "back into the spirit" before you read or write, and to engage my own questions and responses to begin a dialogue.
- At least in the beginning, you will hear me say that you now need to go back and say more about a previous entry in your journal, either because you have been vague or because some later work bears directly on what you yourself might have said earlier. My questions do not mean, necessarily, that I disagree with you, but are meant to initiate and continue our dialogue.
- Bring your journal to each class as we will do some writing in class.
- Date each entry.
- Write on one side of the page only.
- Use $8^1/_2 \times 11''$ paper.
- Either a notebook or loose-leaf binder is fine.
- You are free to show me your journal anytime for feedback, but I will ask to see it once a week on a regular schedule. I'll respond to various things you have written in the spirit of participating in the dialogue you have initiated with a particular text. To say it once again: this is writing *you* are doing for *yourself* as a way of learning about what you are reading. If you write regularly and energetically, following these guidelines, I'll be satisfied.

---

active participation with a text or a problem, and also to promote collaborative learning. To put it most simply, students write important observations, quotations, or "facts" about what they are reading on one page of the notebook. On the facing page, they record thoughts they are having about those observations, hypotheses, or connections with what they have read earlier, or questions, or summaries. When I read their journals, I can respond to their writing and encourage other questions or connections, or wonder further about their hypotheses and observations. One could also divide each page into two columns. Column 1 would contain the "facts." Column 2 would contain the "hypotheses." Column 3 on the facing page, could be used by another student to comment on her or his partner's writing. When I collect the journals, I could respond to all of the writing by using Column 4.

These techniques for responding to text can be used in class or for homework assignments. Frequent modeling of the process in class helps students over the first hurdle: not knowing what kind of response "the teacher wants." Many students have never been given permission to respond to a text, and they need to learn how to give themselves that permission. My own responses to them are very generous and encouraging, because I hope to develop a dialogue with them as we go. When it works well, the student and I fill the facing page with written conversation.

It is sometimes difficult for students and teachers to learn how to frame generous responses. It is difficult not to be judgmental. At times, after writing my own observations on a difficult text during a workshop, I have exchanged my notebook with another participant only to be told that I had been misunderstanding the text all along. Of course, at that moment, I felt misunderstood and attacked. It is also difficult to avoid correcting every mistake and trying to tell what *we* know. I do not appreciate struggling to respond to a difficult text, trying to define its mysteries in my own way, only to have my partner write out a quick lecture to show me "the point" of the text. The purpose of responding to students is not to tell them what they have missed, but to help them to discover that on their own!

There are times when I wish to share my interpretations, solutions, and confusions with students, but I find that such responses do not encourage dialogue. They are most valuable when dialogue is happening already. Most of my initial comments express agreement, or ask questions that seek other openings. "Telling" too soon seems to close off openings, and often encourages the student to make lists of questions that I am expected to answer. While I love their questions, I also want them to try out some answers on their own. Sharing questions, responses, and tentative answers from the journals can be a useful way to start a class.

Writing About Process: Thinking About Thinking

When we say that we wish students would think more critically, in part we are asking that they be more aware of their own thinking so that they can test it as they go. We teach them methods to help them catch their own mistakes. We exhort them to keep asking themselves if what they are doing is making sense to them. Process writing involves recording reactions to past experience or predicting reactions to future experience to facilitate an inspection of our own thoughts.

Students could be asked to write in their journals about a problem:

• How is this problem like or unlike others you have seen?
• How will you attempt to solve it? What strategies will you use?
• What happened during your attempt to solve it?
• Did your actual strategy match your intended strategy?

Writing about the process of solving a problem begins to exercise the capacity of thinking about thought in addition to providing material and questions for small group or class discussion. I have often used process writing to elicit from students their strategies for completing many tasks including reading assignments, exam preparation, and paper-writing assignments. When such writing is shared early and often, success or failure during the tasks takes on a different meaning because each can be assessed against an articulated plan that can then, itself, become the object of inspection.

Integration: When and How

Modeling takes significant time, especially in the first week and a half, but afterwards, in-class writing takes up no more than five or ten minutes of each period, and sometimes, no writing is done at all. I might only take a moment or two to write in order to rejuvenate a sagging discussion. Giving the students a chance to write also gives them time to discover that they have something to say. Taking the time to share is critical, and I devote more time to that in the beginning of a course. If someone does not share often, I can still begin a dialogue when I read his or her journal.

When I have a journal component, I expect that students will respond to text whether or not we are doing a lot of in-class writing on a particular topic. I collect journals once a week and divide the load evenly depending on the frequency of class meetings. I try to impress upon the students that a journal is not something that one can "make up" but rather should be begun at any point. I find I can skim a journal and write appropriate comments in five or ten minutes. When the class is too large for journals, I try to elicit some written dialogue surrounding my comments on their examinations and papers. I try to comment extensively, and before putting a grade on the work I require that they write a brief response to each of my comments. At least I can tell if my comments are making any sense to them, and, often enough, I discover that I write a clarifying comment in response to what they have written.

I find that I look forward to reading journals and responses. It rarely becomes a chore because I enjoy the more personal relationship that such exchange brings. Many times I find myself incorporating references to ideas and questions begun in the journals into my remarks during class. Often, when reminded of a comment, I will ask the student to read from his or her journal.

CONCLUSION

Integrating writing into my own classroom has been an evolutionary process, perhaps punctuated by breakthroughs, but I, too, have had to confront the conflicts between old and new styles, and demands on time both in and out of class. My experiences with informal writing began in a very different setting: freshman writing programs conducted prior to the beginning of regular classes. I found that I did not immediately embrace all of what I knew to be possible, and that when the semester began it was far easier to do what I had long been accustomed to doing. Yet, for the past two years I have used journals and some of the aforementioned techniques in every course where I have had fewer than 20 students. I have not yet discovered ways of using journals in larger classes. I do know that I miss being able to use the journal because that once-new style has become the "old."

I do not wish to create the impression that writing is a panacea for all of the ills of education. It will work if one can create a climate in which writing is used often enough for your students to discover its benefits. It will not turn everyone into creative, "A" students. There will always be students who are not motivated to learn what we have to offer, and not all successful learning styles will involve writing. Perhaps in the beginning, using writing will require some sacrifice of content, but I think we are worrying most about those students who do not seem to be mastering content. I am often asked whether the use of writing will frustrate those who can master content. It may for those who are not used to questioning what it is they think they know. Socrates was, after all, put to death for provoking those who were content to live an unexamined life.

REFERENCES

Elbow, P. (1973). *Writing without teachers*. New York: Oxford.
Heisenberg, W. (1974). *Across the frontiers* (P. Heath, Trans.). New York: Harper & Row. (Original work published 1971)
Plato. (1977). *Meno*. (W. R. M. Lamb, Trans.). Cambridge, MA: Harvard University Press. (Original translation published 1924)
Plato. (1982). *Phaedrus*. (H. N. Fowler, Trans.). Cambridge, MA: Harvard University Press. (Original translation published 1914)

Part II

WRITING AS PROBLEM SOLVING

In a college course in mathematics, writing should enhance the level of mathematical ability, argues William Berlinghoff. It should not be "extra composition assignments appended to the course material." His essay describes writing to teach problem-solving tactics and to engage nonmajors in independent exploration of mathematical ideas that are new to them.

Russel Kenyon surveys many other applications of writing in the mathematics classroom, and details how to implement "writing to learn" in a high school math course.

David White and Katie Dunn report on a four-year National Science Foundation project, begun in 1986, that uses writing as an agent for changing teachers' beliefs about what is possible in their classrooms.

All three essayists in this section discuss how written language helps to make students and teachers more confident and capable of solving problems. Writing can be a natural complement to mathematics when (1) it consolidates and extends understanding by helping students to articulate what they know; and (2) it records and monitors the process of solving problems. Writing can also be a natural complement to teaching, as White and Dunn describe, when it enables teachers to see their classrooms and themselves more clearly and to form a stronger learning community.

CHAPTER 6

Writing *Is* Problem Solving

Russel W. Kenyon

The development of cognitive theory in the 1960s and 1970s has led to the structuring of the general area in mathematics called problem solving. Several educational institutions have followed the National Council of Teachers of Mathematics' (NCTM, 1980a) policy statement that "problem solving be the focus of school mathematics in the 1980s" (p. 1). Only recently, however, have mathematics educators, educational psychologists, and cognitive psychologists begun to work together to develop meaningful programs of study that deal with the cognitive learning skills. These skills can be acquired in mathematics learning through the use of several methods of problem solving, including group problem solving, writing, and various uses of the computer and manipulatives. Of these methods, writing has been used the least in mathematics classrooms.

Why would anyone want to use writing in a mathematics classroom? I shall attempt to answer that question by first defining cognitive learning and then examining its relationship to problem solving. I shall look at writing as an important problem-solving method and show that the use of writing in mathematics classrooms will result in cognitive learning.

We will then consider several long-term and short-term techniques for promoting cognitive learning using writing in the mathematics classroom.

WRITING FOR PROBLEM SOLVING: A COGNITIVE PROCESS

Mathematics instructors have traditionally seen their task as one of presenting material to their students in a clear and precise manner. The model student, having heard the truth from the "expert" standing before him or her, copies the rules and definitions, and memorizes them. This has

Portions of this chapter have been published as "Writing in the Mathematics Classroom," *New England Mathematics Journal*, 87(5), 3–19.

been referred to as the "copy theory" of learning. In general, students feel very comfortable with this strategy. However, students' adherence to this strategy "may be the single most important deterrent to effective education" (Lochhead, 1985, p. 109).

Significant changes are being made in mathematics classrooms around the nation. New methods are proving effective in making passive students active, thereby increasing the efficiency of their learning. Students who simply copy and memorize are being replaced by those who are actively involved in the learning process and are "constructing" their own knowledge structure as they proceed. This active involvement is readily observable. In a recent study (Konold, 1986), time-on-task measurements were taken on students while they were learning by using the lecture method, and while they were learning by using the "pair" or "small group" problem-solving approach. (In pair problem solving, one student is the problem solver, and the other is the listener-observer who asks for explanations of the problem-solving process while the problem solver is solving a word problem.) The pair–problem-solving method yielded a much more sustained student effort ($r = -.142$) than did the lecture method ($r = -.424$).

Active students also have a different attitude toward their work. They are more willing to look for new approaches to problems, to develop new algorithms, and in general, to spend more time on a task. Passive students, on the other hand, are ready to give up if the solution is not immediately at hand. They believe that you either know the solution or you don't. Bloom and Broder (1950) report that the major difference between successful and unsuccessful problem solvers is the degree to which they are active or passive in their approach to a problem.

Verbalization is a technique that requires the learner to report on the thinking process during problem solving. It is based on the assumption that the problem-solving process will be understood by the learner only when he or she can explain it to others. In the case of small or large group problem solving, most of the verbalization is spoken. Thus, the processing is available to both the problem solver and to others to observe and evaluate. Higher level skills are called upon to explain each step in the process coherently so that all will understand the solution.

Writing down the thoughts and procedures involved for each of the steps of a problem solution adds yet another dimension to the processing. The problem solver can now clearly "see" the steps of the solution described in written words and has immediate feedback for review and reflection. Writing encourages the evaluation and modification of each of the steps. Learning is thus enhanced as mathematical facts and theorems are recalled and organized on paper. This allows for further analysis, evaluation, and possible modification to take place. This learning process needs to be further investigated to understand how it is affected by verbalization, writing, and other problem-solving methods.

Cognitive Learning

Cognitive scientists have recently studied learning by constructing a complex model of the human memory system (Anderson, 1983). Some of the modern technologies, such as computer science, information processing, and linguistics, have been applied to this work. The model has been tested and modified, and is a relatively good representation of the human memory system. Based on this model, called Adaptive Control of Thought (ACT), learning can now be defined in terms of two different types of information acquisition. The first type involves the addition of propositions to declarative memory, and the second, the construction and addition to production memory of procedures that originate from other procedures and from propositions. The following definition of learning is based on this ACT model: Learning is the acquisition of knowledge and skills, where knowledge refers to the propositions, spatial images, and temporal strings stored in declarative memory, and skills refer to the procedures stored in production memory.

Process of Problem Solving

Cognitive learning and problem solving are closely related. Now that we have a definition for learning, let us carefully define problem solving. First, we need to understand what a "problem" is. Bell (1978) gives four characteristics of a problem:

1. A person must be aware of a situation.
2. The person must recognize that the situation requires action.
3. The person must either want or need to act upon the situation and must actually take some action.
4. The resolution of the situation must not be immediately obvious to the person acting on it.

It is important to note that in this definition, the person does not have an algorithm available to resolve the situation. Expressing it in cognitive theory terms, there is no propositional knowledge in declarative memory, or procedural knowledge in production memory that would allow the person to move directly from the problem state to the goal state. Problem solving can now be defined as the process by which a person uses previously acquired knowledge and skills to attempt to find a resolution, not immediately apparent, to a situation (problem) that confronts him or her.

Note that problem solving is not simply obtaining the final answer. Rather, it is the entire process, starting with the original confrontation of the situation, through the various steps in the general problem-solving procedure, to a conclusion. Problem solving utilizes knowledge and skills in declarative and production memory to compile new knowledge, which is then added to memory. Therefore, problem solving always yields to cognitive learning.

Problem solving involves application of learned knowledge and skills in order to move through the process of resolving a situation that confronts a person and that the person needs or wants to resolve. The person, when confronted with a situation, first needs to determine what he or she knows about the situation and then determine how to get from this knowledge base to the goal. The next step would be to carry out the plan. The final step would be to evaluate the results and the procedure (Polya, 1957). Learning takes place during the problem-solving process since the new information combines with the existing knowledge and is stored in memory in this new form.

Several rules and procedures, often referred to as heuristics, have been compiled to aid the problem solver in the planning stage (Wickelgren, 1974). General problem-solving strategies have also been developed. It is not entirely clear at this time just what problem-solving strategies and procedures should be taught or at what level. Certainly, domain-based knowledge can be taught, as can some of the general problem-solving strategies. It appears that at least some problem-solving skills are acquired by simply doing problem solving (Schoenfeld, 1982, 1985).

Writing and Problem Solving

Although problem solving has been the watchword of the 1980s in mathematics education, the method for problem solving in mathematics that has garnered the least attention is writing. The Writing Across the Curriculum (WAC) program, which has received support from many school systems in this country and abroad, has not been supported by the mathematics educational community, in my opinion. The WAC literature is clear on the purpose of the program: to teach learning through writing (Tchudi & Yates, 1983). Some of the stages in the WAC program, which will be discussed in the next section, are similar to the steps in problem solving. It becomes evident when the definition for problem solving is examined and compared to the writing stages in WAC that writing *is* problem solving.

In the mathematics classroom writing can be used effectively for the acquisition of knowledge and skills through the problem-solving process.

Asking students to write about a problem requires them to clarify thoughts about how they will approach the problem. Concepts are identified more clearly and sharply. The writing process then becomes an integral part of the thought process (McMillen, 1986). In this writing process, students begin to gather, formulate, and organize old and new knowledge, concepts, and strategies, and to synthesize this information as a new structure that becomes a part of their own knowledge network (Nahrgang & Petersen, 1986). Of equal importance to cognitive learning is the acquisition of the metacognitive skills that allow students to perform the self-monitoring functions in problem solving. As students write down, reflect on, and react to their thoughts and ideas, they enhance the executive problem-solving abilities, and the problem-solving process becomes more effective.

TECHNIQUES FOR USING WRITING IN MATHEMATICS

To promote this thought-processing, activities should be designed to assure that writing becomes a normal part of the daily routine in the mathematics classroom. Students should begin to gain the necessary writing skills as the writing takes place. They should also begin to expect writing to be a standard part of the mathematics program. The following ideas should help the mathematics teacher make writing an integral part of that program.

Long-Term Writing Techniques

We will briefly consider the stages of writing from the Writing Across the Curriculum (WAC) program. WAC does not directly address the issues of cognitive learning, nor does it appear to contain the applications for mathematics that are specifically designed to encourage higher level thinking in mathematics processing. However, some WAC techniques may be adapted so as to encourage problem solving, and therefore, cognitive learning.

Writing is normally described as being divided into several stages. Most authors agree on three main stages, while others add additional ones. The first stage is the prewriting or planning stage. The prewriting phase probably requires more cognitive processing than any of the other stages. The student is involved in the initial state of the process of problem solving, and is attempting to understand the conditions of the problem so as to achieve a goal (or the goal state). A memory search takes place, looking for data, strategies, and techniques to aid in the solution. Ideas for possible solutions are generated and organized during this process using notetaking and exploratory freewriting. In the final phase of this stage, all the possible ideas are evaluated and the final candidate(s) are selected.

The next stage is the writing or composition stage. At this point, the ideas are translated into an extended text. The student should not be concerned about mechanics, that is, spelling and punctuation, at this time. If the ideas were all completely formed in the first stage, the writing should be quite automatic. Otherwise, the student must return to the first stage. The last stage, according to some authors is the revising or rewriting stage. This is the point at which the copy should be carefully read and rewritten for clarity and focus. Ideas can be moved around, redundant material removed, and needed information added (Anderson, 1985; Gagné, 1985). The WAC program adds to these stages the copyediting and the presenting and publishing stages (Tchudi & Yates, 1983). Several ideas for long-term writing will now be presented, as well as an adaptation of a method from the Writing for Learning program that can be applied to the mathematics program.

Writing Projects.   After the writing program is well established, the teacher may want to assign a writing project that will require several days or weeks to complete. The project should be carefully designed to assure that it meets the course/unit objectives and is within the students' technical and writing capabilities. Several of these projects require access to libraries, banking information, and other records. The following is a list of ideas for long-term projects in the mathematics classroom:

- Paper on a career in a mathematics-related field.
- Book report on a mathematics- or computer-related book or paper; e.g., *Mindstorms*, papers from *The Mathematics Experience, Men of Mathematics,* or *The World of Mathematics.*
- Letter to a national testing service, offering suggestions on methods to evaluate and measure intelligence.
- Document outlining a plan to form a financial planning group that would give advice to students on how to earn, save, and manage money.
- Report on statistics as used in the insurance field.
- Paper on a famous mathematician.
- Report on mathematics anxiety.
- Report on how mathematics is used to measure and evaluate intelligence, reading skills, mathematical abilities, and other aptitudes.
- Report on the historical development of some area of mathematics such as algebra.
- Report on a chapter from a mathematics book on a topic not covered in the course this year. Study it, keeping a journal of your thoughts and feelings as you progress through the unit. Summarize your journal in a report.

- Report on new developments in computer technology.
- Letter to a friend/peer on how you feel about mathematics.
- Letter to a friend/peer offering advice on solving a certain problem.
- Discussion of a retired person's budget, considering various expenses and sources of income.
- Paper presenting a solution to a longer mathematics problem. Write out the solution in words (no mathematics), describing each step with its reason.
- Report on the origins of a particular measurement; e.g., length of a day.
- Letter taking the role of a lawyer, dentist, or stockbroker, for example, explaining why one should master the concepts of Algebra I.

A Writing for Learning Application. At the end of a major unit, the main concepts usually need to be brought together and organized. A method from the *Writing for Learning* manual (Wolfe & Reising, 1983) is particularly suitable for this review application. Below is an adaptation of "A Process Approach to Writing for Learning" from that manual. The review of a unit using this technique will require a full 40-minute class period and a follow-up homework assignment. The method is suitable for a variety of applications. The assumption is that a unit on solving linear equations by various methods has just been completed. The class period today will be devoted to a review to prepare for a test that is scheduled for the day after tomorrow. The following is the schedule for today's class period:

1. *The reflection stage.* 10 minutes. Students work individually, brainstorming on the various methods for solving linear equations. They try to outline the material and to draw any pictures that come to mind. This is the time to jot down all the questions they can think of, and to write out phrases, clauses, and full sentences about the various methods.
2. *The clarification stage.* 5 minutes. The students come together with the teacher to make sure that all understand the procedure and to ask final questions before going on. The teacher then gives the instructions for the next stage.
3. *The first draft stage.* 15 minutes. The students again work individually. Everything they know about solving linear equations and about the different methods is written down. There is some time for rewriting, for adding, for deleting, for modifying. Some of the original chaos becomes order.
4. *The peer inquiry stage.* 10 minutes. Groups of two to five students are formed to share the work from the last stage. Each student's work is read in the group, and the group gives two positive, concrete comments

about the writing and then makes two suggestions for revising or editing.

5. *The revision stage.* The homework assignment for the next day is to rewrite the paper considering peer comments. This stage brings together the methods of solving linear equations in a concrete form.

During the next class, the teacher reads the papers, making complimentary remarks and offering suggestions. Any misconceptions are corrected. A second revision stage is often valuable; however, for a mathematics program, this is an optional step.

Short-Term Writing Techniques

Ideas for using writing in mathematics have been offered in several recent papers (Birken, 1986; Geeslin, 1977; Johnson, L., 1985; Johnson, M., 1983; King, 1982; Lubatkin, 1986; McMillen, 1986; Nahrgang & Petersen, 1986; Salem, 1982; and Tchudi & Yates, 1983). These short-term techniques fall into several broad categories that make them adaptable to a variety of teaching styles, grade levels, and class sizes. They can be used as writing exercises that require just a few minutes of class time each day, or they may require the whole period.

Explain How. This procedure is similar to the pair–problem-solving method (Whimbey & Lochhead, 1980, 1984), except that each step is written rather than spoken. Students will need some practice to develop this technique, but it is well worth the effort. See Figure 6.1 (general writing instructions) and Figure 6.2 (writing probes) for ideas to help students become more proficient in this technique. Discuss the general writing instructions at the beginning of the writing program, and encourage students to use the writing probes whenever using this writing technique. Salem (1982) refers to this technique as "chatter: students talk to themselves on paper as they do a problem" (p. 129).

As an example, say to the students: "Consider that solving an equation is undoing what has been done to a variable. Write what has been done to the variable in the following equation. Then state what must be done to reverse that."

$X/3+7=-13$	"X is divided by 3, then 7 is added."
Subtract 7	This is the first step to undo that.
$X/3=-20$	"X is divided by 3."
Multiply by 3	To undo that.
$X=-60$	

Figure 6.1   General writing instructions

---

* Try to write down everything you are thinking.
* Write down each step as if you were explaining your thoughts to a friend.
* If you have done pair problem solving, think of the questioner sitting next to you, asking you to explain each step.
* Your writing is not right or wrong; it is what you are thinking at that time.
* Don't worry about spelling; try to make your writing grammatically correct so that others can understand it.
* Rephrase thoughts so that you will be sure others will understand them.
* Review the writing probes (Fig. 6.2) often to look for new ideas that will help you.
* Draw diagrams whenever possible.
* Describe preliminary ideas, discuss why you accepted or rejected each one, and then explain how you expanded on the final one(s).
* When you have completed your work, go back and review it. Record your final impressions.

A similar technique is to ask students to write the steps to a problem solution. Nonmathematical problems work as well as mathematical ones here. For example, ask students to describe how to build a tower using blocks of different sizes and colors. Then have the students exchange their solutions and attempt to rebuild the tower using only the given instructions. Finally, have the students evaluate their solution by discussing the results of the tower construction. The same procedure can be used with a mathematical solution.

Another alternative to this technique is to require that only the solution steps be written out; that is, leave out all reference to the numbers and/or variables. For example, explain how to add $1/3$ and $1/4$ without mentioning the $1/3$ or $1/4$. It is usually a good idea to add something to the instructions like "assume you are explaining this process to a sixth grader." The "explain how" technique is a good one to start the writing program with.

Compare Two Concepts.   This technique requires students first to define the meanings of various terms in their own words. They may start by constructing rather poorly written paragraphs. As they are able to express themselves more precisely, the paragraphs will shorten to one or two sentences. After students are able to explain the meaning of individual terms in one or two sentences, they are given pairs of terms representing either similar or contrasting concepts. For example, explain how the following concepts are related: equation/graph, line/plane, number line/

Figure 6.2   Writing probes: Ideas to help you form your thoughts as you are writing

---

GENERAL PROBES

- What are you thinking?
- Can you say more about that?
- Explain that so that a fifth grader would understand it.
- Write that again in a different way.
- Are you sure about that?
- Check the accuracy of that last step.
- What were you thinking about to get that?
- What did you mean by "it"?
- Label that step so you can refer to it.
- What does the X stand for?
- What does that equation say in plain English?
- Could you draw a picture of that?
- Why did you write that equation?
- Tell why that last step makes sense.

WHEN YOU ARE STUCK

- Why are you stuck?
- What other information do you need to get unstuck?
- How can you get needed information?
- Do you need to go back and review some of your steps?
- What makes this problem difficult?

WHEN YOU THINK YOU ARE FINISHED

- Do you have other ideas that you have not written about?
- What were you thinking about when you did step X?
- How can you show that you did this correctly?
- Could this have been done another way (more eloquently)?

---

coordinates, point/line, linear equation/quadratic equation, fraction/ decimal number, circle/ellipse, function/relation, and geometry/algebra. When starting to use this technique, students may need to write a paragraph or more. Discourage the use of memorized definitions and concepts. As the technique develops, students should be able to formulate ideas more succinctly, and the paragraph will be reduced to one or two sentences (Geeslin, 1977).

Explain Why.   This is a more advanced technique and requires more preparation on the teacher's part. The student should have done some form of writing, for example, the "explain how" method, before using this technique. This technique uses the open-ended question format, so that a final, definitive solution is never possible. After the students are able to explain how to add two fractions with some degree of proficiency, ask, "Why would you do it this way?" Plan this activity carefully and be prepared for some chaos.

Word Problems. Although there are those who believe that "doing word problems is problem solving," there is much more to problem solving than this. Once the algorithm is acquired for a particular type of "problem," it is no longer a problem, but rather an exercise. Problem solving is not occurring at this point. There are many good references for word problems and for methods of generating problems appropriate to the goals of the instructional unit (see Whimbey & Lochhead, 1980, 1984; Mathematics Council of the Alberta Teachers' Association, 1982; NCTM, 1980b).

Students should be required to have complete headings, carefully defining every variable used for each problem solution. Each item in the heading should contain the words "number of." For example, rather than write "N=nickels," students should write "N=number of nickels," or "N=number of cents represented by the nickels." Suggest that they draw diagrams whenever possible. As the students acquire the skills to "solve" a particular type of problem (i.e., they have learned the algorithm), give them other problems using the same solution method, but varied enough to require some additional thought process. For example, make the solution a part of a larger procedure, change the "setting," or add extraneous information.

Outline the Chapter. Use this technique for introducing new material or for reviewing for a test. This is a good way for students to learn to organize information. Some instruction in outlining methods will probably be needed.

Test Questions. Asking the student to write test questions requires not only a good understanding of the material involved but also the ability to organize and synthesize information. When the student has formulated a tentative problem, it must be evaluated to determine its suitability as a test question. This technique, utilized at the end of an instructional unit, brings together the knowledge of the unit at a high level of mental processing. Many of the higher level cognitive processes are utilized. Problem solving and cognitive learning are taking place. Begin this technique by dividing the chapter or chapters into parts and assigning each part to one or two students. Ask each student to prepare two or three problems. Finally, evaluate the questions that have been submitted, require rewriting as necessary, and compile the questions into a review test and the official test.

Replace Two-Column Proofs with Prose.   The rigor of a formal two-column proof in geometry often causes students to develop mental blocks so they are unable to complete the proof. The prose form allows students to write out their thoughts (and frustrations) and to examine and evaluate them. Because the thoughts are written down, they do not have to be held in short-term memory. This "unloading" of memory makes room for more pertinent information to be activated. After some successes with the prose form, students are usually able to organize information more effectively, and to meet with more success with the two-column proof.

Notebook.   The notebook has two primary purposes: for taking daily class notes during the formal class time, and as a journal for keeping a personal record of thoughts and reflections at the end of the class period. At times the two overlap. For example, students may be asked to write out all of the steps of a problem solution in their notebooks during the class period. However, at the end of the period, they could express in their journals displeasure (or pleasure) at having to write out all of the steps of that problem solution.

During class the teacher should be posing problems at the proper level for learning to be effective. The solutions should be recorded in the notebook as examples. The lecture notes and notes on any class discussion should be rephrased in the student's own words and recorded. A method used successfully by Lubatkin (1986) has been the teacher-led class discussion to arrive at a definition of an important term. The class discussion continues until the appropriate level of precision in the definition is obtained and is understood by the class. Vocabulary lists with synonyms and definitions derived in this fashion should be recorded.

The last five to ten minutes of each class period should be devoted to journal writing. This time for writing is usually designated for reflection on what was learned in class, on a difficult concept that needs some attention, on applications of day's material, on feelings about the material, the teacher, or the classmates. An exercise, supplied by the teacher for the purpose, may be used to evaluate a critical concept. For example, after completing a unit on factoring, ask the students to discuss the following statement: "Factoring and finding a product are reverse processes." The journal writing time gives students time to think at their own rate and to internalize new concepts by relating them to their own experiences. As students become familiar and comfortable with journal writing, their responses will show definite improvements in their organizational skills. As a result, their work becomes easier to read (Nahrgang & Petersen, 1986). Students should also be able to ask the teacher questions in the journal that may be difficult to ask in class.

GETTING STARTED WITH WRITING

The large number of techniques compiled in this paper may be a bit overwhelming to the teacher contemplating the introduction of writing in the mathematics classroom. What follows is an approach for getting started with a writing program.

Every student should have a notebook, and the notebook should be used every day. The teacher should develop or obtain one *simple* daily problem and have the students use the "explain how" or "chatter" technique on the problem during the class period. Expect to see very little real progress for two to three weeks. Recognizing and recording all the thoughts on each step in each problem takes practice. When some progress is noted, increase the complexity of the problem a little.

Notebooks are also used each day to record daily class notes. Time should be given to allow the student to rework each new definition into their own words. Examples of problems worked in class should be recorded also.

The last five to ten minutes of the class period should be reflection time for writing in the journal. Start this part as simply as possible. Ask the students to respond to the following questions:

What were the important points in today's lesson?
What did I understand from the lesson?
What did I not understand from the lesson?
What questions would I like to ask (the teacher the next day) about the lesson?

Often, when students respond to these questions, they are aware of them while doing homework, and they find answers themselves. However, start the next day's class by responding to any unanswered questions.

The teacher should collect these notebooks and respond to the students' work. He or she should make appropriate comments on the written problem solutions. Students will probably demonstrate some misconceptions to the teacher in this way that would never be seen on an achievement test. This is the place to correct these misconceptions. The students may make comments or ask questions in the notebooks that they would not make or ask in class. This should become a valuable communications tool. Careful responses will be important.

As the program develops, other techniques may be added, one at a time. "Outline the Chapter" should help students arrange the topics of the chapter into a form which makes sense to them. Another good review technique is "Test Questions." The better students should benefit from writing their own questions. Time will be needed to present and develop this technique. Use the short-term techniques section above as a "shopping list" to look for ideas that may fit your students and your style. The long-term techniques may only apply after an extended time with the writing program, and then only to the more advanced students. Start with the Writing for Learning Application as a full class review of a major unit.

The use of writing as a problem-solving method allows the student to assume a more active role in the problem-solving process, and cognitive learning becomes more effective. Problem solving requires the utilization and restructuring of higher level cognitive skills and knowledge. Actual cognitive learning may be somewhat difficult to observe and measure; however, the teacher should begin to see increased student performance on word problem solving and in other critical thinking exercises. Persistence is important as it may take some time to observe improvement in the critical thinking skills that are acquired as a result of a writing program.

REFERENCES

Anderson, J. R. (1983). *The architecture of cognition.* Cambridge, MA: Harvard University Press.
Anderson, J. R. (1985). *Cognitive psychology and its implications.* New York: W. H. Freeman and Co.
Bell, F. (1978). *Teaching and learning mathematics (in secondary schools).* Dubuque, IA: Wm. C. Brown Co.
Bloom, B., & Broder, L. (1950). *Problem-solving processes of college students.* Chicago: Chicago University Press.
Birken, M. (1986). Teaching students how to study mathematics: A classroom approach. *Mathematics Teacher, 79*(6), 410–413.
Gagné, E. (1985). *The cognitive psychology of school learning.* Boston: Little, Brown.
Geeslin, W. (1977). Using writing about mathematics as a teaching technique. *Mathematics Teacher, 77*(2), 112–115.
Johnson, L. (1985). What! Write in math class, ugh! Development of a writing project for an algebra 2 class. *New England Mathematics Journal, 85*(11), 12–15.
Johnson, M. (1983). Writing in mathematics classes: A valuable tool for learning. *Mathematics Teacher, 76,* 117–119.
King, B. (1982). Using writing in the mathematics class. In C. Griffin (Ed.), *Teaching writing in all disciplines* (pp. 39–44). San Francisco: Jossey-Bass.
Konold, C. (1986). *Evaluating and modifying a teaching assistant training program for a workshop-style mathematics course.* Unpublished paper, Cognitive Process Research Group, University of Massachusetts.

Lochhead, J. (1985). Teaching analytic reasoning skills through pair problem solving. In J. W. Segal, S. F. Chipman, & R. Glaser (Eds.), *Thinking and learning skills: Relating instruction to research* (pp. 109-131). Hillsdale, NJ: Lawrence Erlbaum Associates.

Lubatkin, H. (1986). *Writing is an integral part of learning math.* Unpublished paper, University of Massachusetts.

Mathematics Council of the Alberta Teachers' Association (1982). *Problem solving in the mathematics classroom.* Edmonton, Alberta: Alberta Teachers' Association.

McMillen, L. (1986, January 22). Science and math professors are assigning writing drills to focus students' thinking. *Chronicle of Higher Education*, p. 19.

Mett, C. (1987). Writing as a learning device in calculus. *Mathematics Teacher, 80*, 534-537.

Nahrgang, C., & Petersen, B. (1986). Using writing to learn mathematics. *Mathematics Teacher, 79*, 461-465.

National Council of Teachers of Mathematics (1980a). *An agenda for action: Recommendations for school mathematics of the 1980s.* Reston, VA: Author.

National Council of Teachers of Mathematics (1980b). *Problem solving in school mathematics.* Reston, VA: Author.

Newman, J. (1956). *The world of mathematics.* New York: Simon and Schuster.

Papert, S. (1980). *Mindstorms: Children, computers, and powerful ideas.* New York: Basic Books.

Polya, G. (1957). *How to solve it.* Princeton, NJ: Princeton University Press.

Salem, J. (1982). Using writing in teaching mathematics. In M. Bart, P. D'Arcy, & M. Healy (Eds.), *What's going on?* (pp. 123-134). Upper Montclair, NJ: Boynton/Cook.

Schoenfeld, A. (1982). Recent advances in mathematics education: Ideas and implications. In S. Rachlin (Ed.), *Problem solving in the mathematics classroom* (pp. 127-140). Edmonton, Alberta: The Alberta Teachers' Association.

Schoenfeld, A. (1985). *Mathematical problem solving.* New York: Academic Press.

Tchudi, S., & Yates, J. (1983). *Teaching writing in the content areas: Senior high school.* Washington, DC: National Education Association.

Whimbey, A., & Lochhead, J. (1980). *Problem solving and comprehension: A short course in analytical reasoning* (2nd ed.). Philadelphia: Franklin Institute Press.

Whimbey, A., & Lochhead, J. (1984). *Beyond problem solving and comprehension: An exploration of quantitative reasoning.* Philadelphia: Franklin Institute Press.

Wickelgren, W. (1974). *How to solve problems — Elements of a theory of problems and problem solving.* San Francisco: W. H. Freeman and Co.

Wolfe, D., & Reising, R. (1983). *Writing for learning in the content area.* Portland, ME: J. Weston Walch.

CHAPTER 7

Locally Original Mathematics Through Writing

William P. Berlinghoff

This paper focuses on writing as a way to get non-science majors to do "locally original" mathematics, that is, to engage in independent exploration of mathematical ideas that are new to them. The setting is a freshman-level mathematics course for students who do not need specific mathematical techniques for their chosen fields of study. The students are in this course sometimes by choice but more often by obligation or default. Their mathematical background is varied and may in some cases be weak, perhaps as little as two years of high school mathematics of uncertain content. Many of them "think" they dislike mathematics, "know" they are not good at it, and "are sure" that they will never need mathematical thinking in the future.

Despite these initial student attitudes, I believe such a course must not just be *about* mathematics but must have the students doing some hands-on mathematics so that they may gain a better appreciation for the so-called "mathematical way of thinking." The challenge of that objective has led me to try many different approaches during the past two decades, including the assignment of short (five-page) papers of various sorts. From that experience I shall report on some kinds of paper topics that have worked well for me and some that have not.

My main objective is to develop worthwhile writing projects that form an integral part of the students' mathematical experience, not just extra composition assignments appended to the course material. Writing is a familiar task for students, especially those majoring in humanities disciplines, but that very familiarity often traps students into thinking they can write papers in any subject merely by stringing together generalities, opinions and references to the literature. While such an attitude is seldom justified in any serious discipline, it is especially pernicious in mathemat-

This paper was presented at the 71st Annual Meeting of the Mathematical Association of America, January 1988.

ics. Moreover, I learned swiftly but painfully that it turns tempting assignments into pitfalls for the instructor. In an effort to spare others some of the pain of this discovery, let me first describe three kinds of writing assignments that have not worked well for me.

1. *Write about a famous mathematician, mathematical event, or historical period.* These topics frequently invited indeliberate plagiarism in the form of an undigested patchwork from several encyclopedias or other handy references. Occasionally they provoked deliberate plagiarism from disguised sources (or commercial term-paper mills). Moreover, such papers, even when well done, usually concentrated almost exclusively on interesting personal anecdotes rather than on mathematical ideas.
2. *Report on an article.* A far too common result of this type of topic was five pages of "I liked it" or "I didn't like it." If the article involved any substantive mathematics, the papers became "I didn't understand it" or occasionally "I don't even know that I didn't understand it."
3. *Solve a problem.* In order to be of sufficient substance, the assigned problems usually required a level of mathematical sophistication and/ or perseverance beyond many of the students in the class. Those students had nothing to say on their own, so some would get what information they could from me during office hours and faithfully reproduce it without absorption, while others used friends, relatives, or other sources with the same end result.

Now for the good news: It is possible to avoid most of these pitfalls by making each student paper focus on the *process of solving* a particular problem or examining a particular mathematical object, a problem or object assigned to that student alone. To prepare the students for this process, I now begin my course by introducing a dozen problem-solving tactics (Berlinghoff & Grant, 1988):

> Check the definitions.
> Restate the problem.
> Draw a diagram.
> Introduce appropriate notation.
> Look for a pattern.
> Construct examples.
> Argue by analogy.
> Solve a simpler problem.
> Approximate the answer.
> Reason backwards from the desired conclusion.
> See if you used all the data.
> Generalize the solution. (p. 7)

The tactics themselves are not new. They are drawn from the elegantly simple approach to problem-solving described by George Polya in *How to Solve It* (1957). I refer to them often in class lectures while developing each new topic so that students become familiar with their use. The key to their use in writing assignments is this: When a writing topic is assigned, the student is asked to describe how he or she used these problem-solving tactics to attack a particular question. Thus, there is always something to write about, regardless of whether or not the student can "solve" the problem. Even a dead end is worthwhile, provided the path to it can be described. Moreover, by paying careful attention to the problem-solving tactics (because they provide a guaranteed source of material for their papers), students often succeed in doing a lot more mathematics than they think they can.

In my experience, this approach has worked best when each student has had his or her own topic to explore. Ideally, all the topics for an assignment should be different, should be similar to each other, and should be closely related to the concept development presented in class lectures. The generating of enough distinct topics to cover an entire class often poses a non-trivial obstacle for the instructor, but it is one that can be overcome with a little extra time and effort. A necessary ingredient in this process is a great deal of out-of-class consultation. For me, the assignment of individual topics entails, on average, about 15 minutes of office-hour time per student, in addition to the usual time needed to help some students overcome difficulties as they write their papers. A corollary benefit of this is the chance to interact with even the most reticent students in the class.

Let us look at a particular instance of this technique, one that has been consistently successful for me during the past four years. It is a topic family based on Chapter 2 of Berlinghoff and Grant (1988), an exploration of perfect numbers, which is covered in class just prior to the paper assignment. Early in that chapter the students are taught how to compute the prime factorization of a number n, the number $D(n)$ of its divisors, the sum $S(n)$ of its divisors, and the sum $P(n)$ of its proper divisors. They construct a table listing the divisors, $D(n)$, $S(n)$ and $P(n)$, for all the numbers from 1 through 30. This table provides a data source in which patterns may be sought (see Table 7.1). The assignment reads like this:

> This is a mathematical research paper on numbers. In class we have developed several ways of describing some properties of natural numbers: Prime factorization, $D(n)$, $S(n)$, $P(n)$. You have made a table of these items for the numbers from 1 through 30.
>
> By the end of this week, you are to see me in my office. Together we shall define a "new" type of number based on the material listed

Table 7.1 Divisors and their characteristics, for the numbers 1 through 30

n	List of Divisors	Number of Divisors *D(n)*	Sum of Divisors *S(n)*	Sum, Proper Divisors *P(n)*
1	1	1	1	0
2	1,2	2	3	1
3	1,3	2	4	1
4	1,2,4	3	7	3
5	1,5	2	6	1
6	1,2,3,6	4	12	6
7	1,7	2	8	1
8	1,2,4,8	4	15	7
9	1,3,9	3	13	4
10	1,2,5,10	4	18	8
11	1,11	2	12	1
12	1,2,3,4,6,12	6	28	16
13	1,13	2	14	1
14	1,2,7,14	4	24	10
15	1,3,5,15	4	24	9
16	1,2,4,8,16	5	31	15
17	1,17	2	18	1
18	1,2,3,6,9,18	6	39	21
19	1,19	2	20	1
20	1,2,4,5,10,20	6	42	22
21	1,3,7,21	4	32	11
22	1,2,11,22	4	36	14
23	1,23	2	24	1
24	1,2,3,4,6,8,12,24	8	60	36
25	1,5,25	3	31	6
26	1,2,13,26	4	42	16
27	1,3,9,27	4	40	13
28	1,2,4,7,14,28	6	56	28
29	1,29	2	30	1
30	1,2,3,5,6,10,15,30	8	72	42

above and find two or three examples of such a number. That type of number will be yours to name and to investigate for a week or so, using as many of the problem-solving tactics from Chapter 1 as you find helpful.

Your paper is to be a description of that investigation, telling me what specific questions you asked yourself, describing the tactics you pursued, showing where they led, etc. (In this type of investigation even a blind alley is something to report, provided you can describe the alley.)

   You may consult with me on this project as much as you wish and may also discuss your topic with other members of the class (if they'll put up with it). However, the paper itself is to be your own writing and is to describe the results of your own investigation.

When a student comes to pick a topic, we examine the table together, looking for patterns or common properties of several numbers that might strike that student as interesting. Often I ask the student to pick his or her favorite number; we then search the list for numbers that have similar characteristics of some sort. For example, suppose the student picks 18. We first write down the relevant data about 18:

$$18 = 2 \cdot 3^2 \qquad D(18) = 6 \qquad S(18) = 39 \qquad P(18) = 21$$

Next, we look for relationships among these numbers; in this case, $D(18)$, $S(18)$ and $P(18)$ all are divisible by 3. Searching the list for other numbers with that property, we find none, so the property seems to be rare. That's a promising avenue of investigation for a good student, but an average student might need something with a few more easy examples in hand. We might modify the property by just requiring $D(n)$ and $S(n)$ to be divisible by 3. Now there is another example in the list:

$$20 = 2^2 \cdot 5 \qquad D(20) = 6 \qquad S(20) = 42$$

Exploring a few numbers just beyond the list, we find another number with this property:

$$32 = 2^5 \qquad D(32) = 6 \qquad S(32) = 63$$

The student is then told to pick a name for numbers of this kind and find five pages of things to say about them.

   At that point (or within the next few days), a common response is "I don't know where to start" or "I don't know what to do." This is where the problem-solving tactics take over. I point out that among those tactics are such items as "construct examples," "solve a simpler problem," "look for a pattern," etc., and suggest some specific questions along those lines:

- Can you find a few more beyond 30? How?
- What about patterns from prime factorizations? (A key question!)
- Does this only happen when $D(n) = 6$?

- What about other powers of 2? Can you characterize when it happens for them?
- What about powers of other primes?
- Are all such numbers even?
- What about $2^2 \cdot p$ for various primes p?
- What about $3^2 \cdot p$ for various primes p?
- What about $q^2 \cdot p$ for various primes p, q?

Questions like these generate lots of easy patterns and theorems (which are left to the reader to discover), and the pursuit of their answers can always be described, regardless of its outcome.

I hear a skeptical voice saying, "But what if the student picks a number like 7, whose table entries are trivial?" In that event, here are some possible patterns and questions:

7 is a factor of $S(n) - 4$, 13, 20, 26, 28
  Which primes work?
  Are the others all even?
  Which multiples of 7 work?
7 is a factor of $P(n) - 8$, 18, 22, 28, 30
  Which powers of 2 work?
  Always even?
  Do all numbers that end in 8 work?
7 is a factor of $P(n) + D(n) - 9$, 14, 20
  Which multiples of 7 work?
  Do any powers of 2 work?
  Which powers of 3 work?

A typical list of student topics, taken from last year's class, is as follows (as usual, "|" means "is a factor of"):

$D(n) | S(n) + P(n)$
$k | P(n)$ for various k
$k | S(n)$ for various k
$D(n) = 4$ and $3 | S(n)$
$3 | D(n)$ and $3 | S(n)$
$D(n) | S(n)$
$S(n) - D(n) + 1 = 3n/2$
$5 | S(n) + D(n)$
$5 | S(n) - D(n)$
$5 | D(n) + P(n)$
$7 | D(n) + P(n)$

Occasionally a student will come in with a topic already chosen, sometimes with surprising consequences. My most memorable instance of this happened three years ago, when a student (a sophomore geography major) proposed to investigate numbers that satisfied the condition

$$\frac{n \cdot S(n)}{P(n) \cdot D(n)} \text{ is divisible by 5.}$$

Despite my voiced concerns that this might be difficult (and much silent skepticism), she went off on her own and characterized all primes that fit this definition, found one non-prime that works (24), proved that no square of a prime can work, proved a general set of necessary conditions for composite numbers, proved a necessary condition for doubles of primes (which could be used to eliminate that type of number entirely), and posed some interesting questions for future investigation!

Work of this caliber is not the usual result of these assignments, but neither is it unique. Successful proofs of theorems are rare, but it is common to see correct conjectures based on perceptive pattern recognition, often accompanied by some comment of pleasant surprise. The main point is that the students do what is for them original mathematical research, most of them get some satisfaction out of it, and many of them actually like it! Thus, the writing assignments actually enhance the level of student mathematical activity in the course, giving the students a much better appreciation of what the so-called "mathematical way of thinking" is all about.

REFERENCES

Berlinghoff, W. P., & Grant, K. E. (1988). *A mathematics sampler* (2nd ed.). New York: Ardsley House.

Polya, G. (1957). *How to solve it* (2nd ed.). Princeton, NJ: Princeton University Press.

CHAPTER 8

Writing and the
Teacher of Mathematics

David L. White and Katie Dunn

Mathematics teachers often feel that problem solving and the tools for problem solving (such as application, estimation, mental computation, and the use of calculators and computers) are important, but they do not often include these topics in their classroom instruction. Instead, many teachers find themselves teaching to objectives and tests that emphasize minimum competencies in mathematics, especially algorithmic computation. In turn, many classrooms are currently occupied with addressing step-by-step algorithmic procedures without regard to conceptual development, applications of mathematics, or problem-solving tools and situations.

In interviews we have conducted, teachers often state that they teach rote computational algorithms because they had been taught that way in their own college mathematics classes and therefore believe that this is the desired way to teach mathematics. Early in our work with problem solving in the classroom, one teacher stated to us, "Problem solving has always been an area that I have tread with dread. I was never that good in this area of mathematics. . . . Philosophically, I suppose that I know deep inside that problem solving should be the only way that upper elementary math should be taught." Another stated, "The area that math students fear most is word problems. Even though I have tried various approaches to teaching problem solving in my seventh- and eighth-grade classes, I have

The study reported here is based upon work supported in part by the National Science Foundation under Grant No. TEI-8554433. The authors wish to thank the National Science Foundation for funding the project from which the study grew and their respective institutions for their support. The views expressed do not necessarily reflect the policy or position of the funding agency. The authors also wish to thank Dixie Dellinger for her extremely helpful responses to early drafts.

yet to discover an approach that I could recommend to other teachers." In short, despite their stated belief that problem solving is an important component of mathematics, few teachers believe they can use problem solving in meaningful ways in their classroom. We attempted to address beliefs embodied in statements such as these by helping teachers find ways to teach problem solving. In designing our project, we chose writing as a way to help teachers focus on their beliefs about the teaching and learning of mathematics.

DESCRIPTION OF THE *MATHCAPS* PROJECT

Conceived in 1985 and initiated in the summer of 1986, the Mathematics Consortium for Applications and Problem Solving (MATHCAPS) Project has as one of its goals the improvement of the teaching and learning of mathematics in schools. In the first phase of this four-year project, 30 selected middle school teachers were chosen from eastern Tennessee and southwestern Virginia to participate as "leader teachers."

Selected middle school teachers attended a rigorous eight-week summer institute at East Tennessee State University conducted by respected visiting scholars in mathematics and mathematics education from throughout the country. These visiting scholars were assisted by project staff, representatives from businesses and industries, and educators from other content areas. Teachers then returned to their home schools where they attempted to use the knowledge, philosophy, goals, and materials from the project. In addition, they were placed in a leadership role where they met weekly during the academic year with a cadre of three to five peer teachers to share goals, knowledge, philosophies, methodologies, and materials gained from the summer institute. Assisting them in this were staff members from the project who followed them into their classrooms and visited and supported the leader teachers and the peer teachers. This follow-up continued during the remainder of the academic year. Leader teachers returned during the subsequent summer for a four-week summer workshop designed to further reinforce the teachers' newfound knowledge and beliefs. During their second summer, teachers refined and modified project products, reviewed and analyzed the year's experiences as recorded in the academic-year journal entries, rethought the problem-solving strategies and materials by writing about them, and refined their understandings of the project, its goals, and its philosophies by writing additional pieces for publication.

We were especially interested in what changes in attitudes, beliefs, and instructional practices occurred in the leader teachers and their peer teachers as a result of participation in the project. We also were interested in the factors influencing the changes. These seemed to be

1. A strong support system established for the leader teachers – the committed support of the local school systems for the participants, and the collegiality developed among the leader teachers, their peers, the project staff, and the visiting scholars
2. A personal commitment secured from the leader teachers prior to being accepted for participation in the project
3. Prestige factors – the reputation of the project and the status of the visiting scholars
4. The intensity and duration of the project
5. Increased opportunities for leadership roles in the home school system
6. Successful implementation of content and strategies into the classroom
7. Writing – journals and the other forms sponsored by the project

While following and documenting the changes in beliefs that our teachers were experiencing, we wanted to ascertain the middle school teachers' beliefs about what was important in the teaching and learning of mathematics, including views of problem solving and whether these views reflected classroom instructional practices. We accomplished this in several ways including preassessments, formal and informal personal interviews conducted by the project staff, and analyses of various writings.

Most of the middle school teachers viewed problem solving as the solving of "word problems" and included "word problems" about once a week in their homework assignments. Most of the teachers never used strategies such as small-group problem-solving sessions or hands-on activities. The majority of the teachers did not make use of calculators, and none used the computer except for games or drill and practice. In general, participants came to the project believing that problem solving should be implemented but did not do so. They seemed to believe, instead, that state mandates and the objectives and tests of mathematical computation were stronger pushes. Problem solving was relegated to an unimportant position, and problem solving often consisted of story or word problems.

THE USE OF WRITING IN THE *MATHCAPS* PROJECT

A major component of the MATHCAPS Project, writing proved an agent of change in teachers' beliefs about the learning and teaching of mathematics. The teachers were introduced to the principal purposes of writing in mathematics, including the following:

1. To foster reflective thinking among the participants in order to modify their beliefs about the teaching and learning of problem solving and applications of mathematics
2. To develop a deeper conceptualization of mathematics
3. To provide a vehicle for dissemination of some of the project products, including modules on specific areas (e.g., rational numbers), articles on the teaching and learning of mathematics, and problem sets
4. To establish working relationships with peer teachers, principals, supervisors, and others
5. To make revisions in the project itself
6. To serve as documentation of changes in teachers' beliefs during teachers' participation with the project.

The writings took many forms.

1. Daily journal entries were made by the participants during the summer institute, and weekly entries were made during the academic year. These were generally initiated by the prompt, "What happened today (or this week) and what did you think about it?"
2. Leader teachers also maintained a double-entry notebook where they kept notes from the visiting scholar presentations and from assigned readings. Later, the leader teachers used their initial notes as a basis for more reflective writing.
3. Participants wrote modules for use with their peer teachers on specific mathematical content areas. Teachers worked in "writing groups," and first rough drafts of the modules were completed during the summer institute. Leader teachers were asked to write comments and modifications during the academic year as they used these modules with their peer teachers. These modules served as a focus of discussion with the peer teachers in the weekly meetings during the academic year. The modules were then revised during the follow-up summer workshop by the leader teachers based upon their academic year experience.
4. Leader teachers wrote problem sets weekly during the summer institute and monthly during the academic year. Here, they posed a "good" problem, one which involved problem solving and applications with a discussion about extensions, applications for the classroom, and possible solutions.
5. During the follow-up summer workshop, leader teachers were asked to

write an article to be submitted for publication in a professional journal for an audience of practitioners based upon a review of literature, classroom practice, or classroom research.

6. Leader teachers were also asked to write a position paper on some aspect of the teaching and learning of mathematics reflecting their own development. Many of these were submitted by the teachers for publication.

7. During the summer institute and throughout the academic year, leader teachers were asked to correspond through letters with their peer teachers, principals, superintendents, congressmen, and others about the project goals and their experiences in the implementation of these goals.

In sum, teachers wrote in a wide variety of forms, for various immediate and removed audiences, and for a variety of purposes.

Thus, we saw writing in the MATHCAPS Project as one of the driving forces to improve the quality of the teaching and learning of mathematics. We felt that if teachers' beliefs didn't change, neither would their practice; furthermore, we felt that if any change in practice were to be long-lived after the project, then teachers would need a set of beliefs that would sustain practice. The design of the MATHCAPS Project provided an opportunity for the teachers to reflect in writing (Burton, 1985) upon proposed innovations in their classrooms. Because the project views teachers as informed, well-intentioned decision-makers, we encouraged them to construct for themselves and through writing a complex and coherent set of beliefs and ideas about problem solving and applications in the mathematics classroom. Seen in this framework, writing became a tool not merely for checking knowledge (cf. Applebee, 1981) but for helping the writer define, clarify, construct, and return to and reshape that knowledge and those beliefs which are growing, developing, and shifting.

EVIDENCE OF TEACHER CHANGE

About halfway through the middle school teachers' experience with the project, they were asked to write a self-report about what changes had occurred as a result of MATHCAPS. From the self-reports and from quantitative reports from weekly logs, we saw changes in the teachers, their beliefs, and their instructional practices during their MATHCAPS experience.

All 28 leader teachers reported that their views of mathematics had expanded, and the majority believed problem solving to be at the heart of mathematics. All said they were better problem solvers themselves. In their classroom they were focusing on problem solving and applications of mathematics by teaching students to look at the reasonableness of their answers, to estimate and to develop mental computation skills, to use patterns, to develop through estimation good number sense, and other problem-solving strategies. Teachers reported that changes in their students included an improvement in attitudes toward mathematics, loss of mathematics anxiety, the use of problem-solving strategies, an increase in the number and quality of questions, an increase in their communication with each other, and the development of good problem-solving skills.

One of the most evident changes in the leader teachers is the growth of their self-confidence. They feel better prepared to teach problem solving and more complete in their content knowledge. In addition, they feel competent to utilize many of the teaching strategies gained from the summer institute of the project.

We feel that writing played an important role in enabling these changes to come about. The journals are one form of writing sustained by the project over a fairly extended period of time and one which helped teachers in rethinking and reshaping their beliefs about the teaching and learning of mathematics. Moreover, for the project staff, the journals became both the bane of our existence (there were so many of them) and one of the joys of the project (they reveal human beings grappling with the immediate, real-life problems set before them).

THE JOURNAL ENTRIES

In the journals, teachers were encouraged to explore, to think, to reflect and to analyze their own responses to the ideas presented by the project. Writing for a minimum of 30 minutes each day during the summer, and for at least 30 minutes once each week during the academic year follow-up, teachers reflected upon and wrote about the event of the time just past. In both cases, the usual prompt was to write about "What happened, and what do you think about it?" During the summer the teachers were sometimes given more focused, more specific prompts including:

- What do you see as the most important theme of the summer institute thus far and what is your feeling about it?
- What problem-solving processes did you engage in as you attempted to solve [a specific] problem?
- What has been a significant experience to you during the project thus far and how will it change what you do in your classroom?

I (White) read and responded to all journal entries. I responded to summer journal entries with marginal notes and end notes on each journal entry, and to the academic year follow-up journals with letters. In both the summer and the academic-year journal entries, my responses to the journal entries took the form of asking for clarification, elaboration, examples, or further support of the content (e.g., "What do you mean by 'the students will be better able to perform'?"). At certain points, I also challenged participants to give rationales, to take a stand and defend it, or to declare themselves more openly in the journal. Some teachers went on to make guesses as to the soundness of ideas or their application to their own classrooms, while others began to write about the principles involved and their applications. Of course, there were also journal entries which bemoaned the exhausted state of the writer or which wandered far afield.

In work reported elsewhere (White, 1987), I analyzed the audience, length, and topics of the journals. Here I will merely report the results of that work as a way to describe the journal entries themselves. The journals sampled from those written during the summer varied in length from a low of 52 words per entry to a high of 349 words per entry. The mean number of words per journal entry was 105. Of these examined journals written during the summer, all but two (or 92 percent) had as their audience a trusted other. The remaining audiences for the journal were self (one instance) and examiner (one instance). Thus, teachers seemed to be unencumbered by the constraint of feeling themselves examined by their audience (the project staff) and instead saw themselves as being relatively free to use the journals as a place where they could write to a trusted other and expect to have their writing seen as a worthy and worthwhile endeavor. This became an important factor in building a sense of trust between writer and reader and helped teachers to devote their energies to thinking and rethinking their understandings and beliefs.

The journal entries written during the academic year were similar in audience and length to those written during the summer. For the academic year, most journal entries frequently mentioned changes in the relationship between the teacher and his or her peer teachers. That this is the case is not surprising considering the leadership role that we asked teachers to take in their home schools with peer teachers and other teachers in their building and districts and the strong professional and personal interaction that developed during the yearlong relationship. Teachers commented on the ways peer teachers reacted to them as sources of knowledge about the teaching and learning of mathematics and about the ways other teachers in their home schools came to see them as "experts" in teaching mathematics.

The journals also frequently discussed the teachers' use of materials and activities suggested by the modules. Teachers were making extensive use of the materials they produced under the sponsorship of the project; indeed, they developed an intense ownership of what they had gleaned from the visiting scholars' presentations and had made the ideas their own. We feel that this ownership of materials and methods, brought about in large part by the use of writing, was the cause for success on the part of the teachers. It seems that of all the writing activities, the journal entries had the greatest impact, so far as changing the materials and procedures teachers use in their classrooms and in strengthening their role as professionals interacting with peers.

The writing that teachers did both documented these changes and fostered them. The relationship between writing and change in teacher beliefs is more complex and circular than it is linear. Teachers used their journals as a place to think about and reflect upon a number of topics. Certainly, we cannot say that writing has forced these changes upon them. But just as certainly, we *can* say that writing documents these changes as teachers discuss the ways that their teaching and learning of mathematics have changed as an outgrowth of the project. We can further say that writing gave teachers a place to think about and to assess tentatively the changes that were taking place in their thinking and beliefs both during the summer and during the academic year when the demands of the classroom are even more exacting.

In addition to allowing teachers to think and rethink their ideas and beliefs, analyze and re-analyze their beliefs, writing also allows teachers to construct for themselves alternate, diverse, and divergent views of the teaching and learning that goes on in their classrooms. This function of writing can be of value to teachers who are undergoing rapid changes similar to the changes experienced by teachers in the project.

Throughout our dealings with the teachers and the writings, we have made the assumption that what teachers wrote in their journals was honest, straightforward, and without intention to deceive. An analysis of the audience of the journal entries supports this contention. The changes teachers reported in their journal entries do not seem to be fabrications; the changes teachers wrote about seem genuinely to be the changes teachers perceived in themselves and their classrooms. To the extent that sustained, lengthy, and multiple self-report data can be accurate, the journals seem to be so. In addition, the journal entries are substantiated by other evidence including more than 200 on-site visits by project staff, by the postassessment data, by other writings, and by weekly and monthly reports containing quantitative data. In short, we found that writing not only fostered change but also documented that change, for both the project staff and the teachers.

WRITING AS AN AGENT FOR CHANGE

We have mentioned several changes that have occurred in teachers' beliefs. One important additional change is that the teachers began to see themselves as agents of change. As one participant wrote, "If I am to be a professional, I must be aware of the changes in content and methods. Furthermore, I must be instrumental in trying to influence future changes." The writing itself changed; teachers grew in fluency; they became more at ease and produced greater amounts of analysis and reflection as the year progressed. Often it was only when their deeply held beliefs were made explicit that they actually began to talk productively about learning and teaching mathematics. Without the writing, beliefs and conceptions about teaching and learning mathematics remained hazy; the teachers and the project staff could not reach towards those deeply held and unarticulated beliefs until they became articulated.

Writing helped teachers to see inconsistencies in their beliefs. In writing for extended periods of time, teachers had to push themselves to elaborate and detail what it was that they thought. They could not continue to state truisms about mathematics or teaching or brush aside the difficulties they had encountered in teaching or learning mathematics. Because extended writing about the same topic demands delving, sifting through ideas, and lengthy analysis, it forced teachers to examine what was seldom examined.

Writing helped teachers to learn new mathematical knowledge. In the few freewrites in which teachers wrote about their solving of particular mathematics problems, several were heard to exclaim in the midst of their writing, "*Now* I see." It takes only one "I see it" from fellow participants to convince many teachers that writing can actually help in learning mathematics.

Writing helped teachers hold in stasis what they were thinking. As such it served as a document to themselves of what they thought or believed at particular times. One of our participants, for example, told us at the end of the summer institute that she had made little change that summer, that although she had learned much in the way of mathematics, she had not changed much in what she believed about the teaching of mathematics, nor had she really enjoyed the summer. Later, she went back to read her journals. "Absolutely flabbergasted" were her words. She saw what she was thinking during the summer and was astounded. She had made tremendous changes in what she believed although she had not realized it until her re-reading of her journals. After re-reading her journals, things began to click; she said she saw for the first time what the visiting scholars were trying to do, what they were really saying. Other teachers related similar experiences. Writing helped teachers to make changes in what they believed and, just as importantly, helped them to see that those changes were real, substantive, and that the changes could be articulated and discussed with other teachers.

There is much to consider in attempting to enable teachers to think most productively about change through their journal writing. We found the following concerns central to planning for writing as an agent for change:

1. Writing tasks or assignments should be standing and consistent; we found once-a-day or once-a-week journal writing routines worked well for us. Making the assignment systematic gives teachers the knowledge that they will be writing on a consistent schedule, thereby stimulating them to come up with ideas for the writing. Often teachers told us that they gave much thought hours or days before actually writing the journals in order to begin to write particular entries. This brings about what Donald Graves calls "composing without writing": thinking between occasions for writing about what will be said in the next journal, a continual process of considering, generating, choosing, and contemplating ideas.

2. Journals must be part of a reading/writing cycle. Writers need to be read and responded to; they cannot continually write into a void. They need responses that assist them in their conversations with their topics. In our case, the project staff read and responded; peers read and responded. Our responses were primarily written but took other forms as well, including conversations, phone calls, individual and small-group conferences, and impromptu dialogues.

3. Responses to the journals must emphasize the content being communicated. Responses shape the journals and so should focus on the most important matters at hand. For instance, we are a project dealing with problem solving and applications in mathematics; as such, tangential topics were interesting but not the usual focus of comments and responses. Likewise, we placed explicit emphasis on thinking and writing about ideas concerning teaching and learning mathematics. As a result, responding to journals never took the form of response to surface features; instead, responses were made to content issues.

4. Writers often need a push to make generalizations based on the understandings and ideas being dealt with. Teachers rarely have the occasion to do this and are often somewhat reticent to do so, usually waiting for "expert" opinions before making pronouncements about ideas they are dealing with. We responded to the journals with questions that pushed for generalizations: Why is this so? How do you know? What does all this add up to? What does it mean? Teachers rose to the occasion in their writing

and replied with generalizations about teaching and learning mathematics.

5. To help teachers make full use of the journals, ways need to be found that encourage them to see their journals with new eyes, to see their ideas in a different light. Such ways include having the teachers going back to earlier entries and revisit the same ideas, re-thinking, re-envisioning, re-reading, re-writing. The same purpose can be accomplished by juxtaposing what they say with what they do: the inconsistencies between professed belief and action, between visiting scholars' principles and journal report, between statements of "should" and statements of "is" about the mathematics classroom.

6. As the year drags on and as enthusiasm for teaching in general wanes, response to the journals needs to be encouraging when that is appropriate. Some parts of the daily grind of teaching involve acting without thinking: getting through the day in the midst of spring fever, trying to keep some sanity in the face of difficult and demanding schedules. The journals sometimes reflect this. Responses then become empathic, sympathetic, and sometimes almost a form of cheerleading. One kind word of understanding often enabled a teacher to deal with a difficulty, and then dispense with bemoaning currently unresolvable classroom conditions and get on with the task of thinking about learning and teaching mathematics.

Much of what we were able to accomplish in the journal writing was an outgrowth of the audience teachers perceived for their journals. The teachers knew their writing was addressed to a select and knowing audience, an audience already quite well informed of the context (including prior knowledge, shared goals, and common beliefs) from which the teachers wrote. Thus, teachers as writers were able to use their journals for analysis rather than merely description or report.

When teachers write for analysis, make guesses, rise to abstraction, and attempt to discuss principles, as they did in their journals, they are dealing in generalizations and ideas, not merely in the particularities or vagaries of isolated events. The journal entries become a place where teachers were encouraged to take chances with these kinds of thinking. And, as such kinds of writing may be a new and unconsolidated affair for them, teachers devoted more attention to the ideas they were developing and less to the formal aspects of writing. The journals themselves are messy, often lacking in some of the conventions of standard written English: the emphasis is on thinking and reaching, not on observing form, conventions, or mechanics. But instead of cleaning up surface features and forms in their journals, most teachers engaged in the rough, difficult, and demanding job of analytical thinking. Again we believe that this came about because of the relationship of trust they had established with their reader/responders.

Trust was built up through the long give-and-take of writing back to teachers about the topics they raised, legitimizing their interest in the topics they wrote about but also pushing them to more analysis of the topics considered most important by us as project staff (those relating to problem solving and applications of mathematics in the context of the teachers' particular classrooms and schools). Balancing the need to push for more analysis with the need to conserve teachers' trust (while still maintaining a mutual respect and collegiality) often required a negotiation by all parties that was sensitive to the roles and needs of both the teachers and the reader/responders.

Another important issue grows out of the trust and resulting frankness found in the journals. Because the teachers were using their own language to make sense of the changes going on in their thinking (cf. Bertoff, 1981), and because the journal entries provided a forum for them to initiate topics that they themselves were interested in, the journal entries gave a different perspective from which to observe the participants and from which to make a general assessment of how they fulfilled the goals of the project or changed and modified those goals. The views of teachers that we received from the journals, moreover, were views quite different from those we developed without the journals; what we saw in participants outside the journals was often not as insightful as what we saw in their journals. Since we as responders pushed teachers to defend their opinions and ideas, and since we were all working toward a common purpose, teachers often pushed us as well to defend our own stances. We were pleased to see this but sometimes unprepared for the depth of resistance often seen in the journals. But this, too, was an important function of the journals: revealing how deeply teachers held their beliefs about the teaching and learning of mathematics and giving us a relatively "safe" forum from which to discuss those beliefs.

CONCLUSION

Writing worked very well for us in our teacher-training project. In fact, teachers saw that writing did for the project what we had set out for it to do. Although we did not concentrate on writing as a tool for teachers themselves to use in their own classroom, several decided to use journal writing with their students. One teacher used journal writing once a week in her pre-algebra classroom as a review of content by asking, "What did we do this week, and what did you learn from it?" Another used journal writing before each new mathematics topic was introduced, asking her seventh-grade students to respond to such journal starters as, "What have you done before with mixed numbers?" "Tell me in your own words what a fraction *really* is?" or "Explain for a younger brother or sister what you know about dividing fractions." A third teacher had her students pick out the most difficult question on a test and explain what they did to answer it. Still another asked students to write letters home about what is going on in mathematics class; this same teacher also assigns report writing for outside enrichment about the history of mathematics.

Although we did not see writing as a tool for learning in mathematics as the focus of the project and although we did not specifically suggest to teachers that they use writing in their own mathematics classrooms, we were of course pleased that they did so and that they thought writing useful in the mathematics classroom. Moreover, it seemed to us an indication of teachers' beliefs about the power of writing that many of them incorporated it into their own classrooms.

As powerful a tool as writing is and as effective as it is in allowing us to talk about deeply held beliefs and understandings, it does have its limitations. First, it did not seem to "work" for every participant. Those mathematics teachers for whom it did not work seemed resistant to the idea of writing as a force for thinking. Many who were technically proficient in the formal aspects of writing did not embrace the task of writing as an important activity, did not see that writing helped to clarify or to aid thinking, and did not engage in what we thought of as reflective or deep analysis in their writing. Those participants for whom it did not work also appeared to distance themselves from the project and did not adopt the goals or philosophy of the project in a wholehearted manner.

Second, writing has limitations in that it focuses attention and thinking on one idea to the exclusion of another. When we focused journal writing in the summer on the *teaching* of mathematics, we did so at the expense of focusing writing on *learning* mathematics. Correspondingly, the number of teachers who used writing as a tool for learning in their own classrooms was much smaller than the number of teachers who used writing in their own classrooms for other purposes. When teachers were asked if writing helped them to learn mathematics, most replied that it had not although they understood that it did help some of the other teachers. Those teachers for whom the freewrites had helped in learning mathematics were, for the most part, those teachers who later used writing to learn mathematics in their own classrooms. (The situation has a parallel in problem solving in mathematics. Those most engaged with problem solving in the summer institute were often those using problem solving the most in their own classrooms. Thus, it seemed that those teachers learning content—whether it be problem solving itself or writing to learn that content—were those most eager to share the same experience with their students.)

Finally, writing has its limitations in that it is an expensive proposition. It takes little in terms of material goods, but it is vastly expensive of time, focus, and energy. It takes much to sustain writing in terms of planning for writing, in the drafting itself, in reading and in responding. We acknowledge the great power for change that writing embodies, but we likewise acknowledge the tremendous effort that must be taken to allow it to take place and to sustain it at levels of thoughtful analysis.

Despite its limitations and expense, writing is powerful and empowering. Perhaps an example of a journal entry that strikes us most as writers and demonstrates the empowering feeling that develops as teachers use writing comes from an eighth-grade teacher from a small town in eastern Tennessee. She wrote,

> I am not a writer. . . . When it is necessary that I write, I write, re-write, read for "sense," read again for spelling, read again for tense, a seemingly endless task. I hate it. When I found we were going to have to actually write every day—keep a journal—did I groan! Why? Why is this necessary? I'm a math person not an English person! Write-Ugh! D. said to write so I wrote—with great difficulty at first. The writing was almost illegible, grammar nearly non-existent, ideas erratic. D. said not to worry about structure and spelling so I didn't. D. said to concentrate on getting my ideas on paper, so I did. Amazingly, changes began to occur. My pen began not to be able to move as fast as my ideas flowed. I was able to write for most of the allotted time. It is getting easier to put my ideas on paper. So my spelling is bad, so my grammar is not always correct, so I'm not as wordy as some people—so what—I am writing!

As dramatic and rewarding to the project staff as this teacher's beliefs about writing and about our own writing in particular may be, it is the actual changes in beliefs where we find our greatest success. The tremendous changes that we have seen in teacher beliefs lead us to view the project and its goals as obtainable, reasonable, and worthwhile objectives and writing a useful tool in helping teachers think and rethink their understandings and beliefs about the teaching and learning of mathematics.

REFERENCES

Applebee, A. N. (1981). *Writing in the secondary school.* Urbana, IL: National Council of Teachers of English.

Bertoff, A. (1981). *The making of meaning: metaphors, models, and maxims for writing teachers.* Upper Montclair, NJ: Boynton/Cook.
Burton, G. M. (1985). Writing as a way of knowing in a mathematics education class. *Arithmetic Teacher, 33,* 40–45.
White, D. L. (1987). Using writing to change teacher beliefs about the teaching and learning of mathematics. *Innovations, 5,* 37–65.

Part III

CLASSROOM APPLICATIONS: WHAT WORKS AND HOW

Physics and mathematics, writes David Layzer, "should be learned and taught not as a collection of facts, formulas, and rules but as a living language, or, more precisely, a family of living languages." This viewpoint is shared by most, probably all, of the authors in this section, indeed, this book. To think as a mathematician or scientist entails learning the community's language — a language that often employs a mathematical symbol system.

"Natural language" — the language we speak and write — is the meta-language of all education, through which we formally teach and learn nonlinguistic symbol systems. Written natural language may not translate exactly the language of mathematics, any more than program notes translate the language of music. But natural language helps us, through conversation in our primary tongue, to acquire and use the symbol system needed to think mathematically.

In his Core science courses for Harvard undergraduates, David Layzer says, "Writing forms the core of the learning process." In Kathryn Martin's biology courses for 100 students in a state university, students write 36 microthemes (described fully in her essay) so that "they come to 'own' the material themselves." Sandra Keith also gives many practical examples of the exploratory writing assignment that "engages the students with the moment of teaching (something which note-taking does not always do), develops trust, and improves the atmosphere in and out of the classroom." She also identifies what she has learned from students' writing about their ways of being wrong. All three emphasize how writing promotes active and collaborative learning, as alternative to frontal lecturing.

Richard Lesnak was skeptical, at first, that writing would help students in his remedial algebra course, but a controlled experiment showed it to be invaluable in achieving cognitive and affective goals. Particularly interesting is his account of integrating objectives, math

111

tasks, and a method of writing. Arthur Powell and his student, José López, designed experiments to evaluate the impact of writing in a developmental math class; their essay reports their positive findings. Especially noteworthy in the Powell/López case study is the collaboration between teacher and student in the research. "Writing to learn mathematics," they concluded, "is transformative not only for learners but for instructors as well." It is a point made again in this section by Mary Bahns, who speaks from her experience in teaching science educators of elementary school students. Through keeping journals of their teaching, she says, teachers may themselves become vital learners.

CHAPTER 9

Writing "Microthemes" to Learn Human Biology

Kathryn H. Martin

At the State University of New York at Oswego, students take three approved courses in the sciences to satisfy one of the requirements for general education. A large number of students have great difficulty with their science requirement in spite of success in their non-science majors. I have taught one of the general education courses, The Human Body and the Natural World, for the last ten years. This course has proven popular as a general education course partly because students perceive a human biology course as less threatening than a physics, chemistry, or earth science course. I have always taught the course as a lecture supported by audiovisual aids. Evaluations of the class indicate a very high level of comfort in class. Students report that they enjoy the lectures, and are particularly excited by the frequent spontaneous discussions (called "tangents").

There are often, however, students who for one reason or another (anxiety or poor background or learning disability?) do not record clear notes, cannot formulate the text material in a clear outline, and do not take objective tests successfully. As a result of my discussions with these students, I feel strongly that some do have a firm grasp of the material but cannot reduce their knowledge to a series of isolated facts. Somehow they "know" the material in a different way than scientists typically present and understand their own subject matter. I have been searching for a method of approaching my course that would allow these special students the opportunity to learn and review the material and to present their knowledge to me in a format that would reflect their unique approach to understanding science.

After attending workshops on the role of writing in learning math and science at the Institute for Writing and Thinking at Bard College, I came upon an idea for the restructuring of my course to accommodate the struggling students. I have been concerned that when lecture notes are the object of a student's study, the material is still "owned" by the instructor. Notes from my lectures reflect my own mental organization and understanding of the material. But if students write about the material, especially from some personal vantage point, they come to "own" the material themselves. I decided to try assigning short papers that would require a student to examine the material from a new perspective. The assignments are sufficiently broad to allow for great individuality and creativity, yet specific enough to demand that certain biological concepts be included. My goal is to increase their recall by associating the material with images or ideas of their own creation. I frequently ask them to draw useful analogies to explain the material. My assumption is that the analogy, if created by the student, will be easily recalled.

Thus, my students now have the option of writing on a daily basis as a means of reviewing biological concepts. These optional assignments, called "microthemes" substitute for part of the value of objective exams. I usually have a total of 100 students enrolled in two sections of the course. I anticipated an interest from about 10 percent of the students. But during the spring 1988 semester, more than half of the students completed at least 20 microthemes, and about one-third completed all 36 microthemes. Since I did not correct grammar and spelling, I was able to read through the microthemes very quickly. I spent an average of two to three additional hours per week reading the microthemes from both classes.

Students seemed to be liberated by the fact that I did not consider structure, grammar, or style. The level of creativity was exciting! Although I had originally planned to place only a checkmark on acceptable papers. I enjoyed reading the microthemes so much that I often added written comments to papers. My written reactions were received enthusiastically and provided an added incentive to students to continue their efforts. Because of this positive response, I now attempt to write at least one brief comment on each microtheme to reinforce student interest and enthusiasm.

The microthemes have also broadened my own imagery of many biological concepts. Covalent bonds have never been better illustrated for me than by two jugglers each with three balls sharing the fourth ball between them. A Pez candy dispenser illustrates perfectly the position of the epiglottis relative to the esophagus. The notes of the octave scale serve well for analogies involving the outer orbit of atoms and interactions between two atoms. The skin resembles the layers of the earth's crust. One student wrote about her narrow escape from anorexia. Students described a cell as a university campus, or a hot fudge sundae, or a pepperoni pizza, or a fortress bounded by a moat. Granulocytic white blood cells are infantrymen with polka-dotted uniforms and dented helmets. One student wrote a compelling theme on dangers of smoking; his mother had died of lung cancer earlier in the semester. I feel that I know this group of students better than I ever have any group in the past.

At the beginning of the course, students receive a complete syllabus with course announcements and an explanation of the microtheme option. The following is a portion of that syllabus including introductory notes, lecture topics, and microtheme assignments.

A SAMPLE SYLLABUS

Course Announcements and Assignments

Students learn in different ways. Many students internalize material better by reading the text, listening to the lecture, and then writing short essays about it. Sometimes this type of learner has great difficulty with objective exams. Other students have no difficulty in taking excellent notes, and in outlining chapters. This latter type of student often does well on objective exams after frequent rereading of notes and outlines. Still others have difficulty in taking lecture notes and reducing the chapters' contents to a series of isolated facts. These students have the greatest difficulty with objective exams. In order to accommodate different types of learners, I am offering a writing option during this course. It will not totally substitute for objective testing, but if all writing assignments are successfully completed, only 46% of the final grade will depend on objective testing.

The writing assignments are carefully designed to assist you in learning the material. They allow you to look at the material in a different way. While working on an assignment, you will easily find the trouble spots in a chapter and will have ample opportunity to gain understanding and insight into the topic. Often rereading notes does not allow you to realize areas of difficulty. Thus, with the writing option, you will likely learn class material more easily than if you attempted to simply memorize notes and outlines.

These writing assignments are called *Microthemes*. Please limit each microtheme paper to one page of typewritten material, or two pages of neatly handwritten material. Your microthemes must include biological concepts presented accurately. If the assignment is complete and acceptable, it will be returned with a checkmark. If no checkmark is present, you may rewrite the assignment. Rewrites will be accepted throughout the semester. However, you must attempt the assignment for the first time prior to the exam that covers the same material. Although good sentence structure and correct grammar will help me in reading your written efforts, I will only be checking for the accuracy of the biology. The assignments are designed as a means of your learning the material more easily than if you memorized notes and reread chapters. By writing about the material, you are re-creating it in your mind in a novel fashion. It is perfectly acceptable (and even wise) to talk with other students about the assignments, but the writing should be done independently.

Microthemes are not required but are encouraged as a tool for learning and as an acceptable substitute for part of the grade, especially for those students who do not take objective exams easily. They are not meant to be complete substitute for exams however. Thus, the grading scheme is a complex one in order to reward students for using microthemes without hurting those who do not choose to use them.

Determination of Grades

Exams: There will be 4 exams on chapter material as well as a comprehensive final. All exams will consist of about 35–60 objective questions (multiple choice). Each exam, including the comprehensive final, counts up to 200 points toward your final grade. Grades will be based on a potential total of 1000 points.

Students find that it is difficult to obtain meaningful notes from other students in the event of an absence. Many of the spontaneous class discussions can never be duplicated in a set of borrowed notes. I am therefore encouraging you to attend all classes.

Effect of Microthemes on Final Grade

There are 36 microthemes, one for each class session. You may elect to use the microthemes as a substitution for some of the points allotted to the four exams. Each microtheme, when accepted, has a value of 15 points. The final will count the full 200 points for all students.

Example: Completion and acceptance of all 36 microthemes means that 540 points of your grade have been fully earned. Instead of 800 points (1000 minus the 200 points reserved for the final exam), the first four exams will count a total of 260 points (800 minus 540). Each will therefore count only 65 points (260 divided by 4) toward your final grade.

Topic Outline and Microtheme Assignments

1. *Introduction.* Type T persons, as described on pages 4 and 5 in your text, are daredevils, risk-takers, those who "live on the edge." Do you think you are a type T person? Support your answer with examples of your

behavior patterns. (This first theme has no right or wrong answer. It is simply designed to get you started in this type of assignment.)

2. *Atomic structure, bonding, hydrolysis and synthesis of life molecules, water, acids and bases, ATP.* Describe an atom of chlorine, an atom of sodium, and a molecule of sodium chloride using a descriptive analogy. Continue with your analogy to compare ionic and covalent bonds.

3. *Chemistry of life molecules.* You have been asked to explain life molecules (carbohydrates, lipids, proteins, nucleic acids) to a classroom of students. Select an age group, decide what is *most important* about these molecules for that age group and attempt to explain it in language and symbols that the class would understand.

4. *Cell structure and function, enzymes, diffusion and osmosis, protein synthesis, energy reactions.* Describe the structure and function of parts of the cell to an audience that knows NO biology! Use a descriptive analogy. Include cell membrane, cytoplasm, nucleus, nuclear membrane, chromosomes, nucleolus, mitochondria, endoplasmic reticulum, ribosomes, lysosomes, and Golgi apparatus. Do not include details of chemical reactions.

5. *Mitosis.* What is the relationship between mitosis and cloning? Do you believe that cloning should be approved as a human method of reproduction? Support your opinion.

6. *Tissues.* Your roommate, who is studying architecture, is having great difficulty with her or his general education biology course. Explain to your roommate the organization of the body using analogies that your roommate would easily understand. Include cells, tissues, and organs.

7. *Organ systems and skin.* Describe the structure of skin. Use an analogy to demonstrate how it is composed of the four basic tissues.

8. *Mouth, esophagus, stomach.* Pizza Hut has asked you to develop an ad campaign that extols the virtues of digesting one of their cheese pizzas. Utilizing catchy media analogies, describe what happens to a Personal Pan cheese pizza as it travels through the mouth, esophagus, and stomach. Use terms and analogies that your audience will understand.

9. *Small intestine, liver, pancreas, large intestine.* Pizza Hut is concerned about the media scare about colon cancer, and wants your ad campaign to include materials that describe what happens to the pizza lunch as it further travels through the small and large intestine. Be sure to include the role of the pancreas and liver.

10. *Nutrition and diets.* Describe a common diet or eating pattern that you have followed or that you have read about. Comment on the effectiveness of the plan (results in short-term weight loss or weight maintenance) and then comment on the positive and negative aspects of the plan.

11. *Anatomy of circulatory system, two circuits, heartbeat.* In the past few years, at least two babies at Loma Linda Hospital have been born with hypoplastic left heart (the left side of the heart is grossly underdeveloped and functions too poorly for survival). At least two of those babies received transplants (the first was a nonhuman heart and the second was a human heart). The editors of a health magazine for general readers have asked you to write a brief article describing the anatomy of a normal heart and explaining why hypoplastic left heart is always fatal. Use whatever analogies you might find helpful to describe the structure and circulatory pathways.

12. *Lymphatics blood pressure, velocity of flow, disorders.* You recently attended a large wedding that lasted over an hour. Just as the ceremony drew to a close, one of the bridesmaids fainted. She had been standing in the same position for the entire ceremony. After she regained consciousness, she asked you to explain to her why she fainted. With your expertise in human biology, you explain to her in comforting tones the role of her circulation in causing fainting spells. Suggest to her how to prevent a similar mishap in the future.

13. *Components of blood, plasma, red cells, blood clotting.* There are two parts to this assignment, Part 1 (counts as 1/3 of assignment): Red blood cells are unusual in that they have no nucleus. Why would this be an advantage for this type of cell? Part 2 (counts as 2/3 of assignment): The National Plumbers Association wishes it could design a plumbing system that would plug leaks just as human blood vessels do. You have been called in as a consultant to talk to them about the possibility. Tell them what would be necessary for a comparable system. Explain why you think it would be possible or impossible for them to produce such a system.

14. *White cells, blood type.* Describe the white cells of the blood using an analogy of military defenders. By using as colorful and detailed an analogy as possible you will find it easier to remember the names of the different cell types, their structures, and their functions.

15. *Immunity, AIDS.* The two Loma Linda babies described in microtheme 11 both received transplants. The first received a nonhuman heart and rejected it after a few weeks. The second received a human heart and is still thriving. Explain to a puzzled friend how the activities of the immune system account for the different responses.

16. *Anatomy of respiratory system, breathing.* There are two parts to this assignment. Part 1 (counts as 1/3 of assignment): Why can't you commit suicide by holding your breath? Part 2 (counts as 2/3 of assignment): Design a board or video game that teaches the parts of the respiratory tract. One wins the game when oxygen has been exchanged for carbon dioxide. Include all parts of the respiratory pathway from nostrils to cellular mitochondria and back.

17. *External and internal respiration, disorders.* Convince yourself or someone else to quit smoking!

18. *Excretion.* You have been asked to design a fictional story (or fairy tale) that utilizes an analogy to describe the functional parts of the kidney. The objective of the tale is to eliminate the dastardly molecule urea. Include the process of filtration, reabsorption, and concentration in the formation of urine by the kidney.

19. *Neurons, action potential.* You are now in a classroom, and your task is to describe to the class a pathway of communication taken by the nervous system. Select an age group. Include in your lesson the structure of a neuron, the process of an action potential, and the production and reception of neurotransmitters. Again, use an analogy that would be understood by your chosen age group. Assume NO prior knowledge of the topic other than the students' awareness of senses and responses. Your analogy can take the form of a story or board game or video game if desired.

20. *Peripheral nervous system.* Some people worry by overstimulating their sympathetic nervous system. Others worry by overstimulating their parasympathetic nervous system. How do you think such patterns developed? What symptoms do you think would characterize each type of worrier? Do you think you fit into either pattern?

21. *Central nervous system and drugs.* Considering the connections between the different parts of the brain, explain why we misinterpret the reality of dangers in our lives (e.g., a piece of paper [quiz] causes stomach pains, diarrhea, chills, or first-class worrying).

22. *Skeletal system.* You have been asked to speak to a school board anticipating an overall change in its sports and extracurricular activities program. Depending on the forces involved in the activity, different bones and joints are frequently damaged, and many become arthritic. For the following sports, *explain* briefly to the school board why you believe certain bones or joints are more likely to be damaged by repeated participation in the sport. Include football, bowling, soccer, chess, horseback riding, basketball, tennis, baseball, golf, bird watching. Feel free to offer advice on the safe sports activities for young people.

23. *Muscles.* Like so many other animals, humans have paired appendages to move about. It is interesting to consider the possibility of a wheel for locomotion instead. Given the limits of existing tissues in humans, do you think it would be possible to move about on a wheel-shaped organ? Support your answer.

24. *General senses, eye.* Your grandmother sees halos around lights because of cataracts (cloudy spots) in her lenses, and she has asked you to explain why. Explain to her how the eye works and why she sees halos. She is very upset at the thought of having the lens removed as a treatment for cataracts. Explain why this is an appropriate procedure to correct her condition.

25. *Ear.* You have been asked to develop a campaign to convince teenagers that loud music permanently damages their hearing. You are to include in your plan how the ear converts soundwaves of rock music to nerve impulses. You may use any analogy that might help your story.

26. *Hormones; pituitary, thyroid, adrenal, sex organs, parathyroid, pancreas.* You are sitting in the same waiting room as two sets of parents. One set has recently given birth to a baby with an enlarged and overactive pituitary. The other has given birth to a baby with a small underactive pituitary. Both babies are girls. Their physician wants them to consider therapeutic intervention, but the physician hasn't explained any details. They see you studying a human biology text, and assume you might be able to help. Explain what you think might happen to both babies without therapeutic intervention.

27. *Hormones* (continued). President Kennedy had Addison's disease. If untreated, how might it have affected his activities? Should the public have been told of this condition while he was a candidate? If a presidential candidate is diabetic and requires insulin injections daily, should the public know about this condition? Should there be any health requirements for candidates for the highest offices?

28. *Karyotype, meiosis.* Your roommate can *not* understand mitosis and meiosis. Explain the difference using an appropriate analogy, with the emphasis on the process of meiosis.

29. *Chromosomal inheritance.* A female patient with symptoms of both Down's syndrome and Turner's syndrome had a quick analysis of chromosomes, and 46 were counted. Since 46 chromosomes are found in the cells of normal individuals, how could this person have symptoms of chromosomal abnormalities? Explain how the chromosome configuration might have come about. Be specific as to when and how the abnormalities likely occurred.

30. *Genetics.* A friend of yours is a distraught mother. She has a daughter who recently miscarried. The daughter was Rh negative and received an injection of Rhogam right after the miscarriage, so she should be able to successfully bear Rh positive children in the future. The mother did not know her own blood type, but knows that her husband is Rh positive. Therefore she is convinced that it is her fault that her daughter is Rh negative. Explain the genetics of the situation to her. Use the terms

introduced in this chapter such as alleles, homozygous, heterozygous, autosome, genotype, phenotype.

31. *Polygenic inheritence, Multiple alleles, incomplete dominance, linkage, crossing over, sex-linked and influenced heredity, inherited diseases.* Why are there no females with Duchenne's muscular dystrophy?

32. *Male and female reproductive anatomy.* Women are often denied the opportunity to play contact sports for fear they will damage their reproductive organs. Referring to the structure and function of male and female genitalia and secondary sexual characteristics, support or refute this policy. Suggest an equitable policy.

33. *Hormonal control of reproduction, birth control, infertility.* You are engaged in a discussion on birth control methods as well as infertility treatments and procedures. The members of the group are comparing the limits each one feels should be imposed financially, ecologically, legally, or morally on the advancing technology. Present your views backed with biological facts behind such technology.

34. *Sexual diseases.* You have been asked to speak to your dorm about having a student with AIDS live on your floor. Give the students the pertinent information needed for them to accept the low level of danger. Include precautions that should be observed.

35. *Fetal development for the first three months.* You are teaching a class to high school students studying sexuality. Their text states that harmful substances are most dangerous to a fetus during the first three months of development. Students ask you to tell them why that is so. Answer them, referring in general to the events of development during those critical months. Use any appropriate analogies that would have meaning to your audience.

36. *Fetal development, birth, childhood.* When do *you* think that a *human* life begins? Word your answer as a response to someone who adamantly feels that a different point in time marks the onset of a *human* life.

CHAPTER 10

The Synergy Between
Writing and Mathematics

David Layzer

Thirty years ago, in a series of radio lectures called "The Two Cultures," the British novelist, applied mathematician, and civil servant C. P.
Snow (1959, 1964) set off a heated public debate over the role of science in
a liberal education. Snow argued that mathematics and the natural sciences define a culture of their own, distinct from the humanistic culture
embodied in literature, philosophy, history, and the arts. He pointed out
that while most scientists understand and appreciate art and literature,
few nonscientists have even a rudimentary knowledge of science. But,
Snow argued, the cultural value of science is just as great as that of literature and art. Snow's critics were scandalized. They conceded that the
second law of thermodynamics had its uses, but they rejected the assertion
that every educated person ought to know what it meant.

In British and most continental European universities, students of the
humanities and students of the natural sciences still pursue non-overlap-
ping courses of study. Someone who "reads" English at Liverpool University doesn't attend lectures in mathematics, physics, or biology; someone
who "reads" physics doesn't attend lectures on Shakespeare or Molière. In
most American universities the situation is different. Students majoring in
math, physics, or biology are required to take courses in the humanities
and social sciences; students in the humanities and the social sciences are
usually required to take some courses in the natural sciences. There is also a
good deal of public interest in science. American newspapers, magazines,
and television stations devote a lot of space and time to science and technology. Stories about the latest discoveries and theories in medicine, astronomy, biology, and physics frequently make the front pages, and some
papers carry weekly sections devoted to news about science and technology. As a result, many nonscientists have read or heard about low-tempera-

ture superconductivity or about the latest theory of how the universe began.

Yet public *understanding* of science is still low. Among the scientifically illiterate are some of the most influential members of our society. For example, a justice of the Supreme Court recently stated in a written opinion that no one has yet proved that "creation science" is not a science. Still more recently, the president of the United States admitted that he doesn't know enough about astrology to assess its validity. Views like these are not merely uninformed: The theory of evolution, which exposes "creation science" as a baseless superstition, is the organizing principle of modern biology. Had the opinion of Justice Scalia — a person with the highest legal qualifications — prevailed, biology courses in the public schools of Louisiana would have been required to accord equal status to "creation science" and evolution, a requirement that no competent teacher or textbook could have met. And President Reagan's inability to understand the fraudulent nature of astrologers' claims is the comic underside of his frightening inability to understand the equally fraudulent nature of claims that technology can in the foreseeable future create an impregnable shield against nuclear missiles.

Why do so few nonscientists achieve an adequate understanding of the scientific enterprise or of the most basic concepts of physics and biology? It isn't because nonscientists don't find science interesting; a glance at the best-seller list is enough to refute that notion. The major barrier to a deeper understanding of science, I suggest, is ignorance of mathematics. Consider the way that science is usually presented to college students who are not majoring in the natural sciences. Although many American colleges require all students to satisfy a natural science requirement, the courses nonscience students may take to satisfy the requirement neither assume nor use any mathematics beyond simple arithmetic. But mathematics is the language of physics. A physics course without math is like vegetarian beef stew. It may be appetizing and nutritious, but it doesn't even resemble the real thing. Trying to understand physics without using math is like trying to understand music without actually listening to any.

Physics, of course, is only a part of natural science. Biology depends much less heavily on mathematics. Nevertheless, a deep understanding of modern biology requires an understanding of certain key facts and ideas in chemistry and physics. The central achievement of twentieth-century biology is the demonstration that life is a natural process, i.e., one governed by physical laws. And physical laws are inherently and untranslatably mathematical. To understand what it means to say that life is a natural process one needs to understand a certain amount of basic physics, and to understand basic physics one needs to understand the language in which it is written. Thus, mathematical literacy is prerequisite to an understanding of modern science.

There's the rub. The heightened public interest in science hasn't been matched by an increase in the level of mathematical literacy among today's high school and college students. Why not? I doubt whether there has been a significant decline in the number of high school and college courses in mathematics or in their enrollments. On the contrary, more of the students I teach take more math courses, and more advanced math courses, than ever before. Not very long ago only a handful of American high schools taught calculus. Today nearly all of the *nonscience* students who enroll in my Core science courses have had at least an elementary calculus course in high school, and most of them have done well in these courses. Yet few of them can understand, much less construct, arguments that use the kinds of mathematics they have been "exposed" to. What has gone wrong?

In most schools and even, at the elementary level, in many colleges, mathematics is taught in the way that foreign languages used to be taught in American schools. The emphasis was on memorizing grammatical rules and word lists. After two or three years of such instruction, few students could use the language they were studying for any practical purpose. Analogously, most courses in algebra, geometry, trigonometry, analytic geometry, and calculus teach students to perform standard operations and to solve stereotyped problems. Rarely do they develop the student's ability to *use* mathematics — to understand or construct mathematical discourse. I wish to argue that the teaching of mathematics in schools and colleges needs to undergo the kind of revolution that has happened in the teaching of foreign languages.

MATHEMATICS AND NATURAL LANGUAGE

Let's begin our revolution by taking a closer look at the analogy between mathematics and a foreign language. That mathematics is *foreign*, few will deny; but is it a *language*? On this point opinions differ, and in ways that reflect the split between Snow's two cultures. Most nonscientists regard mathematics as a collection of definitions and formulas. For physicists, however, mathematics is an essential part of the language in which they think, speak, and write. As Galileo remarked, the book of nature is written in the language of mathematics.

The analogy isn't perfect, however, and the differences are as interesting and important as the similarities. Ordinary or "natural" language is the medium in which we think and speak about the world of ordinary experience. The words and phrases of a natural language derive their meanings, directly or indirectly, from shared experience. A color-blind person knows that "green" is a color name and that green is an attribute shared by leaves and go-signals. Yet the word doesn't carry the same associations for someone who can't distinguish green from red as it does for someone who can. Nor does it carry the same associations for a landscape painter as it does for a person with normal color vision who has never learned to see colors with a painterly eye. Does "green" have *exactly* the same meaning for *any* two people? Probably not, because two people can never fully share even such a "simple" experience as perceiving a patch of color. How much less can they share the experienced contexts of more abstract words such as "beauty" and "justice"!

Mathematics, by contrast, is an unnatural language. It is the medium in which one thinks and speaks of worlds that impinge on but don't coincide with the world of ordinary experience — the world of ideal geometric figures or the world of numbers, for example. Mathematical terms derive their meanings not from experience but from axioms. Axioms are, in a sense, definitions (they are sometimes called implicit definitions), but they differ in a crucial respect from the definitions one finds in a dictionary: they don't refer, directly or indirectly, to ordinary experience.

For example, geometric objects such as points, lines, and planes and relations such as betweenness and incidence (the relation between two distinct points and the line that passes through them, or between two nonparallel lines and their point of intersection) are defined by the axioms that mention them. The axioms completely specify the ways in which the terms that figure in them may legitimately be used. When I read the world "point" I may visualize a dot, but what I happen to visualize doesn't belong to the mathematical meaning of "point." In one system of axioms (the axioms of solid projective geometry), every true statement containing the words "point" and "plane" remains true if these words are interchanged — if "point" is everywhere replaced by "plane" and "plane" by "point." Thus the true statement "Two distinct points are incident with just one line" becomes the true statement "Two distinct planes are incident with just one line." I may visualize "point" either as a dot or as an indefinitely extended flat surface. In another system of geometry (plane projective geometry), "point" and "line" are interchangeable. Thus the true statement "Any two distinct points are incident with just one line" becomes the true statement "Any two distinct lines are incident with just one point." The last statement implies that in plane projective geometry there are no parallel lines. In still another kind of geometry (hyperbolic geometry) there are infinitely many distinct parallels to a given line through a point not on the line. The beginning student of mathematics is tempted to dismiss projective, hyperbolic, and other non-Euclidean geometries as "unreal." But to the experienced mathematician the worlds of projective and hyperbolic geometry are as real as the world of Euclid.

Mathematicians invent logically possible worlds and explore their structure. Physical scientists try to discover the underlying mathematical structure of the phenomenal world. But that structure must be invented before it can be discovered. Thus, recent astronomical evidence, interpreted in the light of Einstein's 1915 theory of gravitation, suggests that physical space is not Euclidean but hyperbolic — a possibility first envisioned early in the nineteenth century as a purely logical possibility by three pure mathematicians, Carl Friedrich Gauss, Nikolay Lobachevsky, and Janos Bolyai.

Because they transcend natural language, mathematics and natural science also transcend specific cultures. We can never hope to understand Euripides's plays in the way they were understood by their original audiences, but Euclid's *Elements* speaks to us as clearly as it did to his contemporaries. Chinese poetry is untranslatable; but T. D. Lee's lectures on particle physics and quantum field theory, originally given in Chinese, lose nothing in translation to English.

Anthropologist Benjamin Lee Whorf (1969), however, dissents from my belief that the language of science is universal. Whorf pointed out that American Indian languages like Hopi embody temporal notions radically different from those of European languages. European languages spatialize time. Speakers of these languages imagine time as a linear continuum. They talk about points in time; they measure and compare time intervals. Hopi and other American Indian languages don't use spatial metaphors to express temporal ideas. These languages have rich and varied means for expressing such temporal concepts as aging, expectation, memory, and desire, but they employ no spatial metaphors. Whorf argued that if the Hopi were to create a physics, it would embody Hopi concepts of time and change. It would therefore be quite different from physics as we know it. Yet, Whorf conjectured, it would be just as effective in describing the external world.

Whorf's argument assumes that natural science derives concepts like time and change from natural language. I think the reverse is more likely to be true. Whorf's thesis suggests that Greek mathematicians invented the time line because the Greek language uses spatial metaphors to describe temporal processes. I think it is more likely that spatial metaphors for temporal processes made their way into Greek and other European languages after Greek mathematicians had invented the time line. This is an issue that classical scholars could perhaps settle. When do spatial metaphors for time make their appearance in classical Greek texts? For example, when did the notion of *distant simultaneity* make its appearance? To educated people in the industrialized world it seems "obvious" that events at widely separated places can take place at the same moment of time. To Aristotle, it was somewhat less than obvious; he discusses the idea carefully and at some length. By then, the time line had been invented; Aristotle uses it to excellent effect in the *Physics*. But would the notion that events not in the consciousness of a single person (or god) may happen at the same instant have made sense to Homer?

The *Odyssey*, composed three centuries before the rise of Greek mathematics, recounts events that occurred at widely separated places during the same period of time. There are two narratives, whose incidents are interspersed with one another. One narrative follows Odysseus and his band as they sail home from Troy and the Trojan war. The other narrative is set in Ithaca, where faithful Penelope is kept busy inventing stratagems to fend off her impatient suitors. Homer's listeners certainly understood that the events in Ithaca were taking place while Odysseus was away. But would it have made sense to them to correlate specific events in the two narratives? Does Homer's Greek contain equivalents to what we would nowadays express by phrases like "at that very moment"? Modern translations do indeed contain phrases like "meanwhile" and "at the same moment," but at least in some cases, these phrases have been used to translate "the simple Greek postpositive δε, which is ordinarily translated 'but'."* The matter deserves to be investigated further.

Mathematics, then, is not solely a medium for lending precision to concepts in a natural language. Rather, it creates concepts that can be adequately expressed only in its own unnatural — and hence universal — idiom. Of course, once these concepts have been created, we can talk about them in ordinary language, just as we can talk about a painting or a piece of music. But words alone can't fully convey a mathematical idea, any more than they can convey a pictorial or musical idea.

MATHEMATICS AND EXPERIENCE

Although the worlds that mathematics creates have no *essential* connection to the world of experience, mathematics began with, and has always drawn inspiration from, efforts to make sense of experience. Consider, for example, the efforts of early Greek thinkers to understand motion. Around the middle of the fifth century b.c., Zeno of Elea propounded four paradoxes, intended to demonstrate that the idea of motion

---

*I am indebted for this information, and for other helpful remarks on an earlier draft of this article, to Dr. Prudence Steiner.

is logically incoherent. In the most famous of the paradoxes, a fast runner (Achilles) forever pursues but never quite catches a much slower runner (the tortoise) who has a head start. Achilles must first reach the tortoise's starting point, then the tortoise's position at that moment, and so on *ad infinitum*. Since even Achilles can't complete an endless series of acts, it seems to follow that he can never overtake the tortoise.

This account of the paradox, a paraphrase of Aristotle's account in the *Physics*, embodies some quite sophisticated mathematical assumptions. Zeno assumes that the racecourse can be represented by a mathematical line and that the positions of the runners can be represented by mathematical points. He takes it for granted that any line segment is infinitely divisible. Indeed, the paradox arises because line segments are assumed to be infinitely divisible. What Zeno considers absurd is that a moving point should be able to traverse infinitely many points. To Aristotle, a century and a half later, the fallacy in Zeno's argument seemed obvious. Aristotle represents the motion of a point along a straight line by a *correspondence* between points on the line and points on a *time line*. In uniform motion, the ratio between two time intervals is equal to the ratio between the corresponding space intervals. Zeno's description of the race defines an infinite sequence of points on the time line and corresponding sequences of points on the racecourse, converging respectively at the moment in time and the point in space at which Achilles overtakes the tortoise.

Underlying Zeno's and Aristotle's discussions of motion are two contrasting attitudes toward the relation between experience and philosophy. Zeno is intent on demonstrating that the commonsense view of motion is logically incoherent. His arguments appeal to logic over experience. Aristotle, on the other hand, takes common sense as his starting point. For him the reality of motion isn't an open question to be settled by a logical argument. Motion is obviously real, so if our account of it is logically incoherent something must be wrong with that account. Zeno's account is half mathematical, half intuitive. It treats space mathematically, but it treats time and motion intuitively. Aristotle resolves the paradox by making the discussion fully mathematical, representing time as a linear continuum and motion as a correspondence between points in space and moments in time. Aristotle's account of motion is perfectly logical but transcends intuition and common sense.

Intuition recoils from the notions that a continuous line is made up of dimensionless and distinct points and that duration, indivisible in experience, is made up of distinct and durationless moments. Some philosophers, such as David Hume and George Berkeley, have taken our inability to visualize or give a complete verbal account of mathematical ideas like infinite divisibility as proof of the unreality of such ideas. Others, such as

Galileo Galilei and Isaac Newton, argued that we need mathematics to understand nature; we cannot rely entirely on intuition, common sense, and purely verbal arguments, however subtle and refined. This difference of opinion, I believe, is at the root of the split between the two cultures.

Despite his mathematical treatment of space, time, and motion, Aristotle's sympathies lay with the nonmathematical tradition. He considered mathematical descriptions to pertain to surface appearances. Like Plato, he believed that the reality hidden beneath appearance was purposeful rather than mathematical and could be apprehended through rigorous verbal arguments based on common sense. The mainstream of Western philosophy continues the tradition of Plato and Aristotle, relying on purely verbal arguments and assigning a secondary role to mathematics.

The founders of the mathematical tradition of natural philosophy were Pythagoras, who held the mystical view that some kind of numerical harmony lies at the heart of reality, and Democritus, a contemporary of Socrates, who was an atomist and a thoroughgoing materialist. Galileo and Newton are philosophical descendants of Democritus. Both were atomists — believers in the then unverified hypothesis that matter consists of indivisible particles whose properties determine, but are qualitatively different from, the properties we apprehend through our senses. Both also believed that natural phenomena are governed by underlying mathematical laws. This belief is the modern version of Pythagoras's mystical doctrine of number. It is the central tenet of natural science.

HOW SHOULD MATHEMATICS BE LEARNED AND TAUGHT?

The preceding considerations suggest a preliminary answer to the question raised at the beginning of this essay: How should mathematics be learned and taught? It should be learned and taught not as a collection of facts, formulas, and rules but as a living language, or, more precisely, a family of living languages. (Even Euclidean geometry and arithmetic, the oldest members of the family, are still growing.) In addition, mathematics should be taught, as much as possible, as part of an effort to understand the external world. Mathematics is the language in which the book of nature is written. To read the book, we must learn the language; no adequate translation exists.

Conventional methods of teaching often fail to supply either a strong motive for learning mathematics or a meaningful context for what is being learned. Curiosity is the strongest of all motives for learning, and everyone is born with a healthy measure of it. The human need to explore new worlds is as natural as a cat's need to explore an unfamiliar room. The teacher and the course that present mathematics as the key to understanding unseen worlds beneath the world of appearance supply both a powerful motive for mastering the new language and a meaningful context for it.

Consider the teaching of elementary algebra. The new element for a beginning student is the occurrence of letters like x in places where the student expects to see a number. The student is typically told that x stands for an unknown number whose value one can find by solving an equation. To this end, the student is required to learn a collection of rules for manipulating equations. Having mastered these rules, the student can use them to solve word problems like "If John and Mary have eight apples between them, and John has three apples, how many does Mary have?" What could be duller?

Perhaps, you may say, that can't be helped. Elementary algebra *is* dull — dull but necessary. I disagree. If a subject is dull, it is either unnecessary or it is badly taught.

Let us reconsider those rules for manipulating equations. I would organize a unit about them along the following lines. Take the equation $5+3=8$. Like an English sentence, it has a meaning. [Question for a written assignment and subsequent classroom discussion: What is that meaning?] The same meaning is also expressed by other equations, such as $3+5=8$ and $5=8-3$. [Why are the meanings the same?] Answering the bracketed questions will teach the student that the reason the three equations mean the same thing has nothing to do with the numbers 3, 5, and 8. If we replace 3 and 5 by any two numbers, positive or negative, and 8 by the sum of these numbers, we will once more get three synonymous equations. We can express this by saying that if a and b are any two numbers and c is their sum (that is, if $a+b=c$), then, $b+a=c$ and $b=c-a$. [Invent and justify as many rules of this kind as you can.] Having completed these written assignments and participated in classroom discussions of them, the student is ready to talk and write about what the whole exercise means. [We started by comparing the equation $5+3=8$ to an English sentence. Can you think of analogies for the "transformation rules" we have been discussing? Are these analogies perfect? Why not?]

Students who have worked through a unit of this kind will have acquired a measure of insight into the syntax of arithmetic and its relation to the syntax of English. They will have had some practice in manipulating and transforming arithmetic statements, and they will understand what they are doing. They will understand one of the reasons why it is sometimes useful to represent numbers by letters. They will have discovered some syntactic rules but will not have been required to memorize any, nor will they need to.

Beginning algebra isn't just about the syntax of arithmetic or solving equations. It also introduces students to *variables* and *relations between variables*. These are deep and difficult ideas. They are best introduced, in my opinion, as concepts that help us gain insight into the workings of nature. Many nonscientists believe that physical laws link effects to their causes. It is true that scientists do sometimes talk about causal explanations, but no physical law has the form "*A* causes *B*." Physical laws are relations between variables like force and acceleration or temperature, volume, and pressure. Students could be introduced to these powerful notions by writing about and discussing questions like, How does the height of a fixed quantity of water in a beaker depend on the beaker's cross-sectional area? How is the height of the mercury in a thermometer related to its temperature? How is the speed of a freely falling object related to the distance through which it has fallen?

Scientific problems also provide an excellent context for studying more advanced kinds of mathematics. Newton invented the differential calculus because he needed a language in which to describe nonuniform motion in three dimensions. The section of Newton's *Mathematical Principles of Natural Philosophy* (1685/1962) in which he describes this language offers a far better (and broader) introduction to differential calculus than most modern textbooks.

A crucial feature of the mode of learning I advocate is its active character. It requires students to think, to write, and to discuss. The teacher acts as a guide rather than a pundit. Writing forms the core of the learning process. Reading assignments give the student something to think and write about. Students' writing provides an indispensable basis for fruitful discussion. My experience has shown that regular and frequent writing assignments based on appropriate readings and followed by structured discussions motivate even nonscience students to make the strenuous efforts needed to learn how to use mathematical language in scientific contexts. (In my courses, students write two-to-three-page essays twice each week and participate in two carefully organized 90-minute discussions.)

There is a peculiar synergy between mathematics and ordinary language. Writing and talking about mathematical subject matter stimulates the efforts needed to master abstract mathematical ideas. Conversely, mastery of these ideas enables students to write and speak more articulately about the contexts in which these ideas figure.

I have found this interaction between ordinary language and mathematical language especially useful in helping students to understand Einstein's special theory of relativity. Here the mathematics is relatively elementary and well within the grasp of high school students who have studied algebra and analytic geometry. Yet the theory isn't easy to understand. Several people who have studied it deeply — among them, the philosopher Henri Bergson (1968) and the physicist and philosopher of science Herbert Dingle (1962, 1967) — have published perfectly reasonable but nevertheless mistaken refutations of special relativity. Bergson's and Dingle's misunderstandings resulted not so much from mistakes of verbal or mathematical reasoning as from a failure to make the right connections between the two levels of discourse.

In one of my Core science courses I use a book by Albert Einstein (1952) called *Relativity: The Special and General Theory*. This isn't, as its title might suggest, a mathematical treatise. It is a book intended for nonmathematical readers, and the main body of the text contains no equations or diagrams. In my course, students, with some guidance, reconstruct the formulas and diagrams that Einstein left out. They end up understanding both the words and the symbols. The two modes of discourse stimulate and reinforce each other. Without adequate verbal support, the formulas and diagrams tend to lose their meaning; without formulas and diagrams, the words and phrases refuse to take on the new meanings that Einstein's radically new notions of space and time demand.

Because mathematics is an unnatural language, it is untranslatable into natural language. At the same time, mathematics requires the support of natural language, whose structure is better attuned to the natural workings of the human brain than mathematics. I have always been struck by the fact that the most original thinkers in mathematical physics and in pure mathematics express themselves with extraordinary lucidity in ordinary language. Dirac, Einstein, and Feynman — three of the most creative physicists of the century — all described their discoveries and inventions in limpid prose. So did the pure mathematician Kurt Gödel (1967), whose 1931 paper on the incompleteness of arithmetic revolutionized the foundations of mathematics and logic. That paper contains one of the most original and complex mathematical arguments ever invented. Yet the argument was set forth so clearly that the mathematical community immediately accepted its revolutionary conclusions. Of course, not everyone who can construct clear and logical verbal arguments is good at math. But my experience as a teacher suggests that accomplished mathematicians usually write clearly and logically.

Obviously, Dirac, Einstein, Feynman, and Gödel couldn't have written so clearly unless they understood perfectly what they were writing about. What I wish to suggest is something like the converse to this truism: that the ability to think and write clearly and logically is an essential ingredient in mathematical creation at its highest levels. If that is true, then it is not surprising that the cultivation of writing skills in mathematical and scientific contexts is such an effective tool for learning and teaching mathematics and mathematical physics.

REFERENCES

Bergson, H. (1968). *Durée et simultanéité*. New York: French and European Publications. (Original work published 1922)

Dingle, H. (1962). Special theory of relativity. *Nature, 195*, 985–988.

Dingle, H. (1967). The case against special relativity. *Nature, 216*, 119–122.

Einstein, A. (1952). *Relativity* (15th ed.) New York: Crown Publishers.

Gödel, K. (1967). On the completeness of the axioms of the functions calculus of logic: Some metamathematical results on completeness and consistency; On completeness and consistency. In J. van Heijenoort (Ed.), *From Frege to Goedel* (pp. 582–591; 592–617). Cambridge, MA: Harvard University Press. (Original work published 1931)

McCrea, W. H. (1967). Why the special theory of relativity is correct. *Nature, 216*, 122–124.

Newton, I. (1962). *The mathematical principles of natural philosophy*. Berkeley, CA: University of California Press. (Original work published 1685)

Snow, C. P. (1959). *The two cultures and the scientific revolution*. New York: Cambridge University Press.

Snow, C. P. (1964). *The two cultures: A second look*. New York: Cambridge University Press.

Whorf, B. L. (1969). *Language, thought, and reality*. Cambridge, MA: MIT Press. See especially the essays entitled "The role of language in habitual thought" and "An American Indian cosmology."

CHAPTER 11

Exploring Mathematics in Writing

Sandra Keith

There is a growing concern among mathematicians that students should be able to communicate, and the mathematical writing of students (as well as professionals) has lately been coming under scrutiny. At the level of college or high school teaching, the trend is perhaps related to the difficulty in attracting and keeping students, the changes in higher education demographics, and the fact that we are having to take more responsibility for teaching a broader cross-section of the population. The typical mathematics classroom is a formal affair, a teacher lecturing precisely on topics and later evaluating student performance in infrequent and anxiety-producing tests. One unintentional, or perhaps intentional, effect of this method has been to "weed out" students, a practice that is becoming less acceptable. Students often find the mathematics classroom cold and the teachers uncaring, while teachers themselves complain when their well-crafted lectures and patience go unappreciated and severely criticized on evaluation materials. The mathematics syllabus is time-constrained, and the teacher may feel there is no way that the syllabus or style of teaching can be changed to keep up with expectations from their department or other departments. Lately, though, because calculators can now do much of what we have spent time teaching, there is some time to explore teaching mathematics for understanding rather than for rote skills. Frustrated by students' inability to achieve our goals, we have come to the point where we would rather study communication in the classroom than automatically blame the student.

Writing-across-the-curriculum workshops have been timely, then, and inspiring, in showing teachers how learning is enhanced by various types of writing assignments, from journals to term papers. In my experience, the form of writing that most easily adapts to syllabus pressures and that seems to offer the most valuable resource for the student is the 15-minute, in-class assignment, which I call an "exploratory" writing assignment. Sometimes collaborative, these exercises are aimed at asking the students to put their understanding down on paper informally, and in the context of the teaching. The assignments may be to define terms, develop procedures, apply definitions, predict what is to come, or assess what is being done. Writing teachers sometimes say that term papers are often condemned to failure because unconscious decisions made in the first hour of work rule out many options on the project. In the same way, in mathematics, students build internal explanations for themselves that may be based on fallacies or uncertainties. Students want so badly to understand what is being said that they can easily convince themselves of what they do on very trivial grounds — the idea looks familiar, looks like something that has made sense before, and so forth. Exploratory writing assignments are pedagogically useful because we can get meaningful, direct, and almost immediate interaction with the students on tactics and strategies for learning. Frequent, open efforts at doing simple things that are part of larger projects, whether they be proofs or homework problems, allow for immediate evaluation of often unexamined or automatic decisions on their part about how to solve or analyze. For these reasons I tend to rely on questions and assignments that can be responded to quickly. Further discussions give students criteria for a meaningful assessment of their own work, which, being short, will be easier to assess.

Besides teaching strategies for understanding, the collaboration in learning that goes along with the use of exploratory writing assignments engages the students with the moment of teaching (something which note-taking does not always do), develops trust, and improves the atmosphere in and out of the classroom. Test results are improved, and not necessarily only on those problems practiced. Most students are happy to have home assignments contribute to their grade and appreciate the chance to be heard and understood. Discussion of the results of these assignments is admittedly often confusing and messy, but from the point of view of many students, it is mathematical elegance that is obfuscating.

Before discussing specific exploratory writing assignments, let us consider the procedures and goals common to all.

PROCEDURES AND GOALS OF
EXPLORATORY WRITING ASSIGNMENTS

In typical math classes, writing is used almost exclusively for testing purposes. Exploratory writing assignments provide the students with techniques for refining their methods of learning, which I will describe here. Along with the gain to the student comes an inseparable benefit for the teacher.

Assessment of Where We Are. When the class looks stupefied or bored, I may ask for an immediate explanation of what we are doing or a term we are using. This break in the classroom situation shows me precisely where the problem lies, and allows me immediately to regroup and redirect my own teaching to address the confusion more efficiently.

Anticipation of New Material. I often use these assignments to introduce or even anticipate the topic. For instance, the assignment to define a "degree" can be followed by a discussion of the need for radians. Students are more alert to the resulting lecture. And, since the evaluation of these assignments frequently requires a re-teaching of the idea, it is useful to assign these exercises before getting locked into teaching the technicalities of a concept.

Discussion. Overnight I often rewrite what students have written onto transparency sheets, or I have the students individually or in groups write directly on the transparencies. Then I show the results, pre-screened or not, on the overhead projector. I give my own reactions, and I try to encourage discussion by asking what the terms within each definition mean. Students could probably be easily humiliated at this stage, but not when efforts are made to understand their writing — what they were thinking of as they wrote their definition, and how it could be made more complete. Because I define the purpose of the writing assignment as a communication with me, I can focus on my own confusion in understanding. (As a result, the need for precision is dramatically illustrated.) With this approach, students are steered away from being embarrassed or ridiculing their peers.

Student answers often go awry in similar ways, and the same unusual answer can be repeated many times over: this is some comfort to the students themselves. Language is not precise and clear at all times, and the language of mathematics is particularly difficult. Strange as some of the answers may be, the input of other students is useful in explaining what was intended: As most of us have seen, students can often communicate with each other more easily than they can with the teacher.

Peer Collaboration. When small groups of students have to produce an answer, they tend to negotiate and analyze their answers more critically. They are more prepared to take risks, they benefit from having to ask and to explain, and they also become confronted by their peers with the need for learning *now*.

Papers written individually can be exchanged and evaluated by specific criteria that provide a means by which students can see their work from a teacher's point of view (for a model for a peer-evaluation worksheet, see Figure 11.1).

Group quizzes, which require certain rules of fairness, are popular in my classes, and any inflation of grades can be counterbalanced by higher expectations on tests.

Revision.   Students often believe that tests and submitted work are terminally judged, and it is important to dispel this notion. One helpful strategy in the pursuit of this goal is creating the expectation that written work is never really "finished" and that an initial effort is always open to revision. Students can revise their initial effort for the next period or during the next period. When the teacher corrects students' work, students may not really understand until they are faced with the need to reconstruct their own answers.

Evaluation.   In these informal assignments the students generally show a control of grammar and mechanics so closely linked with their ability to use logic that I never need to grade separately for correct English. Doing so, at least initially, would probably be counterproductive, as focusing on correctness in spelling and grammar might intimidate students into using a smaller vocabulary and taking fewer risks. Again, the focus is on communicating.

TOPICS FOR WRITING ACTIVITIES

Once one gets in the habit of using exploratory writing assignments, topics bubble up everywhere. I have favorite types of assignments, however, which are presented here according the types of reasoning required of the mathematics student.

Explanation.   Students are asked to respond informally to a concept. This can be used to test students' understanding of something already explained or to see where a class stands early in the unit.

- Discuss why the label "Mean Value Theorem" is appropriate for Theorem 2.1.
- Explain in writing, informally but clearly, how we multiply matrices.

Formal Definition or Statement of a Theorem.   Students are given experience in using formal and precise mathematical language.

Figure 11.1   Peer evaluation worksheets

Name _____

Definition Worksheet

DEFINE:

5 — A completely adequate definition. Clear and accurate vocabulary and
     notation. Maximum of mathematical vocabulary. Minimum redundancy.
4 — Minor problems with clarity or notation or vocabulary or wordiness.
3 — Basic concept is clear (writer seems to know what he or she is defining) but
     significant confusion in notation or vocabulary.
2 — Basic concept shows significant confusion, with major problems in notation or
     vocabulary.
1 — Definition does not relate to concept asked for, or merely an example has been
     provided.

. . . .

Name _____

Theorem Worksheet

STATE:

5 — A completely adequate theorem. Clear and accurate vocabulary and notation.
     Complete hypothesis and conclusion. Maximum of mathematical vocabulary
     and minimum redundancy.
4 — Minor problems with clarity or notation or vocabulary. Minor incompleteness
     in hypothesis or conclusion.
3 — Basic concept of theorem is clear (writer seems to understand the theorem),
     but significant confusion or error in vocabulary or notation.
2 — Basic concept of theorem shows significant confusion about hypothesis or
     conclusion, with major errors in notation or vocabulary.
1 — Theorem does not relate to concept asked for.

138

- Define precisely, in mathematical language, the notion of a "periodic function." To say "the function repeats itself" is vague, but there is a way of saying this in functional notation.

Generalization of a Concept. Students develop an overview of the unit or section.

- Mathematicians invent definitions when a clear need arises. In your own study of polynomials, what definitions might you invent? (Example: Define a polynomial with real roots as a "double-r-nomial." Where could this be useful?) Where in "real life" do you come across modular arithmetic?

Translation of a Visual Image into Words. Students often do not think they need to put together verbal and visual explanations in their minds; they usually wait passively for something to "click." In undermining that learning pattern, this kind of exercise can be very empowering.

- Describe the graph of this function, in as accurate mathematical vocabulary as possible, as if you were explaining it to a friend on the phone.
- How do the graphs of $y = \sin x$ and $y = \cos x$ relate? How could you predict the behavior of the second from that of the first, and vice versa?
- [The class is divided into pairs.] One of you must describe to the other a graph in as accurate and precise language as possible ("as x approaches positive infinity the function descends and approaches $y = 0$ as an asymptote"). The other student must attempt to draw the function, with no chance to see the graph as it is being drawn. (The describer and drawer are then switched.)

Summarization of Tactics. Students are made aware of tactical choices they have in problem solving.

- Describe a method for solving distance-time-rate problems. Do not merely provide an example.
- Give four rules for combining fractions (or working with square roots or logarithms) that would be illegitimate, and explain why they are wrong.
- What is the difference between combinations and permutations, and by what clues do you distinguish problems involving the one or the other?

Writing of an Algorithm. Students practice and analyze algorithmic thinking.

- Write out an explicit algorithm for dividing (factoring) polynomials.

Communication of Thought to a Specific Audience. Students learn to "translate" one explanation into another and generally assume the burden of communicating. Many writing problems demand that students communicate something to someone who knows the subject better than they do. Sometimes, however, the best learning takes place when we are explaining at a very elementary level.

- Write to the head of a company to which you are applying for a job. She doesn't like math and doesn't know any, but she needs the solution to Problem #31. Remember, she will not be familiar with all the terminology you may be inclined to use. Be brief but don't sound as if you're "finessing" it!
- Write a procedure for finding the number "m modulo n" that a fifth grader could understand.
- Write the author of your book a critique of one of the sections in this chapter. Tell him or her what you found confusing, and how it could be improved.
- Edit this proof that I am giving you for the student who is the author. Make corrections, and explain why they are needed. Give helpful suggestions to the author.

Integration of the Reading and Writing Experience. Students are offered a way around blocks created by textual explanations which are difficult to understand.

- Many of you did not understand the concept on page 12 of the text. What was wrong with the text's explanation? Rewrite this explanation as you would have liked to see it written.
- In a few pages, write a "crib sheet" for a friend who is seriously behind in this course. List important concepts, definitions, and theorems, and briefly explain any methods of this unit that you might be tested on.
- Using the book, rewrite and submit your classroom notes on Section 3.1.

Invention of a Problem. Students learn to create their own illustrations and to predict what the teacher expects from them. Asking questions is the key to research in mathematics. Perhaps this assignment won't create researchers, but it can help develop a technique of asking.

- You have 4 brothers, 5 sisters, 2 dogs, and 30 cats. Invent 5 combinatorics problems. For example, in how many ways can the 2 dogs be fed by you and your siblings each day? In how many ways can you line up for soup if you refuse to stand next to a brother?
- Write a reasonable test question for this unit. Explain briefly why the questions are included. (A good group project.)

Collaboration on a Group Project. Students are allowed, through exchange of language and ideas, to take risks they would not take working alone, as collaboration often enhances confidence and productivity. Because students enjoy this activity as if it were a sport, it is a good way to introduce writing assignments.

- Now that you have seen my graphical description on the board of maxima and minima, can you formally write an explanation of how the first derivative can indicate where a relative maximum or minimum occurs? If so, you have invented the "First Derivative Test."

Evaluation of Understanding. Students are taught to build a self-critiquing system into their learning and to be more precise in coming to understand what they don't know and what they need to know.

- Write out the most important (difficult) concept in your opinion that we have studied so far, and why you felt it was important (difficult).
- Interview the person next to you about what methods he or she found most difficult in this section, and why. (A question list can be provided.)
- Explain to me, the teacher, what methods (problem solving in class, writing assignments, on-the-board exercises, formal lectures) most enhance learning for you and why.

WAYS IN WHICH EXPLORATORY WRITING ASSIGNMENTS EXPOSE LEARNING PROBLEMS

I want to finish this discussion by trying to re-create some of the experience of using writing exercises, along with a loose taxonomy of types of problems. From one perspective, I suppose, this is a handlist of horrors, but on the other hand it shows what sort of strategies the students are using, and it forces one to come to terms with the real effort that students are making. This seems to me to be a crucial point about the use of writing assignments: The responses are wrong, but they can be seen as misdirections that can be redirected, as presuppositions that can be resupposed.

In a college trigonometry class I asked the students to write briefly in class on "What is a reference angle?"* If I had drawn Figure 11.2 and had asked them to show me the reference angle, no one would have had any difficulty. But by asking them to produce a self-contained definition, I created a situation that invited them to fall into various sorts of strategic traps, and the resulting material proved very useful for a general workshop on definitions. The discussion allows one to get not just at the definition of a reference angle, but at the two problems of how definitions work and how students can get confused about definitions. When the sentences are *their* sentences, sentences they have just written, I have their interest and attention to an extent that is difficult to achieve with any other teaching device.

An adequate definition would be something like the following, with the illustration in Figure 11.2 included: A reference angle for a given angle α is an acute angle θ, which is formed by the x-axis and the terminal side of

---

*This example and its accompanying illustration are also included in S. Keith, "Exploratory Writing and Teaching Mathematics," *The Mathematics Teacher* (in press).

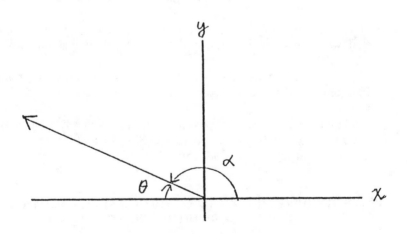

Figure 11.2　Illustration of a reference angle

α, as shown in the illustration. The students' answers fall into a few specific patterns. Few answers are completely wrong.

1. Some students merely give an *example* alone (which of course is a start).
   - An angle like if you have 400 degrees on the unit circle, your reference angle would be 40 degrees.
2. Others use imprecise vocabulary or fail to recognize the conditions of *necessity and sufficiency* that a definition requires. They define by characteristics or properties which follow from a proper definition.
   - Another angle that is the same as your first angle but in simpler terms. (The words "same," "first," and "simpler" are vague, and what the "simpler terms" are is the essence of this definition.)
   - The acute angle with the same terminal side.
   - An angle closer to the x-axis than the original angle.
3. Some try to define by simply stating *how* the construct (here the reference angle) is used.
   - The angle that has to measure up supplementary with the angle given that tells which quadrant it is in.
   - The angle that makes it easier to compute trig functions for the first angle.
4. Frequently, students opt for a "damage control" strategy, where the object is to use technical-sounding words vaguely, or to say as much as possible, with the objective of maximizing partial credit.
   - An angle for which measurements of less than 90 are made in relationship to the x-axis only. The angle is smaller than the original and has equivalent trig functions, like 30, 60, 45, etc.
5. Surprisingly, very few students *draw pictures*. They will ignore the possibility of using a figure to explain or will simply reconstruct an illustration without labeling it or writing about how it has been used. While picture-drawing may not properly be a part of definition writing, it is much easier for students to discuss or write about a concept if they have learned to draw an accurate picture first. Some students may first grasp a concept visually or tactilely, rather than verbally.

In a class discussion/workshop, these error types offer a systematic perspective on definition-making. There are other problem areas that have come up in other exercises, however, and I will finish by looking at several of these that I have found important and interesting.

1. A problem in definition that appears widely is a blindness to the need for categories in defining, for *nominalizing*. For instance, one might "partition" integers into evens and odds, but "a partition" is a *collection* of sets with certain properties (here, evens and odds). My students seemed intent on clinging to a "procedural" sense of the word.
   - A partition is when . . .
   - A partition divides . . .
   - A partition gives an equivalence relation . . .
   - When we have a partition, we can . . .
   - We can get a partition by dividing . . .
   - A partition is a division, a breakdown, a separation, a listing . . .

   Some of these are almost acceptable; however, we have to consider whether we could move on to the next stage of proving something is a partition with these definitions.

2. Another type of difficulty is with subscripting, superscripting, and *conventions of notation*. Perhaps students have had this provided for them, or they have never had to work with terms at this level, only with examples. But the following exercise has produced arresting results in all my calculus classes (some near completion of the full year's sequence). The question is "What is a polynomial?" This concept has been around since ninth grade. In calculus much of the theory centers on polynomials, and differentiation and integration are introduced with these functions. Their importance in calculus can not be overstressed. There is no better way to define a polynomial than as a function $f(x)$ of the form:

$$f(x) = a_n x^n + a_{n-1} x^{n-1} + . . . + a_1 x + a_0,$$

where a_i are elements of the real numbers and n is a positive integer. Here is a collection of students' answers:
   - A function that you can differentiate and integrate and factor.
   - A multiple addition and subtraction with different powers of x for each part.
   - An equation in which some constants are multiplied by variables which are sometimes raised to powers. These are then added or subtracted.
   - A polynomial is like $3x^2 + 5x + 7$
   - $f(x)$ is a polynomial if it is a number raised to some power which makes it a many-numbered function. It is not a straight line.

- $a^x + a^{x-1} + \ldots$
- $a_x^n + a_x^{n-1} + \ldots$ (These latter two students have only remembered that something is superscripted or subscripted. Contrast these with the proper definition.)

3. Often, when students *presume that the reader already knows the answer*, the act of explaining or analyzing feels false. When caught in this pattern, the students may, however, be hiding from their own uncertainty. Here the assignment was to describe the procedure for computing the determinant of a 3×3 matrix.
   - Take the row 1 column 1 position and multiply it by the determinant of the 2×2 matrix.
   - Do not use the whole expansion, use cofactors, which is just telling what sign we give it. A plus or minus times the minor.

4. Other problems show up when students fall short in *giving an algorithm*. Here they were asked to explain the procedure for dividing polynomials, as they might see it in a text. When assigned this project in one of my recent classes in calculus, some students merely showed an example; some students showed an example and explained confusingly what was going on as a sideline to the example (done well, this may actually be the preferred method); and only one student could actually generalize sufficiently to give a good algorithm and then an example for illustration.

5. The situation becomes more critical still when the question is not merely to state a definition or algorithm, but to *write a proof*. Formidable problems arise: the students don't understand what constitutes an explanation, and they are insecure about their ability to communicate with the teacher. We hear, "But I didn't know that's what you *wanted*." The examples below from an upper-level abstract algebra course probably will not surprise teachers of the subject.
   - Prove that if H and K are normal subgroups of a group G, then $H \cap K$ is a normal subgroup of G.
     Proof: Since H and K are subgroups, $H \cap K$ is normal by a THEOREM.
   - Prove that LCM $(m,n) = mn/\text{GCD}(m,n)$.
     Proof: We must have that LCM $(m,n) = mn/\text{GCD}(m,n)$ because assume this is not true. But that can't be because we know that LCM $(m,n) = mn/\text{GCD}(m,n)$. Therefore this is a true statement.
   - If f and g are functions, and $f \circ g$ is onto, prove f is onto.
     Proof: Assume $f \circ g$ is onto, i.e. for all y there exists x such that (x,y) belongs to $f \circ g$. Let (x,y) be arbitrary. After *universal gen-*

eralizations, $(x,y)\epsilon f$ and $(y,z)\epsilon g$, and after *simplifications* we get $(x,y)\epsilon f$, which is what we want to prove after *universal generalizations*.

- Prove $f(x)=x^3-4$ is a well-defined, one-to-one, and onto function on the reals.

  Proof: Given a function $f(x)=x^3-4$, we wish to show it is a function, one-to-one and onto. Since any x in R there exists y such that there is no other value equal to y. Therefore f is a function. It also follows that f is one-to-one and onto in order for f to be a function.

  This proof is enough to make teachers throw up their hands, but in the spirit of tackling a problem, it actually makes a nice proof for students to edit.

For a final example that demonstrates the difference between writing-based teaching and test-based teaching, an upper-level course take-home problem follows: "Below is the fictional city of X, with its layout of streets. A postman wants to pass through the city, walking on the right side of the street the first time around, and then passing through the city on the left side of the street. Will this be possible?" At the upper levels, it is assumed that a take-home question of this sort requires an explanation beyond a "yes" or "no"; while the problem does not specifically say to "explain", it is clearly testing the students' understanding of an Eulerian path. Ideally, we are training the mathematics student to learn, eventually, to ask and answer his or her own questions in a productive way for other practitioners in the field. Students must become "explainers," and "proponents," rather than merely, "answerers," as they move into the complex world of mathematical research. The failure of so many of our students to "prove" or "propose" further raises the question of how well they "construe" (read) or can "ask." There might be some useful research to be done in that question, but for right now, working with the writing process through class workshops offers the most plausible way to help with such problems.

CHAPTER 12

Writing to Learn:
An Experiment in Remedial Algebra

Richard J. Lesnak

When the Robert Morris College writing-across-the-curriculum program was proposed in 1984, I volunteered to be a participant in the initial implementation — a somewhat doubting, skeptical participant. At the time I had taught mathematics for 25 years with what I considered to be a great deal of success. In fact, I had serious doubts as to whether writing-to-learn strategies could improve the learning process in my math classes. At that time I was only cautiously optimistic that my students' attitudes toward mathematics might also be changed in the process. I am no longer a skeptic. I have no doubt that writing-to-learn activities can be a valuable tool not only in improving academic achievement but in eliminating the negative attitudes of many of our students with respect to mathematics in general, and beginning or remedial algebra in particular.

Our initial group of volunteers at Robert Morris were trained in a seminar-type program under the direction of Richard Young of Carnegie-Mellon University and JoAnn Sipple of Robert Morris College. It was proposed that writing-to-learn activities were particularly effective in upper-division courses where course objectives emphasize analysis, synthesis, and evaluation. Since my area of specialization at Robert Morris had been in entry-level or basic algebra, I hoped to develop and use writing strategies for use in basic algebra, where the objectives are principally in the areas of knowledge, comprehension, and application. In reality, basic algebra at Robert Morris is a remedial course for students with virtually no algebra background and for students whose previous experiences with algebra have created negative attitudes and virtually no confidence in their abilities to learn algebra. Using terminology I am not particularly fond of, many students sincerely believe they have "math blocks" and suffer from "math anxiety." Thus, I concentrated my efforts in developing and using writing-to-learn strategies to promote attitudinal change as well as to strengthen basic algebraic computational skills.

COURSE DESIGN

The ability of a teacher to use writing-to-learn activities in a classroom with confidence and competence depends upon the skill with which the teacher incorporates writing activities into his or her course design. An instructor could use isolated writing activities within the framework of a present course design, but a more creative approach is achieved through the planning of a new course design. Planning a course should involve analyzing the objectives, methods to achieve the objectives, and the writing-to-learn techniques to be incorporated into these methods, before preparing the syllabus of instruction.

A cross-sectional chart, commonly referred to as the Henderson (1965) matrix, is a very useful device. One of the axes lists the objectives the instructor seeks to accomplish. The objectives should include both cognitive and affective goals. In a basic algebra course the cognitive objectives involving knowledge of facts and computational skills are too often uppermost in the teacher's mind. The affective objectives, such as increased confidence and improved attitudes, must be given proper attention. The failure to define and attack these affective objectives results in mediocre course designs and teaching.

The second axis of the matrix consists of a list of the subdivisions of content that form the basis of the course. Objectives come first, for the instructor must know what he wants to accomplish before he can choose the content wisely (Bloom, 1956). The intersections of the axes form "cell blocks." Specific tasks expected of the students are inserted into these cell blocks. Having defined these outcomes carefully, the instructor is now in a position to choose those methods that will best accomplish the outcomes. Figure 12.1 illustrates my course design for beginning algebra, incorporating writing-to-learn activities within the cells of the matrix design as valuable tools in accomplishing desired course objectives.

The final step in the course-planning procedure is to bring together in orderly form the results of the analyses of the detailed matrix design. For the instructor, this becomes a plan of action, a teaching syllabus. There is a tendency to make the syllabus nothing more than a brief course outline. However, a syllabus that contains a day-by-day description of the topics to be covered and the methods used to achieve the desired outcomes clearly illustrates to the instructor where and how he or she will use writing-to-learn activities in achieving course objectives.

EXPERIMENTAL DESIGN

My statistics background influenced my decision to design an experiment in which I could quantitatively measure the benefits of using writing-to-learn in the teaching of basic algebra. When the experiment was designed, I was considering increased academic achievement as the principal measure of success. It was during implementation and final evaluation that I realized qualitative benefits involving changes in attitudes, confidence levels, and self-images might be taking place. These qualitative findings will be discussed later.

My experimental design involved teaching four basic algebra classes consisting of 26 students in each class. Two of the classes (the control group) were taught using the same methods and techniques I had been using for more than 25 years. The other two classes (the experimental group) were taught using a teaching syllabus prepared from the course design incorporating the writing-to-learn strategies (refer to Figure 12.1). The registrar's office at Robert Morris cooperated by placing incoming freshmen students in the four classes in a purely random manner. Over 90 percent of these students previously had at least one year of algebra at the secondary level with little or no academic success. The other 10 percent were taking algebra for the first time. This is not uncommon at Robert Morris College. Thus, the basic algebra course is really a remedial algebra course. My goal with this experimental design was to statistically compare the final mean average for the control group versus that of the experimental group. The results of this statistical comparison are presented later in this discussion.

IMPLEMENTATION

In an attempt to isolate the value of writing to learn, I taught the two classes in my control group using the same techniques and methods I had been using in the past, while in the two classes in my experimental group I used these same techniques plus the writing-to-learn activities described in the course design. The students' initial reactions were discouraging to say the least. The two writing classes were not only unimpressed with the plan, they were depressed and discouraged to the point of hostility. To quote the typical student, "I've never been able to learn algebra the regular way, now you're making things worse by making me also worry about writing." It was at this point I realized I had to sell the plan to the students before I could hope to be successful. My "sales pitch" focused on three points. First, I was not going to teach them to write or evaluate their grammar, but to

(*text continues on p. 152*)

Figure 12.1 Course design for Beginning Algebra

Instructional Objectives \ Topics	From Arithmetic to Algebra (2 weeks)	Simplifying Algebraic Expressions (3 weeks)
Knowledge of basic algebraic computations for more advanced study of algebra	Discuss and have students write order of operations for all arithmetic problems Discuss and have students write procedures for evaluating expressions Discuss and have students write the rules for signed numbers	Discuss and have students write rules for addition of algebraic terms Discuss and have students write rules for multiplication of algebraic terms Discuss and have students write laws of exponents used in multiplication and division Define a radical and demonstrate the simplifying of a radical
Ability to identify problems and select proper computational technique	Identify the arithmetic operations in a multi-step problem Write the proper order of operations that apply to a problem before completing solution	Discuss the importance of distinguishing multiplication from addition in the simplifying of algebraic expressions Have students write a detailed procedure for simplifying any and all algebraic expressions Test #1
Improvement in problem-solving techniques and in the ability to think analytically	Illustrate that as number of steps increase, writing of step-by-step procedure helps in problem solving Have students attempt multi-step problems without writing and then with writing to judge improvement	Demonstrate and assign multi-step problems that are combinations of previously acquired basic algebraic skills Have students list the individual problems that make up the total problem before continuing to final solution Have students write the question a radical asks before simplifying
Ability to analyze an incorrect solution for the purpose of determining the error in the solution	Present students with completed "incorrect" solutions and require a written description of the procedural error before the problem is redone correctly	Present students with completed "incorrect" solution and require a written description of the procedural error before the problem is redone correctly
Realization that algebra is the generalization of previously learned arithmetic	Demonstrate that order of operations does not change when numbers are replaced by letters in algebraic expressions Demonstrate that order of operations does not change when signed numbers are introduced into problems	Demonstrate that rules governing basic arithmetic operations of addition and multiplication do not change and are applied to letters as well as numbers in the simplification of algebraic expressions
Awareness that problem-solving techniques in basic algebra are applicable in future problem-solving situations	Have students write correct order of operations for advanced algebra problems even though they cannot yet continue to a final solution	Discuss and demonstrate how simplifying algebraic expressions is a first step in future, more complex algebraic computations
Increased confidence in one's ability to understand algebra and a desire to learn more	Re-assign multi-step problems presented on first day of class that most students could not do then, but can do now with the knowledge of order of operations	After going over test #1, have students write a summary of those computations they feel confident with and those that they do not yet fully understand Discuss students' comments before proceeding to next topic

Figure 12.1 *Continued.*

Factoring (3 weeks)	Solving Equations and Inequalities (4 weeks)	Word Problems—Applications (2 weeks)
Discuss and demonstrate greatest common factor Discuss and demonstrate difference of two perfect squares Discuss and demonstrate factoring of a quadratic polynomial Discuss and demonstrate concept of a prime factor and factoring completely	Define and discuss an equation: statement of equality Define and discuss a "solution" Define and discuss how to "check" Define and discuss a literal equation Define and discuss algebraic inequalities Define and discuss "first-degree"	Discuss and demonstrate that practical applications in various subject areas can be represented by equations Discuss and demonstrate the fact that an algebraic equation results from a statement of equality in words Have students write equations given a statement of equality in words
Discuss and demonstrate the proper procedure for factoring using two or more techniques Have students write a detailed procedure for factoring an expression completely Test #2	Illustrate that all first degree equations and inequalities can be solved if four procedural steps are followed Have students write the four steps in their notebooks and refer to these steps in every solution of an equation or inequality Test #3	Discuss and demonstrate the value and importance of a written statement of equality before writing an algebraic equation Have students write statements of equality from various practical applications Final exam
Discuss and demonstrate the fact that factoring is to "un-multiply" Assign problems requiring the student to "check" every factoring problem by multiplication	Every time students claim that they do not know how to proceed in the solution of an equation, require them to write the four steps they have learned in order to get themselves moving again toward a solution	Discuss practical applications (word problems) as the ultimate problem-solving exercise of this course Assign problems of varying difficulty, requiring a written statement of equality before translation into an algebraic equation
Present students with completed "incorrect" solutions and require a written description of the procedural error before the problem is redone correctly	Present students with completed "incorrect" solutions and require a written description of the procedural error before the problem is redone correctly	Present students with completed "incorrect" solutions and require a written description of the procedural error before the problem is redone correctly
Discuss and demonstrate the factoring of arithmetic numbers Demonstrate that the factoring of algebraic expressions is exactly the same concept	Discuss and demonstrate that the four steps in solving equations and inequalities are previously learned algebraic skills that were generalizations of arithmetic	Discuss and demonstrate that once the equation is written the problem of solving the equation is another combination of basic algebraic skills that were generalizations of arithmetic
Discuss and demonstrate importance of factoring in finding least common denominators when working with algebraic fractions Have students write a brief statement predicting how this LCD process will be used in solving equations	Ask students to respond in writing to the question, "Where do the equations we have been solving come from?"	Discuss applications (word problems) that the students will encounter in business related courses they will be taking in the future. Have students write a summary of applications they foresee that were not discussed in class
After going over test #2, have students write a summary of those computations they feel confident with and those that they do not yet fully understand Discuss students' comments before proceeding to next topic	After going over test #3, have students write a summary of those computations they feel confident with and those that they do not yet fully understand Discuss students' comments before proceeding to next topic	Have students write a brief evaluation of the course focusing on their attitudes toward algebra and the degree of confidence they have in their abilities

use writing to help them overcome the "math blocks" they perceived themselves as having. Second, the methods they had used in the past to learn math must not have worked very well or they wouldn't be in a remedial algebra class as college freshmen. Finally, my personal enthusiasm for the program had to convince them to give my theory a chance; that is, the use of writing would help them overcome the "math blocks" they perceived themselves as having.

Students in a remedial algebra class who claim they have "math blocks" must be trained to handle two questions that really matter: What is making this problem difficult for me, and more important, what can *I* do to make it easier for myself? Author Sheila Tobias (1988) believes that posing these questions and figuring out possible responses is precisely what distinguishes those who do well in mathematics from those who don't. There are ability differences in mathematics, and such differences will always exist, but these can be narrowed significantly if students are given the time, opportunity, and means to incorporate these questions into their thinking. The first topic I discuss in a basic algebra course is the fact that there is an order of operations that must be followed in any mathematics problem involving more than one step. What better way to incorporate this order of operations into problem-solving techniques than by *writing* the step-by-step procedure? What better way to understand what is making the problem difficult and how to get over the "block," than to be able to refer back to this written step-by-step procedure? Whenever students in my writing classes failed to use the order of operations properly or hit one of their "blocks," they were expected to use their written procedures not only to find their mistakes but also to proceed correctly. The students began to believe in my "sales pitch" for writing-to-learn activities, and actually seemed eager for more.

The actual writing of step-by-step procedures and the referring back to these written procedures in problem solving was the only difference in my teaching methods in the control (non-writing) and experimental (writing) classes. In the non-writing classes I taught and emphasized the same procedures and problem-solving techniques as in the writing classes, except for the explicit demand that the writing be done. One of these writing tasks turned out to be very effective, much more so than I expected. Before the first exam I informed the students that a "ticket" would be required for admission to the exam. This "ticket" was to be a list of the written step-by-step procedures for each of the different kinds of problems I announced were to appear on the test. The "ticket" would not be graded or evaluated in any way, but must be turned in at the beginning of the exam period in order to sit for the exam. Were there grumblings? Yes, but everyone turned in a "ticket"; they had no choice! Some students had the procedures written perfectly, some not so perfectly, some downright carelessly, some awfully. I separated the "tickets" into two categories. In group A were those that were written perfectly or nearly so, the others were included in group B. After I graded the exams, I found that *every* student who scored from 80% to 100% had turned in a "ticket" that was in group A and *every* student who scored less than 80% had a "ticket" in group B. Also of significance, the only students who failed the exam were those whose "tickets" I had evaluated as awful. I presented the classes with this documented evidence. They exchanged their exams and "tickets" with one another to verify my contention that their exam score and their ability to write the correct procedure appeared to be directly correlated. They were impressed. How impressed? A few weeks later I announced the second exam and the topics to appear on the exam. I deliberately said nothing about a ticket. Almost in unison, the class responded, "What about a ticket?" They were asking me to force them to write! I was no longer a skeptic. It was at this point that I became totally confident that writing-to-learn activities not only might help my students achieve higher academic goals, but could also be a valuable weapon in the attack on the "math blocks" many of them perceived themselves to have.

Throughout the remainder of the semester the students in the writing-to-learn classes continued to grow more enthusiastic and confident with the writing assignments. Their enthusiasm and confidence seemed to peak when they realized that once they were able to write in words the step-by-step procedure for solving any first-degree equation or inequality, no equation's solution was beyond their abilities. However, they felt there remained one "math block" to be challenged. How could writing help them to do the dreaded *word problems?* In a remedial algebra class I find that most students believe they are victims of the "insider/outsider" dichotomy described by Sheila Tobias (1988). Students feel "insiders" can read a problem and write the corresponding algebraic equation, while they, as "outsiders," do not have the intellectual skills to do so. In the experimental writing classes I illustrated that a desired algebraic equation is easily obtained once a statement of equality is written out in words. Very few remedial algebra students realize that the key to solving a word problem is the written statement of equality. I insisted they search out and write this statement of equality before attempting to write the algebraic equation. Most students felt this writing exercise gave them a chance at successfully solving word problems, something they never thought was possible.

RESULTS, OBSERVATIONS, COMMENTS

The results of this experiment with writing-to-learn in basic algebra are both quantitative and qualitative in form. Since my original evaluative tool was to be a statistical analysis of the differences in academic achievement between the control and experimental groups, I will summarize the quantitative results first.

The 52 students in the control group, those not exposed to the writing-to-learn activities, completed the course with a mean average of 74.5%. The 52 students in the experimental group, those who were taught using the writing-to-learn activities, averaged 77.7%. Using a statistical test of the difference between two means, this difference of 3.2% in their final averages is significant at a level of significance of 4.6%. Very briefly, this means that if all variables in the two groups were equal except for the use of writing-to-learn activities, then the probability of this difference occurring by chance is less than 4.6%.

I prefer to downplay these quantitative results for two reasons. First, I believe the qualitative results to be presented are far more significant than this statistical analysis of the students' academic performance. Second, I believe that educators, administrators in particular, tend to be obsessed with quantitative statistical documentation to the extent that qualitative research is discouraged.

I want now to consider the qualitative results of this experiment as a measure of the success of using writing-to-learn activities in a remedial algebra class. In my previous discussions I indicated that as the course progressed the students not only accepted the writing-to-learn assignments but seemed to acknowledge that the writing assignments helped them overcome some of their "math blocks." The final writing assignment in which the 52 students in the writing classes were asked to evaluate the course and the writing-to-learn activities provided positive indications of success beyond all expectations. All 52 responses were positive! The grumblings that had bordered on hostility at the beginning of the semester were totally gone. The 52 students who commented favorably included eight students who did not pass the course, but still felt that the writing activities helped them to do the best they could. The following are some of the comments made by these students:

> Writing helped me most in the very first set of problems when we had to write the order of operations. I realized you could not do the problems then or in the future if you did not know the order of operations.

> The writing process made doing out-of-class assignments easier by not having to rely on total memory of what was explained in class to solve problems. It also was an excellent way to prepare for a test. Writing helped me to determine in which areas I was weak. If I couldn't explain the steps and procedures in how to solve a particular problem clearly in writing, I knew that was an area in which I was weak and had to study more.

Writing the steps made it easier to remember them. Usually when I see a "bunch of numbers" as examples, I get confused and don't remember; but now that I've written the steps, I can explain the procedure to myself instead of just trying to do the problem and hope it comes out right.

When you write something on paper, you remember it better. When I was doing a problem or equation, if I got stuck, it was easier to remember the step-by-step procedure because I had it written down.

Writing helped me to organize my thoughts rather than memorizing problems.

The positive reactions of the students along with my personal qualitative evaluations were the determining factors that led me to conclude that the writing-to-learn experiment in basic algebra was a success. These results were much more important to me than the statistical data that seemed to indicate an increase in academic achievement due to the writing-to-learn activities. I am not positive I was able to control all the variables, nor can I be sure I eliminated all bias in my teaching of the control and experimental groups. Yet I am absolutely positive that 52 students felt the writing-to-learn activities not only helped their academic skills but also raised their levels of confidence and created more positive attitudes toward the learning of algebra. I would have been just as enthusiastic with the results of this experiment even if the quantitative statistical analysis had not indicated a significant increase in academic achievement. David Layzer, a member of the core science subcommittee at Harvard, has studied how writing influenced students' cognitive learning. He has discussed with me his theory that "students with the most severe 'math blocks' are the ones that dissociate mathematical reasoning most completely from verbal reasoning. Establishing a bridge between the two is often enough to dissolve the block." Writing-to-learn activities certainly appeared to be that bridge for the students involved in this experiment with the teaching of remedial algebra. The qualitative results of this experiment provided me with the most rewarding experiences of my 25 years of teaching basic and remedial courses: I know I achieved success in helping students attack their "math blocks" and reduce their "math anxiety."

Three final comments. First, not all teachers will be able to achieve the same degrees of success incorporating and using writing-to-learn activities in their classes. Writing to learn will not work in a pure lecture-type classroom. The instructor must be committed to the theory of writing to learn if he hopes to "sell" the learning process to his class. Especially in a remedial situation, the students must be motivated by the enthusiasm of the instructor. Second, since this experiment with basic algebra, I have incorporated writing-to-learn activities into new course designs for my classes in college algebra, analytic methods, and statistics. I have found writing-to-learn strategies to be equally effective in achieving higher level objectives involving analysis, synthesis, and evaluation. Finally, I would urge all instructors to experiment with innovative teaching techniques even if the results of such experimentation can be evaluated only in qualitative terms. Do not be intimidated by higher education's obsession with quantitative research data that must be subjected to formal statistical analysis. The main objective is to improve the learning environment through improved teaching and teaching techniques. If the only means by which this objective can be accomplished is through qualitative research, then this type of research should be encouraged at all levels of instruction.

REFERENCES

Bloom, B. (1956). *Taxonomy of educational objectives: Cognitive domain*. New York: Longman.

Henderson, A. D. (1965). The design of superior courses. *Improving College and University Teaching, 13*, 106–109.

Tobias, S. (1988, Winter). Insiders/Outsiders. *Academic Connections*, 1–5.

CHAPTER 13

Writing as a Vehicle to Learn Mathematics: A Case Study

Arthur B. Powell and José A. López

There is a dangerous myth going around that people learn from experience.
. . . the best that can be claimed is the *possibility* of learning from *reflecting* on experience.

> D. Pimm (1987, p. 60, emphasis original)

One learns from reflecting on experiences—a sensible and uncontroversial correction of the well-known adage. Because of its very familiarity, Pimm's statement is in danger of stimulating only momentary thought rather than enduring, fundamental transformations of our perspectives on learning and teaching. In the prevailing model of mathematics teaching, referred to by some as the "chalk-and-talk" method, there are few, if any, situations in which students are asked explicitly to reflect on the mathematics they are doing, their feelings about mathematics, or themselves in relation to the discipline. Instead, the results of others' reflections are narrated to students who are simply asked to memorize these results. This method of teaching incorporates assumptions about teaching and learning that Freire (1970, 1973) characterizes as the "banking" method and Gattegno (1971) describes as the traditional method of schooling.

In the prevailing model, the absence of explicit requests for students to reflect suggests that learning occurs as one moves along a linear sequence of experiences. This view is depicted in Figure 13.1. In this model, "experiences" are didactic situations in which mathematics is presented in a precognized, atomized, and rule-bound form. As a consequence, learning is

A version of this paper was presented at the 71st annual meeting of the Mathematical Association of America, Atlanta, Georgia, 9 January 1988.

EXPERIENCE₁ ⟶ EXPERIENCE₂ ⟶ EXPERIENCE₃ ⟶ ···

Figure 13.1 The prevailing model of mathematics education, which assumes that learning occurs as one is simply transported from one experience to the next

largely an intellectually passive activity in which the need to construct meaning is minimized. Furthermore, since within this model mathematics is believed to yield objective answers to quantitative questions, feelings are excluded from consideration.

On the other hand, the reality of learning suggests a more complex, dynamic model, one which captures the interconnections between experiences and reflections. The model in Figure 13.2 portrays dialectical movement between experiences and reflections, as well as among them and another type of reflection — critical reflection. In the didactic moments of this model, "experiences" are situations in which one perceives, feels, and acts on aspects of one's environment. Reflections on experiences are thoughts about ideas, things or objects, and feelings. These reflections are descriptive, comparative, inferential, interpretive, and evaluative. Such reflections also involve awareness of one's affective responses to experiences. Reflections, then, have two components: thoughts and feelings. These components of reflections are interconnected in that affect influences thoughts and thoughts impinge on affect.[1]

Thoughts and affectivity are also aspects of the third component of this model of learning. Critical reflections are reflections removed from the immediacy of particular experiences. Such reflections are thoughts about thoughts directed toward planning, monitoring, reviewing, and revising. While cognition is a component of reflections, metacognition is a component of critical reflections. The second component of critical reflections is what could be termed "meta-affectivity," monitoring and controlling one's

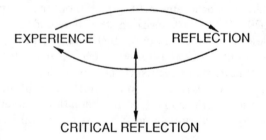

EXPERIENCE   REFLECTION

CRITICAL REFLECTION

Figure 13.2 A model of learning depicting the dynamic, complex interactions among experiences, reflections, and critical reflections

affective responses to experiences. In this model (refer to Figure 13.2), learning is recognized to be a cognitively and affectively interrelated and active enterprise. This view presupposes the existence of learners capable of directing their cognitive and affective resources to learn from experiences.

Writing is a powerful instrument with which to reflect on experiences and, like mathematics, is a major tool for thought. Two decades ago, Bruner (1968) advised that both writing and mathematics were "devices for ordering thoughts about things and thoughts about thoughts" (p. 112). This instrumental notion of writing and mathematics can be extended to include the ordering of both thoughts about affect and thoughts directed toward monitoring affect. It is, therefore, reasonable that there be pedagogical techniques in which these instruments together function to augment learning.

For a number of years, mathematics educators have explored pedagogical connections between writing and mathematics, specifically, writing as a support to mathematics learning. The rationales and purposes for, as well as implementations of, writing in the curricula have varied. From among this variety, two categories of approaches can be distinguished: product and process-product. In the former approach, writing is used as a way of demonstrating knowledge; in process-product approaches, writing is a way of knowing. In product approaches, mathematics educators engage learners in writing activities for purposes immediately focused on mathematics, rather than on learners. The concern is for what learners know at the moment, not for the evolution of their understanding of mathematical concepts. The reverse is true of approaches in the process-product category, where writing is used first to focus on learners and then as a means to have learners reflect on mathematics. It follows that writing activities in the process-product category tend to have more than one phase or drafting stage. These stages provide learners with opportunities to construct meaning and generate knowledge.

Different approaches require students' writings to have different functions. These functions range between two of three functions of writing categories formulated by Britton et al. (1975), namely expressive and transactional.[2] Transactional writing is chiefly the type of writing students are to do in product approaches. Writing activities in product approaches are used for assessment and diagnosis; to have students complete sentences or to write short, well-developed passages in a response to instructor-supplied questions or topics; and for students to record step-by-step arithmetic procedures (Azzolino & Roth, 1987; Geeslin, 1977; Goldberg, 1983; Johnson, 1983; Nahrgang & Petersen, 1986; Pallmann, 1982; Watson, 1980). Because these activities are mainly for evaluation, students are required to produce writing which is impersonal or transactional, rather than expressive (see also King, 1982).[3]

More pedagogically interesting than product-oriented approaches are ones that foster writing that reflects students' independent thinking. Process-product approaches strive to do this, and as a consequence, reflection and critical reflection are pedagogical foci of writing activities. In process-product approaches, writing activities tend to require exploratory, speculative writing in which the writer externalizes some content of her or his mind. Writing is used primarily as a means to learn mathematics and about oneself, not just as a means to measure information acquisition.

Though not necessarily expressed in terms of the theoretical framework provided by Britton et al., process-product activities move students along the expressive-transactional continuum; that is, expressive writing activities often provide starting points since, according to Britton and others, they are "a kind of matrix from which differentiated forms of mature writing [poetic and transactional] are developed" (1975, p. 83). Students write to articulate their beliefs about the nature of mathematical knowledge and their affective responses to the mathematics they are doing; to construct and negotiate meaning; and to reflect on and monitor their learning and affectivity (Buerk, 1982; Countryman, 1985; Frankenstein, 1983; Powell, 1986). From these starting points and through a process including feedback and revision, students move into a mode of writing about mathematics whose function is transactional (Burton, 1985; Gopen & Smith, 1988; Kenyon, 1987; Mett, 1987; Stempien & Borasi, 1985).

Can writing, in fact, be used as a vehicle to learn mathematics? Drawing on studies in cognitive psychology (Bruner, Luria, Vygotsky), neuropsychology (Gardner), sociolinguistics (Hymes), and philosophy (Dewey, Polanyi), Emig (1977) argued theoretically and convincingly that writing is a unique, multirepresentational, and bi-spheral "languaging process" that also corresponds to other powerful learning strategies; therefore, it ought to be incorporated as a central academic process. A number of mathematics educators have asserted that writing facilitates mathematics learning; however, little evidence of students' conceptual development or increased mathematical maturity has been proffered to support the reasonableness of this assertion. Empirical studies designed to measure the effect of writing on students' achievement in, and attitude toward, mathematics were themselves problematic. Among other technical and pedagogical considerations, either the instructional period was too brief (Bell & Bell, 1985) or the statistical instruments yielded confusing and contradictory information (Selfe, Petersen, & Nahrgang, 1986). As a first approximation toward inquiring into the reasonableness of the claim, the present case study was initiated with the following question in mind: What changes could be observed in students' understanding of and feelings toward mathematics through their writing? The following three questions also drove this study:

1. Do students' writings display their recognition of patterns, relationships, and attributes in mathematics?
2. Is writing a means by which students can construct or negotiate meaning?
3. Do students use writing to draw conclusions, make conjectures, ask questions, and express their feelings about mathematics?

SETTING

During the fall semester of 1987, this study was conducted in one section of a computation course, Developmental Mathematics I, at Rutgers University's Newark College of Arts and Sciences, whose students are primarily commuters. The course, based on a pedagogical model of Hoffman and Powell (1987) that departs in fundamental ways from the chalk-and-talk model, includes the study of fractions, decimals, percents, word problems, and an introduction to elementary algebra. The course met three times a week for fourteen weeks and had an initial enrollment of twenty-four students, out of which eighteen completed the course. Most were first-year students, and all were placed in the course on the basis of their performance on the New Jersey Test of Basic Skills or, on an in-house instrument, the Mathematics Placement Test. The content of both instruments is arithmetic computation and elementary algebra.

Based on previous scholastic experiences, many students in this course have developed negative feelings and beliefs about mathematics and themselves as mathematics learners. A student expressed one such view as, "Mathematics is something you do, not something you understand." Like students in similar settings (Buerk, 1982) and generally (McKnight et al., 1987, pp. 42–49), most students in this course consider mathematics not only as an abstruse symbol system but also as an arcane and fixed body of knowledge whose secrets will not be revealed. Students have developed an estranged relationship with academic mathematics: This estrangement is manifested in strategies of avoidance which include learning passivity, inappropriate study routines, and reluctance to participate actively in class.

Developmental Mathematics I was chosen for two important reasons:

It is the first of a three-course sequence, the last of which is an intermediate algebra course, College Algebra, for which successful completion satisfies a degree requirement. Approximately 50% of the entering students correctly answer less than 40% of the items on either placement examination. These students are placed into one of the first two courses in the sequence. In any given semester, the failure rate in College Algebra is approximately 40 percent. This figure is as true of students who place directly into that course as for those who are required first to take one or two developmental mathematics courses. Consequently, there is college-wide concern for the retention of students who do not meet the college mathematics proficiency standard upon matriculation.

There was a second, equally compelling reason for selecting this research setting. Students in Developmental Mathematics I come from among the most disadvantaged sectors of our society and are victims of racial, gender, and class oppressions. The aggregate effect of these impact negatively on students' academic performance, generally, and on their mathematics performance, specifically. (For an elaboration of a model that attempts to explain differences in mathematics achievement based on students' race, sex, and socioeconomic status, see Reyes & Stanic, 1988). The prevailing chalk-and-talk method of mathematics teaching contributes to students' estranged relationship with the discipline and, as such, is another element of oppression. As writing requires an active rather than a passive involvement of learners, this project aimed to empower students in two ways: (1) to promote students' awareness of and facility in the use of writing as a vehicle for learning, and (2) to put students at the center and in control of their own learning by engaging them in reflection and critical reflection on mathematical experiences.

METHOD

During the second week of the semester, the nature and objectives of this study were discussed with the class verbally and in writing (see Figure 13.3), and research collaborators were solicited. Students were asked to respond in writing, explaining whether they wished to be a research partner and why. From among the affirmative respondents, two students were selected; one, José, is a co-author of this paper and his work is the basis of this case study.

A number of writing activities were used in the course, two of which, freewriting and journal writing, have been analyzed for this study. For five minutes, at the start of each class and each examination, students were

Figure 13.3   Letter to Developmental Mathematics I students

Dear Developmental Mathematics I Student:

This semester, I will conduct a research project for which I am looking for student collaborators. The goal of the research project is to discover whether writing about the mathematics that one is learning and doing can be helpful in learning mathematics. Let me tell what the project is about.

In this course, I will ask each of you to keep a journal about your learning and to do other types of short writing assignments related to the course. Most of the writings that you do I will collect and analyze, and to some writings I will respond. Those who collaborate with me may be asked to do a bit more writing than others. Each week, collaborators and I will meet as a research team to help me analyze their writings.

The central research question that I hope to answer by the end of this research project is: What types of thinking about mathematics are displayed in students' writing? In addition, there are three subquestions that I will be asking about the writing that you do.

1. Do students' writings display their recognition of patterns, relationships, and attributes in mathematics?
2. Is writing a means by which students can construct or negotiate meaning?
3. Do students use writing to draw conclusions, make conjectures, ask questions, and express their feelings about mathematics?

Why do I ask students to write in a mathematics class? I believe that writing can be a powerful tool for developing or improving your critical and reflective thinking about mathematics. By critical thinking, I mean the type of thinking that is careful and reasoned. And by reflective thinking, I mean thinking that is inquisitive, thoughtful, and deliberate. Reflective thinking also can lead one to think about how one thinks. Both critical and reflective thinking can lead one to search for and find meaning and understanding. These, I believe, can be the benefits to you of this research project.

I intend to co-author a paper, with those who collaborate with me, on the results and findings of this project. Let me know if you would like to work with me. The first meeting of the research team will be held in my office during the free period (1 p.m.) on Wednesday, 16 September.

Sincerely,

Arthur B. Powell

asked to freewrite. Freewriting topics were of their choosing; when none came to mind readily, they could write about that. Students were made aware that these writings were neither to be evaluated nor collected. It was suggested, though, that they maintain a collection of these writings for their own purposes. It was hypothesized that freewriting would promote reflection and provide a meditative period in which to collect and give oneself perspective. As we shall see, freewriting served another, unexpected purpose. No attempt was made to monitor the freewriting, but although the instructor also freewrote, students were observed to be freewriting during the allotted time.

Journal writing was the central, more substantive activity; indeed it was initially conceived as the only writing-to-learn activity upon which this case study was to be based. Students were asked to write daily, or at least for each class or assignment, on any topic or issue related to their learning of, or feelings about, the mathematics of the course or the course itself. To help remove the chore-like conception some have of writing and to relieve anxieties many associate with the quantity to be produced, students were advised that five minutes of writing was sufficient for each journal entry. After becoming accustomed to journal writing, most found themselves spending more time than this to express their thoughts. A list of topics was offered only to stimulate thought and reflection (see Figure 13.4).

Journals were collected weekly and returned with comments on the substance of what was written. The comments were intended to be non-judgmental and most often took the form of questions about or suggestions on issues, ideas, and so on to encourage further exploration. The objective was to use journal writing as a tool for learning mathematics. Therefore, it was emphasized to students that neither their grammar nor syntax were of concern, only what they had to say. Aside from moral and other intrinsic incentives, neither penalties nor rewards, in the form of grades or otherwise, were given. To have done so would have indirectly communicated to students that there was a way in which they were to process concepts and feelings. The eighteen students who completed the course submitted journals 93 percent of the time.

Freewritings and journals were two of three processes-products of this research project. The third process-product entailed student–instructor collaboration in the analysis of the student's writings and mathematics as well as in writing this case study. As co-authors, we held periodic meetings to discuss and analyze José's journal and, eventually, freewriting entries. Notes of these discussions were kept; later they were discussed, elaborated, and revised. At the end of the semester, we met several times to decide on the shape of this report and to write drafts of it.

Figure 13.4   Instructions to students on writing journals

You are asked to keep a journal on $8^1/2'' \times 11''$ sheets of loose-leaf paper. Generally, one or two sheets will be sufficient for a week's worth of journal writing. Neither your syntax nor grammar will be a concern or checked; my only concern and interest is what you say, not how you say it. You are asked to make, at least, one journal entry for each meeting that we have, and, as a rule of thumb, you need not spend more than five to ten minutes writing each entry. Each week, the latest journal entries will be collected and returned with comments.

The focus of your journal entries should be on *your learning* of mathematics or on the mathematics of the course. That is, your reflections should be on what *you* do, feel, discover, or invent. Within this context, you may write on any topic or issue you choose. To stimulate your thoughts and reflections, here are some questions and suggestions.

1. What did *you* learn from the class activity and discussion or the assignment?
2. What questions do *you* have about the work *you* are doing or not able to do?
3. Describe any discoveries *you* make about mathematics (patterns, relationships, procedures, and so on) or yourself.
4. Describe the process *you* undertook to solve a problem.
5. What attributes, patterns, or relationships have *you* found?
6. How do *you* feel about *your* work, discoveries, the class or the assignment?
7. What confused *you* today? What did *you* especially like? What did *you* not especially like?
8. Describe any computational procedure *you* invent.

RESULTS

Freewriting

In the original design of this study, we did not intend to analyze José's freewriting entries. At the end of the course, however, he suggested that an examination of selected entries could be informative. Indeed it was, and we found that freewriting served four purposes for José, each within the category of expressive writing. First, it focused one; it was a meditative activity, allowing one to make contact with and to take control of one's inner reality and gain a degree of confidence. Second, freewriting provided a way to clear the mind of preoccupations. These preoccupations were varied, and entries included discussions of feelings, related and unrelated to the course and mathematics; concerns about chores to be accomplished; the anxiety of making presentations in front of the class; career choices and future life; evaluations of the course's content, structure and teaching ap-

proach; and issues involving social interactions. Third, freewriting func-
tioned as a means to reflect on mathematical processes. The following
entry illustrates these three functions of freewriting (this entry and all
others, unless otherwise indicated, are from the writings of the student-
author):

> Oh Boy! Here I am again. I think the page hates when I write on it. What
> else. What else. What? I made various observations of the patterns in the
> multiplication chart. It was helpful to hear the feedback from the group.
> Start on Jones' assignment tonight, study for chem exam, outline psych.

Written during the sixth week of the semester and after the same number
of weeks of freewriting, this was the first entry to contain a specific reference to mathematics or a mathematical process of the mind (recognizing
patterns). Later, the following entry was written. José details a specific
observation and the insight it engendered.

> Here we go again. Today in class I observed that when working with expo-
> nents when one moves to the right the value of the exponent increases by one.
> Oh! Oh! I ran out of room. Where was I? Oh! So what I said on the previous
> page and then the reverse is true when moving to the left. Also, the # of
> multiplication steps is the same as the exponent when moving to the left one
> takes the reciprocal of the pos. [positive] value found when moving to the
> right. Wow! I wonder if what I just said sounds confusing.

At times, the stream-of-consciousness nature of some freewriting requires that one read entries carefully, a few times, to extract meaning.
While referring to a chart similar to the one in Figure 13.5 below, several
interesting observations are mentioned in the entry above. There, the comparative statement that the number of "multiplication steps" (really factors
of the base) "is the same as the exponent," demonstrates that knowledge
brought to the situation was synthesized with information observed directly in the chart. This was an act of looking and seeing beyond the mere

...	2^{-3}	2^{-2}	2^{-1}	2^0	2^1	2^2	2^3	2^4	2^5	2^6 ...
	$\|$	$\|$	$\|$	$\|$	$\|$	$\|$	$\|$	$\|$	$\|$	$\|$
...	$\frac{1}{8}$	$\frac{1}{4}$	$\frac{1}{2}$	1	2	4	8	16	32	64 ...

Figure 13.5 Chart showing the relationships and patterns among the negative, zero, and positive powers of 2

appearance of things. It is interesting, however, that no mention was made that this insight does not hold true for expressions left of 2^1. Nevertheless, the above freewriting entry illustrates, in writing, José's wrestling with a new concept, negative exponents, and achieving an understanding from among several layers of meanings of the concept. In addition, the penultimate sentence in the above entry indicates that insight was acquired into the relationship between two concepts: reciprocals and negative exponents.

The fourth purpose freewriting served for José was not initially anticipated. Often a day's freewriting entry was reviewed immediately before writing a journal entry. That is, freewriting entries were used as notes for further elaboration in journal entries. An example of this purpose will be given after some discussion of the general results of journal writing.

Journals

As in the case of freewriting, journal entries were varied, but they were constrained in different ways. Journal entries were to be more like "learning logs" than stream-of-consciousness writings and were public documents, to be read and commented upon. Yet they retained their expressive function, almost always: Journal entries contained expressions of feelings, summaries of learning, commentaries on the course, questions, conjectures, specifications of areas of difficulty or confusion, as well as descriptions of solutions and discoveries. Perhaps because of the particular constraints on journal writing, it provided, more than freewriting, a substantive account of how and what one was learning and feeling. Journals also proved to be a powerful vehicle for dialogue between student and instructor.

Over the course of the semester, the nature of José's journal entries and topics demonstrated growth in his understanding and enjoyment of mathematics as well as confidence in his ability to do mathematics. At first, however, entries dealt with how the class or classmates were reacting to the course, and, as such, these writings were mainly messages to the instructor, as the following excerpt illustrates:

> Also, I see that the more we work with circle expressions [see Hoffman & Powell, in press] the more people feel at ease about working with them. I find or rather it is my opinion that the work groups are helping a lot of people. It gives them some sort of security to work in a group rather than on their own.

It was suggested that journal entries focus on one's own learning, feelings, insights, discoveries, and so on. Afterward, José's entries became largely summaries of class discussions. During the first couple of weeks, these summaries were mostly flat, general narratives of class events.

> Today we worked on the old postage stamp problem. We went over the previous information on the problem, and also we found out some new things about it. . . . Also, some conjectures were suggested.

José's writing was still outwardly focused, but over time it shifted inward and began to include reflections that claimed that patterns were being noticed and that described his feelings in relation to assignments.

> As time goes by, I'm finding it easier to see patterns in the work that I'm doing. I feel confident with the work I'm doing. . . .

Also, there were statements that correlated the relative ease of solving problems with a certain degree of enjoyment.

> I find, as time goes by, that it is becoming easier for me to solve math problems and that I am enjoying math somewhat more than I used to.

At this point in the semester, José's more positive affective response toward mathematics also corresponded both to increased specificity in his summary statements and to movement toward reflecting on mathematics in writing. To some extent, this movement also was stimulated by instructor nudgings at the bottom of a week's journal: "It would be interesting to read about the patterns that you are seeing. If you write about these patterns, then your understanding of the material may also increase." Soon after this nudge, the following entry was written. What is particularly interesting is that it contains an elaboration of an observation first mentioned in a freewriting entry written earlier that week, illustrating that freewriting entries were used, at times, as "starting notes" for journal writings (see the entry related to Figure 13.5). This was an unexpected function of freewritings.

> Today in class, I observed that when working with exponents, when I move to the right the value of the exponential number increases by one. The reverse is true when moving to the left. Also, the number of multiplication steps is the same as the exponential number. When moving to the left, I take the reciprocal of the positive value I found when moving to the right. When multiplying numbers with the bases the same, but different exponential numbers, I can add these exponents. e.g. $5^3 \times 5^1 = 5^4 = 625$. When dividing numbers whose base is the same, but have different exponents, I can subtract the second exponent from the first. e.g.,
>
> $$\frac{5^3}{5^1} = 5^{3-1} = 5^2 = 25.$$

In the above entry, not only does José restate more clearly what he wrote during a freewriting session earlier that week, which itself is indicative of a degree of intellectual engagement with the topic, but he goes on to summarize new material in some detail.

Another shift in the nature of José's journal entries was evident midway into the semester. New elements appeared: detailed summaries and expansive illustrations and explorations of mathematical concepts and relationships. These can be seen in the following entry:

> Today in class, I observed more patterns in exponential properties. There are now six ways to solve exponential equations. They are:
>
> EP1: If a is any number and n and m are exponents, then $a^m \times a^n = a^{m+n}$
>
> EP2: $\dfrac{a^m}{a^n} = a^{m-n}$
>
> EP3: $(a^m)^n = a^{m \times n}$
>
> EP4: $(a \times b)^n = a^n \times b^n$
>
> EP5: $\left(\dfrac{a}{b}\right)^n = a^n / b^n$
>
> EP6: $(a^r \times b^s)^n = a^{r \times n} \times b^{s \times n}$
>
> When working with fractions one can say that taking a reciprocal of a number is the same as raising the number to the negative first power. Also, when raising a negative number to an odd number exponent the result will be negative, and when raising a negative number to an even number exponent the result will be positive. e.g., $(-2)^3 = (-2) \times (-2) \times (-2) = -8$ and $(-2)^2 = (-2) \times (-2) = 4$.

This is one day's journal entry. In the first part, José summaries six properties of exponents (EP) which had been discussed in the previous few days. It was the first evidence that the journal was used to summarize in great detail, rather than simply to state what was learned, and, as with later entries, its purpose was to reassure oneself of what was learned. These restatements of ideas mentioned in class represent ideas with which José is now comfortable and of which he is claiming ownership. The act of restating was used to explore one's thoughts and understandings of new ideas.

In the second part of the above journal entry, two discoveries of José's are mentioned. The first is an interpretation of the meaning of an invariant situation and was made independently. It is interesting that this discovery represents a reentry into the topic of negative exponents. This time another aspect of this topic was uncovered: the relationship between taking the reciprocal of a fraction and raising a fraction to the negative first power. José's second discovery exposes a relationship not discussed in class but discovered while reflecting on an assignment.

Journals also were used to promote critical reflection. Students were asked to review previous entries, look for instances where they used writing to think about mathematics, reflect on those instances, and comment on them in writing. During one such exercise, José's awareness of the equivalence between "taking the reciprocal" and "raising to the negative first power," was extended to include integers, not only fractions whose denominators are other than one.

Just as entries detailed what a student understood from a lesson or an assignment, they also revealed gaps in understanding and misconceptions. Appropriate attention to these indications could turn such entries into dynamic vehicles for challenging and augmenting a student's mathematical awarenesses. An instance in which the journal was used to challenge a misconception occurred when we studied techniques for determining the greatest common factor (GCF) and lowest common multiple (LCM) of a group of integers. In an attempt to clarify and claim ownership of the first of these two concepts, José wrote the following:

> I found that I could find the greatest common factor of two integers by first finding common factors of both integers and then by taking the largest common to both.
> e.g. (24, 30) 1,2,3,6   GCF=6 or $2^1 \times 3^1$

Later, he attempted to internalize both concepts and accommodate them into his understanding of prime factors and prime factorization.

> The way one goes about finding the LCM of a group of integers is by looking at the prime factorization of the integers in the group, then picking out the common prime factorizations thus giving one the LCM. e.g., LCM(28, 36)=2^2, since 28=$2^2 \times 7^1$ and 36=$2^2 \times 3^2$. In this case 2^2 is the LCM.

It appeared that José's confusion was simply a matter of using the wrong group of three letters, LCM for GCF, not one of misconceptualization. The problem was pointed out and a question posed. Subsequently, the question, reiterated in the first sentence of the entry below, was answered and illustrated with a few examples. José described correctly how to determine the GCF of a group of positive integers and even discussed a special case.

> Today, I looked at the prime factorization of a group of numbers to see if I could determine their GCF and LCM just from their prime factorization. I found that both of these answers can in fact be determined by the prime factorizations. The way one goes about determining the GCF of a group of integers is to first see what prime factors the group has in common. The common prime factors of the group is the GCF. Note, if there are no common prime factors among the group their GCF is (1) one.

e.g. $\text{GCF}(60, 12) = 2^2 \times 3^1$ $\text{GCF}(5, 12) = 1$

         $60 = 2^2 \times 3^1 \times 5^1 : 12 = 2^2 \times 3^1$ $5 = 5^1 : 12 = 2^2 \times 3^1$

However, in the second part of this journal entry, presented below, a gap in understanding or a linguistic misconception still was evident.

> The LCM can be determined in a similar fashion. However, when trying to determine the LCM of a group of integers one must take the prime factorizations common to the group.
> e.g. $\text{LCM}(6, 12, 15) = 2^2 \times 3^1 \times 5^1 = 60$
> $6 = 2^1 \times 3^1 : 12 = 2^2 \times 3^1 : 15 = 3^1 \times 5^1$

In this part of the entry, although José computed the LCM correctly, his available language did not permit him to describe accurately his perception and action. On the other hand, part of his confusion related to what the adjective "common" qualifies and what can be seen in the prime factorizations of a group of integers. To find the GCF, the word "common" is related to what one sees directly in the prime factorizations. Given their prime factorizations, however, the LCM of a group of integers is not related to "common" visible elements. That is, the multiples of the integers are not displayed; one cannot see the LCM of a group of integers by simply examining their prime factorizations.

José had to search for language that corresponded to his perceptions and actions. When asked to reflect critically, to review and comment, on a group of journal entries that contained the one above, he eventually did find language to describe correctly the process he actually engaged in to find the LCM. The following is excerpted from that journal entry:

> To find the LCM, least common multiple, of a group of numbers one must take the distinct prime factors of the group that one expressed to the highest power.
> e.g., $\text{LCM}(2^5 \times 5^9 \times 3^3, \ 2^1 \times 5^3 \times 3^1, \ 7^1 \times 19^1 \times 13^1) = 2^5 \times 3^3 \times 5^9 \times 7^1 \times 13^1 \times 19^1$.

There are three fascinating aspects to this journal-entry excerpt. First, integers are represented not in standard form such as 750, but in their prime factored form, $2^1 \times 5^3 \times 3^1$; that is, a level of ease in handling a more abstract representation of integers is evident. Second, José's description of how to determine the LCM is general and concise. He achieved this level of generality and conciseness by reflecting and critically reflecting through writing and revising his written conceptualizations. Third, in the description above, if the word "take" were replaced by "multiply" and the phrase "that one" replaced by "each," which is how they are interpreted in practice, then José's description would appear to have come from an edition of James and James (1963, p. 262)!

Student–Instructor Collaboration

In conventional research models, including classroom-based ones, there is a researcher and objects of research. Even in more progressive models, such as classroom-based research models, the instructor is the researcher and students are the objects. We rejected such models in favor of one that can be called participatory. In the methodological design of this case study, in terms of both processes and products, student and instructor co-labored to analyze the student's writings and to write this report. In the following excerpt, José reflects on several features and benefits of his involvement in the collaborative project:

> I became interested in the study due to my poor math skills. I felt that if I took a more active role in the learning of mathematics I might be able to do better in the course. Throughout the semester I kept a journal detailing my observations of the class, course, and my learning of mathematics. . . . We met after classes and whenever our schedules allowed us to discuss what I felt that I had gained as a result of writing in a mathematics course. I was then asked to comment on the writing experience and the journals that I had kept, to see exactly how it was that I had gained a better understanding of the mathematics I was learning. I found many instances where certain ideas or concepts became clearer to me as a result of writing about them. . . . We then proceeded to put together our paper with the focus being on my learning process and understanding of mathematical concepts through writing.
>
> As a result of the writing that I had done during the course of the semester, I felt more confident in my problem-solving abilities and understood the material better. I was not only more efficient and understood better, but I found that by writing about mathematics I had eliminated some of the anxieties I had once had about mathematics. As a result, I had one of the two highest final exam scores and semester grades in the class. Previously, I *disliked* mathematics and performed poorly.

José's decision to participate in the project was an act directed toward improving his mathematics. Indeed, his insight into and facility in mathematics improved. These improvements occurred as José began to overcome his anxieties of, and estrangement from, mathematics. Explicit attention to reflection and critical reflection were the vehicles for these transformations to occur.

CONCLUSIONS

In this participatory study, we have analyzed select freewriting and journal entries of one first-semester freshman, the student-author, who was enrolled in a developmental computation course. The analysis of these reflections and critical reflections was undertaken to determine the degree of reasonableness of the claim that writing can facilitate the learning of mathematics. As we have seen in this study, writing is a heuristic tool with which one can negotiate meaning; in negotiating meaning, one is generating knowledge and learning. Thus, the claim is more than reasonable. In addition to this, we have derived other conclusions. Though these are stated in general terms below, we will discuss limitations on their interpretations. Finally, we will mention a few questions suggested by this study.

Our conclusions are grouped into three areas: student–instructor communications, students' affectivity, and students' learning. With respect to student–instructor communications, students are encouraged to write expressively and tend do so freely. Journals are a powerful medium for dialogue between instructor and students. Moreover, this means of personal dialogue can serve to reassure students that their concerns are taken into account. Instructors have an opportunity to provide feedback to students' statements, interpretations, questions, discoveries, and misconceptions. Rich opportunities for encouraging students to reconsider their conceptualizations and to extend and deepen them often present themselves. In addition, the revelatory nature of students' expressive writings provides instructors with feedback on important dimensions of their pedagogy.

Reflecting critically in writing about the mathematics they are learning gives students greater potential to control their learning and to develop criteria for monitoring their progress. The development of control and monitoring capabilities engenders in students feelings of accomplishment. These feelings, in turn, have a positive effect on their affective response toward the mathematics they were learning. Finally, from acquiring greater control over their learning, developing criteria for personal standards of progress, and conceptually understanding the mathematics in which they are engaged, students derive a great deal of satisfaction with themselves as learners capable of doing *and* understanding mathematics.

Reflecting critically on one's mathematical experiences in writing presupposes an active, not a passive, learner. This action, coupled with the revelatory nature of reflective writing, suggests that writing can have a significant impact on learners' cognition and meta-cognition. Writing, because the writer and others can see it, allows one to explore relationships, make meaning, and manipulate thoughts; to extend, expand, or drop ideas; and to review, comment upon, and monitor reflections. Expressive writing supports these cognitive and meta-cognitive acts. After one establishes a degree of confidence in one's ideas, it seems almost natural to move from expressive to transactional prose. This is what occurred to José as he wrestled with his ideas on how to determine the least common multiple of a group of integers. He constructed and reconstructed meaning. He wrote and revised his reflections. The process was mediated by external comments. As José began to express his ideas with greater clarity and confidence and selected language that more accurately described his perceptions and actions, his writing shifted from expressive to transactional.

Through this case study, we have also shown that writing helps students to acquire a rich vocabulary and use it in the context of their understanding of mathematics. Mayher, Lester, & Pradl (1983) make this point with regards to learning in general:

> Writing's capacity to place the learner at the center of her own learning can and should make writing an important facilitator of learning anything that involves language. Writing that involves language choice requires each writer to find her own words to express whatever is being learned. Such a process may initially serve to reveal more gaps than mastery of a particular subject, but even that can be of immense diagnostic value for teacher and learner alike. And as the process is repeated, real and lasting mastery of the subject and its technical vocabulary is achieved. (p. 79)

By providing students with opportunities to work with mathematical concepts and terms in their own language and on their own terms, writing also helps students build their confidence in the context of mathematics and become engaged in the material more thoroughly.

Writing to learn mathematics is transformative not only for learners but for instructors as well. Useful writing-to-learn activities are those that engage learners in exploring the contents of their minds; that is, they should maximize the extent to which learners choose language to describe their thoughts, actions, and perceptions. As Mayher, Lester, and Pradl (1983) have claimed, "Writing that involves minimal language choices, such as filling-in-blanks exercises or answering questions with someone else's language — the textbook's or the teacher's — are of limited value in promoting either writing or learning" (p. 78). The more learners are involved in choosing language, the more they are engaged in constructing and reconstructing meaning and making sense of mathematics for themselves. For learners to develop their reflective and critical reflective abilities, learning environments must promote, as Freire has argued, "acts of cognition, not transferrals of information" (1970, p. 67).

What can a case study tell us about the usefulness of writing to learn mathematics generally? It seems likely that most of the conclusions presented above hold true in general. Yet it is also true that one cannot generalize from the case of one to that of many. Broader studies are required to determine precisely for how many other learners our conclusions are true. Conversely, individual learners cannot be known solely on the bases of generalizations derived from the study of groups. A number of our conclusions, however, do point to questions and patterns to look for in the writings of other learners.

This study raises a number of broad questions: How can writing activities best be structured to promote mathematics learning? Do such activities differ in relation to different levels of mathematics? Can writing activities be used to promote collaborative learning? What types of instructor responses prompt students to write more meaningfully and with greater clarity? In what ways can writing be used as an independent, reflective, and meaning-seeking learning tool? We invite others to examine these and other questions that involve students in writing as a vehicle to learn mathematics.

Acknowledgements

We are thankful for support received from the Center for the Study of Writing in New Jersey, the Dean's Office and the Educational Opportunities Fund Program at the Newark College of Arts and Sciences, Rutgers University. We have also benefited from comments from Mark Driscoll, Marilyn Frankenstein, Dixie Goswami, William Jones, Anneli Lax, Paul Perdue, and Molly and Dan Watt.

NOTES

1. The notion that feelings are critical to learning and understanding mathematics is not usually made explicit by mathematics educators or acknowledged by mathematicians. Henderson (1987), a mathematician at Cornell University, has expressed introspectively that feelings are an essential component of understanding mathematics: "When I understand something my perception of my universe of experience has been broadened – deepened. . . . To be complete this understanding (increased perception, changed meaning) must include the components of *knowing, feeling,* and *acting*" (p. 1; author's emphases). Also see Mason, Burton, & Stacey (1985) for practical suggestions on how to attend to affectivity to do mathematics successfully.

2. Transactional writing uses language "to get things done: to inform people (telling them what they need or want to know or what we think they ought to know), to advise or persuade or instruct people." It is used whenever an "accurate and specific reference to what is known about reality" is needed. Expressive writing is "'thinking aloud on paper.' It has the function of revealing the speaker, verbalizing his consciousness . . . submits itself to the free flow of ideas and feelings. . . . " (Britton et al., 1975, pp. 88–90).

3. Some educators, such as King (1982), classify and describe writing activities as being either expressive or transactional. However, this results in a problematic classification scheme principally for two reasons. First, as categories of writing,

expressive and transactional refer to the function of a piece of writing for the writer, not to the characteristics of a writing task or to an instructor's expectations (Britton et al., 1975, pp. 88–91). Though the type of writing to which an instructor gives greater value can be distinguished as expressive and transactional. Second, as described by King, all activities, including those classified as "expressive," are actually product-oriented and, from a developmental perspective, are static. The point is that any of King's activities could be used properly to move from "close-to-the-self" or expressive writing to product-oriented impersonal or transactional writing.

REFERENCES

Azzolino, A., & Roth, R. G. (1987). Questionbooks: Using writing to learn mathematics. *AMATYC Review, 9*(1), 41–49.

Bell, E. S., & Bell, R. N. (1985). Writing and mathematical problem solving: Arguments in favor of synthesis. *School Science and Mathematics, 85*(3), 210–221.

Britton, J., Burgess, T., Martin, N., McLeod, A., & Rosen, H. (1975). *The development of writing abilities (11–18).* London: Macmillan.

Bruner, J. S. (1968). *Toward a theory of instruction.* New York: W. W. Norton.

Buerk, D. (1982). An experience with some able women who avoid mathematics. *For the Learning of Mathematics, 3*(2), 19–24.

Burton, G. M. (1985, December). Writing as a way of knowing in mathematics education class. *Arithmetic Teacher, 32,* 40–45.

Countryman, J. (1985). Writing to Learn Mathematics. In *Woodrow Wilson Foundation Mathematics Institute curriculum module: Focus on functions* (pp. 337–348). Princeton, NJ: Woodrow Wilson Foundation.

Emig, J. (1977). Writing as a mode of learning. *College Composition and Communications, 28,* 122–128.

Frankenstein, M. (1983). Teaching radical math: Taking the numb out of numbers. *Science for the People, 15*(1), 12–17.

Freire, P. (1970). *Pedagogy of the oppressed.* New York: Seabury.

Freire, P. (1973). *Education for critical consciousness.* New York: Seabury.

Gattegno, C. (1971). *What we owe children: The subordination of teaching to learning.* New York: Discus.

Geeslin, W. E. (1977). Using writing about mathematics as a teaching technique. *Mathematics Teacher, 70,* 112–115.

Goldberg, D. (1983). Integrating writing into the mathematics curriculum. *Two-Year College Mathematics Journal, 14*(5), 421–424.

Gopen, G. D., & Smith, D. A. (1988, January). How to respond to students' first efforts at writing mathematics. Paper presented at the 71st annual meeting of the Mathematical Association of America, Atlanta, GA.

Henderson, D. W. (1987). *What does it mean to understand a piece of mathematics?* Unpublished manuscript.

Hoffman, M. R., & Powell, A. B. (1987, July). An alternative model for teaching college students with underdeveloped mathematics potential. Paper presented at the seventh Inter-American Conference on Mathematics Education, Santo Domingo, Dominican Republic.

Hoffman, M. R., & Powell, A. B. (in press). A Multivalent Tool for Teaching Computation. *Mathematics in College.*

James, G., & James, R. C. (Eds.). (1963). *Mathematics dictionary.* Princeton, NJ: D. Van Nostrand.

Johnson, M. (1983). Writing in mathematics class: A valuable tool for learning. *Mathematics Teacher, 76,* 117–119.

Kenyon, R. W. (1987). Writing in the mathematics classroom. *New England Mathematics Journal, 87*(5), 3–19.

King, B. (1982). Using Writing in the Mathematics Class: Theory and Practice. In C. W. Griffin (Ed.), *Teaching writing in all disciplines* (New directions for teaching and learning no. 12, pp. 39–44). San Francisco: Jossey-Bass.

Mason, J., Burton, L., & Stacey, K. (1985). *Thinking mathematically.* Reading, MA: Addison-Wesley.

Mayher, J., Lester, N., & Pradl, G. (1983). *Learning to write/Writing to learn.* Upper Montclair, NJ: Boynton/Cook.

McKnight, C. C., Crosswrite, J. F., Dossey, J. A., Kifer, E., Swafford, J. O., Travers, K. L., & Cooney, T. J. (1987). *The underachieving curriculum: Assessing U.S. school mathematics from an international perspective.* Champaign, IL: Stipes.

Mett, C. L. (1987). Writing as a learning device in calculus. *Mathematics Teacher, 80,* 534–537.

Nahrgang, C. L., & Petersen, B. T. (1986). Using writing to learn mathematics. *Mathematics Teacher, 79,* 461–465.

Pallmann, M. (1982). Verbal language processes in support of learning mathematics. *Mathematics in College,* 49–55.

Pimm, D. (1987). Fear, safety and dangerous things: Reasons for belief. In L. P. Mendoza & E. R. Williams (Eds.), *Proceedings of the Tenth Annual Meeting of the Canadian Mathematics Education Study Group, 29 May–2 June* (pp. 60–61). Queens University, Kingston, Ontario.

Powell, A. B. (1986). Working with "underprepared" mathematics students. In M. Driscoll & J. Confrey (Eds.), *Teaching mathematics: Strategies that work* (2nd ed, pp. 181–192). Portsmouth, NH: Heinemann.

Reyes, L. H., & Stanic, G. M. A. (1988). Race, sex, socioeconomic status and mathematics. *Journal for Research in Mathematics Education, 19*(1), 26–43.

Selfe, C. L., Petersen, B. T., & Nahrgang, C. L. (1986). Journal writing in mathematics. In A. Young & T. Fulwiler (Eds.), *Writing across the disciplines: Research into practice* (pp. 192–207). Upper Montclair, NJ: Boynton/Cook.

Stempien, M., & Borasi, R. (1985). Students' writing in mathematics: Some ideas and experiences. *For the Learning of Mathematics, 5*(3), 14–17.

Watson, M. (1980). Sharing teaching ideas: Writing has a place in a mathematics class. *Mathematics Teacher, 73,* 518–519.

CHAPTER 14

Writing in Science Education Classes for Elementary School Teachers

Mary Bahns

Although science education has enjoyed periods of intense national interest, it has more often been considered, if not expendable, at least decidedly less important than reading and mathematics. Even during post-Sputnik days, when science education enjoyed a great deal of popular support, it was deemed important primarily in terms of its contribution to the pool of professional scientists. But more recently there has evolved a growing awareness that scientific literacy is essential for all citizens in this highly technological world. Business and industry need a competent and knowledgeable work force. Successful competitors in the job market are increasingly in need of technological know-how and a basic understanding of scientific concepts. A democratic nation requires citizens who understand scientific issues — issues that frequently have no easy answers, but affect all of society.

Providing children with a thorough science education is, then, critically important. Furthermore, this education must begin in the elementary grades (K–6). Most students who enter junior high (or middle school) with inadequate or inappropriate science experiences have already developed a hearty dislike for science and find junior high science too difficult. The importance of good science experiences beginning at an early age cannot be overemphasized. It is both my privilege and challenge, then, to teach elementary school science to pre- and in-service teachers. Writing has played an important part in this endeavor.

Not only should science be taught in the elementary grades, but it must be taught appropriately. Research shows that most children at these ages are intuitive or concrete thinkers. They learn by doing, through physical, hands-on experiences. Most cannot handle purely abstract concepts, although they can, of course, memorize if they must. Historically, several different approaches to teaching science have been promoted, but all emphasize the necessity of a process-oriented, problem-solving, investigative approach — one in which concrete, hands-on experiences form the basis. This is not how science is taught in most elementary school classrooms today.

According to three National Science Foundation studies, elementary school science consists primarily of "recitation (discussion), with the teacher in control, supplementing the lesson with new information (lecturing). The key to information and the basis for reading assignments was the textbook" (Smith, 1980, p. 43). As for concrete, hands-on experiences, "'Activity' is apt to be the filling in of workbook exercises" (p. 44). These findings are corroborated by the written reflections of my graduate-level students in their journals. In response to a reading assignment (Mechling & Oliver, 1983), one student wrote:

> The depressing thing about this article is that it confirms my experiences in a year of substitute teaching: the usual science class is a stultifying exercise of reading the textbook and answering the questions. It's rare for children's participation to be much more than planting Lima beans or looking at a few rocks.

Further examples follow:

> I have been allotted $33 to spend on science equipment for my classroom. Many teachers are purchasing duplicating books.

> I just helped my son with his seemingly 40 million worksheets for his science class. No wonder he hates learning it [science] at school.

> At the beginning of the school year I gave each student an interest questionnaire. One question dealt with their least favorite subject — the majority put science. The overwhelming reason was it was boring — "all we ever did last year was read out of the book."

In many cases, teachers themselves have had negative experiences in science and are poorly prepared to teach it. Frequently, they feel inadequate, fearful, and uninterested. They share these feelings in their journals:

> Science is the one subject I teach where I feel totally ill at ease. I believe that I am actually afraid of science. It would be more accurate here to say I'm afraid of failure when it comes to understanding and being able to transfer that understanding to my students. My problem is . . . I don't enjoy those aspects of science that I am unsure of and I have a lack of enthusiasm for it. I'm afraid that this is also communicated to my students.

I'm presently starting the unit on our solar system. All year I've dreaded teaching science. Anyhow, I've begun to ask myself the question, "Am I not teaching mere definitions instead of concepts?" . . . I'm unsure.

The teachers' feelings of inadequacy and dislike for science, which have their roots in elementary and junior high experiences, were reinforced by required high school and college science classes that often neglected to clarify basic concepts effectively. Teachers who have graduated from these classes go into their own classrooms ill-prepared to teach elementary school science. Having had negative (or negligible) science experiences, these teachers are likely to provide the same for their students, and the cycle continues.

Education courses in elementary school science bear, in large part, the burden of breaking this cycle. In achieving that breakthrough, in both the graduate and the undergraduate science education courses I teach, writing is an important component and is used (1) in journals students are asked to keep and (2) for concept clarification following science activities and investigations.

USING JOURNALS FOR REFLECTION

A primary objective of the use of journal writing is to stimulate future and in-service teachers to think about the ways children best learn science and to motivate them to develop teaching strategies that enhance the learning of science. Thinking and writing about effective teaching strategies in elementary school science will convince education students of the importance of an activity-based, inquiry-mode methodology in science education.

The journal assignment consists of a minimum of two two-page entries a week, written, for the most part, outside of class, and turned in weekly. I prefer that these be handwritten, although typed pages are accepted, and some students utilize word processors. I read all journal entries (time is a limiting factor, but science classes usually number not more than twenty-four students), and respond with written comments, questions, or answers to questions posed by the journal writer.

Conditions I have found conducive to effective learning through journal writing include (1) supportive, low-stress writing requirements, (2) thought-provoking stimuli for reflective thinking, and (3) a responsive "audience" (reader).

In order to reduce anxiety and provide an environment that supports spontaneity, risk-taking, and sharing, the free-flow writing of thoughts is encouraged, and journal entries are evaluated in terms of their reflectiveness as "adequate," "could be improved," or "excellent." Although journal writing is not graded for grammar, spelling, sentence-structure, cohesiveness, or other mechanics of good writing, some entries are very well written, and most are adequate for the occasion. In some instances, serious writing deficiencies are observed; in such cases, the difficulties are discussed with the student and appropriate help is recommended.

While the primary goal of the journal is to stimulate the kind of reflectiveness and commitment that will lead to good science teaching, there have been other benefits as well. An unplanned but positive development of the journal assignment is that it has provided a vehicle for dialogue between each student and me on the teaching and learning of science and on science content that requires further clarification.

> I have enjoyed the journal process in this class more than in past experiences for two reasons. One is that the things I reflect and write down can really be applied in my teaching. The second reason this has been successful is your willingness to read and respond to what we write. I don't know how you found the time but it sure makes the writing more meaningful knowing that someone would actually read it and provide feedback. . . .

In their journals, students are asked to reflect on how they have learned (or not learned) science in school or at home, on their observations of children learning science in science classes and in informal settings, on assigned readings in science education publications about the teaching and learning of elementary school science, and on their feelings about science and the teaching of it. The science activities and investigations, which are an integral part of both the graduate and undergraduate science education classes, also provide inspiration for the sharing of thoughts about science, and insights obtained or questions provoked by these experiences.

On Personal Experiences in Science Education

The science experiences recalled in these journals provide insight into some of the reasons many of today's teachers feel ill-prepared to teach science. Several examples follow:

> As an elementary teacher, I do not have a background in science. . . . I remember my school days. My science teachers were coaches whose first love was football. They were teaching (ha!) science just because they *had* to do something else besides coach. During class they would work on football plays and give us busy work instead of making science interesting. From that experi-

ence to college . . . I took several education courses but nothing to help me teach science.

After reading this article [Feynman, 1968], I feel as if I have been "short-changed" in my science education. I always read my assignments, defined my vocabulary, and of course, memorized all the pertinent facts for the "test." I never enjoyed my science classes because most of the time I was either bored or really didn't understand what I had learned. The only time I actually recall learning anything and enjoying it as well was when there was a lab involved. This was in high school and in college. . . . In my own classroom experiences as a student, I blindly accepted all that was told me and memorized what was "important." I doubt if I ever really had a "handle" on any of those abstract concepts.

In high school I was in an honors/advanced program in science and math, yet I managed to finish school with very little knowledge in either area. The main problem I've seen, is that "definitions were taught, not concepts" [Feynman, 1968]. I knew my stuff as long as I had the facts memorized, but I had no real understanding of what was actually going on.

On Observations of How Children Learn Science

While it is helpful for pre-service teachers to reflect on how children learn science, such activities are especially beneficial to in-service teachers, who have often already established an ineffective pattern of teaching science. Seeing the excitement of their students when science class fosters inquiry and process skills provides teachers the motivation to take the extra time needed to plan and prepare for that type of class. The improved behavior of the students is further compensation for their efforts:

My children love it when we do an activity. I've begun to combine my science and social studies time 2 or 3 times a week so I can have a 50-minute block. I have found that my children's observation skills are an untapped resource. Once I get them thinking about what they're seeing, or what is happening, they literally "bubble over" with ideas.

I used one of the activities from our [science education] class. I showed the class 2 large yellow candles. We used our sense of smell, sight, touch and hearing. The children all participated in descriptions of the candles. We made notes on the board of measurements and descriptions. [activity described] . . . The children seemed quite eager and animated. I was acutely aware of how different their attitudes would have been if we'd simply read the introductory pages in our text on observation.

I've added a "science nook," and when they get through with their seatwork two students can go over and "discover." I have rocks, birds' nests, magnifying glass, books, . . . etc. I have observed that they really hurry through their work to get over there. Now they are bringing things in themselves and the enthusiasm is very high. It is really exciting. It has made me realize that I need to teach more science.

My class began a study of magnets. The children were quite eager to join in the discovery process. . . . They listed their predictions (about which things would be picked up by the magnet and which things would not) on paper in chart form. . . . The magnets were passed out and one by one each item was tested and results recorded on a chart. We discussed why certain things were not attracted to the magnet. One interesting thing happened quite by accident. Some of the pins were attracted to the magnet and others weren't. The *children decided* it was because they were not made of the same thing. One of my students suggested that one was made of steel and one of aluminum. The aluminum pin was not attracted to the magnet.

One of the most common misconceptions that elementary school teachers have is that science consists primarily of a body of established facts. They feel intimidated and overwhelmed because they themselves have so little command of all these many "facts." They feel that it is their task to instill into the minds of their charges as much as possible, and they shy away from children's questions if the answers are not readily available in the text or a nearby encyclopedia. What I want my science education students to realize is that questions are the very "stuff" of science, and that investigating questions is what scientists *do* — that although there is indeed an existing body of scientific knowledge, science is very much a process of inquiry and investigation, and even established scientific facts are subject to an ongoing process of questioning, testing, and refinement, modification or even rejection. It is this questioning, exploratory, investigative posture that should be at the core of an elementary school science program and it was with a great deal of pleasure that a graduate student related the following incident:

Yesterday, I got lucky. The students asked, "What is fire?" and I didn't know. If I had known an answer, I would probably have thoughtlessly given it and that would have been the end of it. Instead, we had a wonderful experience. I promised I would find the answer at my TCU science class, so they were primed today to see if I had done my homework. First, I told them how impressed the other teachers and "experts" were that third graders had asked such an interesting question. Then: "Imagine you are sitting by your fireplace at home. Tell me what is happening. What do you see? Hear? Feel? Smell?"

Their answers were marvelous! And they were so excited. "I feel heat." "I see light." "I hear the wood popping and the flames make little s-s-s-s-s sounds." "I smell the smoke," [What state of matter do we breathe?] "Oh, yeah, gas." "I see the smoke." [What does the smoke look like?] "It's gray and it has little bitty pieces of stuff in it." [What are those pieces? Where did they come from?] "They're like little ashes. They came from the wood. They're what the wood is turning into." [Are you saying that the fire is turning the wood into something that's not wood?] "Yes! And I know the word for something that makes something else happen. It's energy!" [Aha! Look at your answers I've written on the board. They're very close to what I heard last night. You've said that fire is an energy process that changes wood into something else: gas and ashes. And that it produces heat and light. Wood is a solid. Does anyone have artificial logs in their fireplace? What's burning there?] "I do, but I don't know what's burning." [What can you remember about it?] "You turn it on with a little handle and if you don't light the match quick, you can hear it and you can smell it. Oh, I know, you can smell it, but you can't see it, it must be gas." [Okay, so we know fire can burn some solids and some gases. What about liquids?] "No, because water puts fire out." "Yeah, but other things are liquids, too." "Liquids can burn. I remember one time my Mom had some grease on the stove and it got too hot and caught on fire."

During all this time, the children's enthusiasm was almost intangible. They were bubbling over with comments and questions and looking things up in dictionaries and encyclopedias. But of course, I was the one who learned a lesson I hope I never forget: *Don't give an answer if the children can "invent" one for themselves.*

On Assigned Readings

Throughout the semester, students are asked to read and reflect on articles in professional journals that discuss subjects such as studies on cognitive development of children, how children best learn science, the history of science education in this country over the past several decades, and science education reforms. It is anticipated that reading, reflecting on, and writing about these matters will further ensure a commitment on the part of each teacher to teach science enthusiastically, asking and encouraging thought-provoking questions, utilizing investigations and inquiry/process skills. Responses to the articles are sometimes refreshing and usually revealing. In response to the publication "What Research Says About Elementary School Science" (Mechling & Oliver, 1983), one student commented:

[A] depressing question: why is it so difficult for schools to make fundamental changes? These research results are not new findings. The education courses I took thirty years ago emphasized that children learn by doing. How come we still teach as if "doing" meant filling in a worksheet?

Responding to the same article, another student expresses her concern about some of the inadequacies of many science textbooks:

> I read an article that despaired of the use of "cookbook experiments" in nine major science texts. I heartily agree. In ours the experiment is given with step-by-step instructions but the results are revealed in questions at the bottom of the page. . . . This is aggravating because the kids try to make the experiment fit the right answers instead of trusting their particular results.

Sometimes an article provokes some discomfort or disagreement, forcing the student to examine her own position more carefully. Following are two responses to the article, "What Is Science?" (Feynman, 1968):

> His second definition of science [belief in the ignorance of experts] I still struggle with a little. I don't like to think that I believe that experts are ignorant. There's not much security in that. However, truth should be testable and, if it is indeed "truth," should come out victorious. If it is not, then we should move on in the search for truth and the sooner, the better!

> After reading the article, "What Is Science?" by Dr. Richard Feynman, I have come to the conclusion that what goes on in my science class must not really be science. . . . I have always believed that children learn faster by experiencing, by doing, than by being told. It just now really hits home that science needs to be activity-centered. . . . I have definitely decided that my methods for teaching science will need to be revised.

In the following entry, the student described, not a personal encounter with conflict, but the idea that addressing conflicts or dilemmas can be productive of creative thinking and problem-solving efforts:

> I read an article on how to use dilemmas in science instruction. This is very similar to the approach you are taking with us as you teach. This author advocates written problematic situations gleaned from imagination or the newspaper or a magazine. All situations "invite participants to get involved and react."

On Feelings About Science and Methods of Teaching It

Through their journal entries students give me insight into their feelings and understandings about science and into the strategies they are employing to teach science in their classrooms. Several such journal anecdotes follow:

Since I started this journal I've really been motivated to do more science in my classroom. My first graders are easily motivated also. They are so "curious" and anxious to learn anything.

Since I have been in this science class, I have discovered 2 things about the way I have been teaching science. These revelations are (1) I have always presented my science lessons through lectures (when I should be lecturing less and letting students explore, discover, wonder & question more), and (2) I have not done half as many experiments in class as I should be doing. Experiments help explain concepts that may take a teacher 2 or 3 hours to explain.

Actually putting down in writing what has happened and then being able to make predictions often gets lost in the time crunch. Because of this course I am beginning to realize that this perhaps is really the intended goal. Being able to predict and to compare and to analyze are essential parts of all our courses of study. I can see science as an excellent way to teach these important skills . . .

WRITING TO CLARIFY CONCEPTS

In addition to the keeping of journals, writing is utilized in my science education classes as a means of concept clarification. In class, the teaching of elementary school science is modeled through an activity/investigation format to help students develop skill and comfort in an inquiry/process teaching mode, and to help them enhance their own understandings of specific science concepts. A puzzling situation or problem is investigated by groups of students in a simple lab-like setting. Observations are made, data collected, tabulated and graphed (when appropriate), and patterns identified; based upon these data, inferences and explanations are made. Immediately following such investigations, especially those which are conceptually more difficult, students may be asked to express in writing their understanding of the concept(s) studied. The format is very simple: essentially, students are asked, What did you observe, and how do you explain your observations? In addition to describing the activity briefly and explaining what they can about it, students are encouraged to ask any questions that they may have, to state anything that is unclear to them, or to suggest a further exploration or investigation that occurs to them. These writing assignments are conducted in class and are diagnostic, not evaluative. The responses are intended to be as candid and as stress-free as possible. For these reasons, grades are not given and students need not identify themselves. I read the responses before the next class so that I can clear up

any misunderstandings that may have surfaced in the writings, and so that
questions and comments can be addressed.

In writing these brief expositions, students become aware of questions
they have, and sometimes they also gain new insights into the problem.
Concepts become clearer and the material easier to recall later.

An unexpected finding of these brief writings has been the variety and
number of misconceptions that exist even after the class discussion that
follows a science activity or investigation. In one class, students were asked
to carefully observe the behavior of a raisin dropped into a glass of 7-Up, to
make a hypothesis about the raisin's behavior, and then to test the hypothesis by first predicting, then testing the behavior of other small objects
(including an unshrunken raisin or grape) in the 7-Up. This was a group
activity and discussion within the groups was shared, as were the conclusions of each group with the entire class following the activity. At the close
of the activity, students were asked to briefly describe and explain their
observations. Some of the explanations were correct, although the term
"buoyancy" was not ventured. Other explanations, however, bordered on
the fantastic, and further discussion was called for during the next class.
Several of the initial explanations follow:

The raisins that were filled with water stayed more to the bottom with little
movement. The raisins that were flattened contained less water which caused
them to go up and down and float.

The raisin accumulated gas and then sank. As the gas escaped it began rising.
When the raisin was full of gas it had more density than the water itself.

In our [investigation], the whole raisin fell straight to the bottom while the
squashed raisin would fall and rise over an interval of time. The raisin may
have sunk due to the density or weight, yet the squashed raisin did not. The
squashed probably rose and fell because there was more surface area for the
bubbles to attach to and cause the raisin to be lighter than it really was and to
rise to the top where the bubbles would then pop and cause the raisin to seem
heavier and fall back down to the bottom to gain more bubbles.

The carbon dioxide which is dissolved in 7-Up when released from pressure of
the bottle, began to escape. Some of the gas bubbles attached themselves to
the surface of the raisin. As the combined density of the raisin and gas became
less than the liquid, it rose to the surface to float. When the raisin broke the
surface of the liquid, the gas escaped into the air. When enough gas escaped
into the air so that the density of the raisin and bubbles was less than the
liquid the raisin sank to repeat the process.

Studies show that previously learned misconceptions interfere with learning and must be displaced before a more accurate understanding can be acquired. Having education students write for clarification reveals some of the misconceptions that they may harbor, and helps me better understand how to re-teach a concept when necessary.

A further benefit of these exercises is that some of the students (inservice teachers) have begun to use writing for concept clarification in their own classrooms:

> Lately as a result of this class, I have begun to check my children's grasp of scientific knowledge or behavior by having them write about what they have done in science. I agree with George Hein (1987) when he assesses current tests in science as rigid and not indicative of what a child really understands. I know immediately after reading my children's notes if they have a clear idea of what was done.

Such reports are especially encouraging since the transference of writing into the classrooms of these elementary school teachers holds promise for renewing the students as I saw it do their teachers.

CONCLUSION

Writing holds great promise, for all levels of science education. One very successful example of the effectiveness of writing in science was demonstrated by a federally funded project carried out in several fourth-grade classrooms in San Antonio, Texas. The children, mostly Hispanics of lower socioeconomic level, described in writing their observations and inferences about science class activities and investigations. Within a period of two to six weeks, their observational skills and use of logical inferences improved markedly, not only in science but in all other classes as well. But perhaps even more important to the personal and intellectual growth of each individual, is the permission and encouragement that writing gives to students to use their own language — to talk the talk of investigators, not mimic the clichés of teacher or text.

REFERENCES

Feynman, R. P. (1968). What is science? *Physics Teacher, 7,* 313–320.
Hein, G. (1987). The right test for hands-on learning? *Science and Children, 25,* 8–12.
Mechling, K. R. and Oliver, D. L. (1983). *What research says about elementary*

school science (Handbook IV, Project for Promoting Science Among Elementary School Principals). Washington, DC: National Science Teachers Association.

Smith, H. A. (1980). A report on the implications for the science community of three NSF-supported studies of the state of precollege science education. In *What are the needs in precollege science, mathematics, and social science education? Views from the field*, (National Science Foundation SE 80-9, p. 43).

Part IV

PROGRAMMATIC POLICIES AND PRACTICES

In Part III, individual teachers described successful classroom practices. In this section, the essayists each describe a course or courses that reflect a broader institutional commitment to the writing-to-learn program.

Joanne Snow explains the Advanced Writing program in mathematics at St. Mary's College, Indiana, where majors compose one substantial paper in each of their last three years. The requirement focuses on production of longer, finished, formal papers outside of class, in contrast to the emphasis on informal, in-class, exploratory writing noted elsewhere throughout this book.

William J. Mullin, for example, a professor of physics and associate director of the Writing Program at the University of Massachusetts at Amherst, claims that writing is a mechanism that stimulates the qualitative, intuitive thinking that physics students need. He describes (1) the rather formal "macrothemes" assigned in a Writing in Physics course required of majors in their junior year; and (2) the less formal "microthemes" written in other physics electives, where the emphasis is primarily on learning rather than writing. Numerous examples of both assignments are appended to his paper. His basic argument is, "Giving the student practice in cutting through the precise stuff to the core qualitative meanings must be a good idea."

George Gopen and David Smith relate their cooperation in an experimental calculus course that requires weekly computer lab reports and uses a new methodology for analyzing and teaching writing. This essay focuses, first, on how and why words and numbers have been dissociated. It then analyzes common problems math students exhibit when asked to write. Finally, it describes Duke University's Writing Across the Curriculum program, which is based on what they call "reader expectation theory." It attends more to formal elements of style than to invention heuristics, in the belief that "Eventually the method transforms itself from a set of revision tactics to a set of invention procedures."

CHAPTER 15

The Advanced Writing Requirement at Saint Mary's College

Joanne Erdman Snow

At Saint Mary's College (Notre Dame, Indiana), there are two requirements in the area of writing proficiency. First, a student must demonstrate proficiency in general writing, for which she earns a "W." The second requirement, called the Advanced W, is to demonstrate writing proficiency within the student's particular major. This second requirement is the topic of this chapter.

The Advanced W program is the result of a proposal submitted to the college about four years ago by the Writing Proficiency Steering Committee. Since that time the departments have been designing programs and experimenting with assignments. The class of 1990 is the first class required to earn the Advanced W.

While each department at Saint Mary's determines its own guidelines for the Advanced W, the Writing Proficiency Steering Committee guides and coordinates department efforts to define their requirements. This committee has brought in lecturers from outside the college, held workshops, and set an agenda for determining the operation of the Advanced W Program. The lecturers are recognized specialists in the subject of writing and have included Maxine Hairston, John Rieff, John Ramage, and Arthur Young. For the mathematics department, these lecturers and workshops have helped us define our goals and determine the operation of the program. While one tries to make the assignments a natural part of the coursework, these papers do mean extra work. From these speakers we have gotten some tips on how to make the papers part of the learning process and how to preserve our sanity while doing all the extra grading. The members of the Writing Proficiency Steering Committee are available as consultants when a department experiences difficulty. They have advised us about evaluation techniques, the number of papers to require, and the presentation of the rules and regulations to the students.

In determining the program for the mathematics department, we were guided by the goals of the requirement, as our department saw them. These goals are (1) to prepare students to write the kinds of reports and papers needed in their professional careers, (2) to monitor the development of students as writers, and (3) to collect student writing to demonstrate the range of their competence. We chose types of assignments we felt represent the goals of this requirement.

We require a total of three papers — one each during the sophomore, junior, and senior years. The sophomore paper is to be expository in nature. It may be part of the coursework from the Calculus III/differential equations sequence or the algebraic structures/linear algebra sequence. Alternately, the student has the option of doing an independent paper under the supervision of her adviser in the department. During the junior year the student does a technical or analytical paper. This paper may come from any of the upper-level courses: real analysis, algebra, probability, statistics, topology, math programming, or graph theory. It may consist of a sequence of related proofs or an analysis of some applied problem. In our applied courses, it is common for the students to do team reports. Such reports are also acceptable papers for the portfolio. The last paper is part of the senior comprehensive project. This project has been in place for years, and so we have had some experience in formally monitoring our students' writing skills. This paper is both expository and technical in nature: It is a summary of a student's independent study of a topic in mathematics on which she gives three lectures. The first part of the paper is a description of the problem and the results she has discussed in her first two talks. The second part is in theorem-proof style and contains the material for the third talk.

Regarding the administrative procedures of this program, we have adopted the following policies. The goal is to complete these three papers, have them approved, and put them in a folder called the portfolio. To achieve this end, we proceed as follows. The first two papers are part of the normal course work (unless the student opts for the independent study paper) and are identified as candidates for the portfolio when the teacher makes the assignment. These papers are thus first graded by the teacher making the assignment. It is suggested that, when reading this first version, the teacher should address major problems. Minor problems are tolerated in this draft to avoid overloading the student with criticism. If the student chooses to submit the paper for her portfolio, the revision process begins.

First, based on the teacher's comments, the student will revise the paper. Then the student has a classmate critique the paper. (This is one of the labor-saving devices mentioned by Maxine Hairston [1982]. There is an additional benefit to this: the critiquing of another's work can be thought of as part of the learning process for the reader.) The student reader must sign a paper to indicate she has reviewed the paper. We are relying on our students' honesty and common sense to take this requirement seriously. After passing through the student reader and subsequent revision based on the fellow student's comments, the paper is again submitted to the teacher of the course. The teacher continues to suggest revisions until she or he feels the paper can be submitted to another teacher for final approval and acceptance for the portfolio.

The senior comprehensive paper is monitored by the student's comprehensive project adviser during the process of preparing the talks. It is thus first approved by this adviser. Then it is approved by a second person — either the senior seminar instructor or another reader if the advisor and senior seminar instructor are the same person. As these papers tend to be lengthy — 30–50 pages — I encourage the students to prepare their paper and talks at the same time. Seniors are required to use a word processor for their papers as it makes constant revisions more feasible. The burden for meeting deadlines and getting the papers finished falls on the student; however, the student's adviser monitors progress, and the portfolio of accepted papers is kept in a department file.

We have devised our own guidelines for writing papers in mathematics and have included them in a pamphlet we give the students that describes the program. We also make available in the library a copy of the booklet by Leonard Gillman (1987) on the writing of mathematical papers.

In closing, I would like to offer some tips we have picked up from our experience. First, it helps to get the students used to writing in small doses. I require the students to use words on their tests; the calculations must be accompanied by reasons and explanations. After a little fuss, students accept this as one of my requirements. It is my experience that this makes a difference in a student's success in writing longer assignments and papers. Second, the instructor should be careful to spell out any assignment in great detail. The goals and expectations of the assignment should be clearly outlined. When a topic is broad, the students like to know how specific you want them to be. Giving them a list of subtopics that should be touched upon or questions that should be answered guides their writing process. One should also specify the length and number of sources required. Providing a model or sample paper is useful. Third, it is advisable to require a few outside sources. In Calculus III, I thought it would be a good idea to have the students describe some notion such as the gradient. My purpose was to have them pull together all the bits and pieces of information I had given them. The first time I tried this, several people gave me a transcription of my lecture notes. The next time I made this assignment, I had already gotten the students used to writing. This subsequent writing experience plus requiring them to read other texts yielded much better results, as the students had more confidence in explaining ideas in their own words. Fourth, it is important when making an assignment to specify the intended audience, so that a student knows what she is allowed to assume is common knowledge and what she must define and explain.

A final suggestion is one made by the chairman of the Writing Proficiency Steering Committee. The chairman suggested that we advise our students to take an advanced writing course offered by our college. The student would then write a paper for this course in her area of interest. The writing course teacher would grade the writing, while a member of the mathematics department would read the paper to check the accuracy of the content.

I have mentioned one of the topics I have tried as a sample assignment in the sophomore courses. Below is a list of a few more suggestions; teachers of real analysis will find that Bartle's *Elements of Real Analysis* (1976) contains many projects that would be suitable for writing assignments.

1. Explain the relation between continuity and partial derivatives.
2. Prove a proposition in geometry using vector methods. For example, show that any angle inscribed in a semicircle is a right angle.
3. Explain the notion of projections and components. Interpret the idea and derive the formulas.
4. Explain the graphing of a quadric surface in terms of intercepts, traces, sections, symmetry, etc.
5. Trace the history of determining a numerical value for π. In particular, discuss the role of series in estimating its value.
6. Discuss the history of series.
7. Determine a function of two or three variables which represents a company's profits. Have the students interpret the level curves or surfaces and the partial derivatives of this function. Lastly, find the point where the function achieves its maximum.
8. Explain the origin of some differential equation, solve the equation, and do a specific problem relating to this equation. Some examples of problems to consider are cooling, interest, and population growth.

My experience with this writing requirement has convinced me that incorporating writing into the class improves the student's understanding and ability to express herself mathematically.

REFERENCES

Bartle, R. G. (1976). *The elements of real analysis* (2nd ed.). New York: John Wiley and Sons.

Gillman, L. (1987). *Writing mathematics well: A manual for authors*. Washington, DC: Mathematical Association of America.

Hairston, M. (1982). The winds of change: Thomas Kuhn and the revolution in the teaching of writing. *College Composition and Communication, 33,* 76–88.

CHAPTER 16

Qualitative Thinking and Writing in the Hard Sciences

William J. Mullin

Physics is described variously as rigorous, quantitative, formal, mathematical, and hard (either as in "hard science" or "hard to do"). All these adjectives do indeed apply; physics students attest to their accuracy. However, there is another side to physics that is well known to professionals in the field. For them the subject is often intuitive, heuristic, nonmathematical, qualitative, conceptual, and fun. An intuitive, qualitative understanding is absolutely necessary if the physicist is to master the field. Personally I don't keep a lot of complicated equations in my head, and yet I consider myself a successful and knowledgeable physicist. While I often do use elaborate mathematical manipulations, I survive as much by a gut feeling for how nature works. Do we as teachers need to pass along this informal mode of understanding to our students? Can writing exercises aid us in this regard? Is such an approach as important for advanced majors as for, say, non-science students? How do these ideas apply to other sciences? Do we have time for yet another pedagogical fad?

NEED FOR QUALITATIVE UNDERSTANDING

Before selling you a new vitamin supplement for your students let me establish that there is indeed malnutrition out there. My observation that physics has a qualitative side is hardly new. Conceptual Physics courses for non-science majors are taught at most universities and colleges. However, my main concern is with science majors—students who are nominally capable in mathematics. In order to show that these individuals also need to learn to function on a heuristic level, let me explain how I see conceptual physics.

Consider the typical textbook treatment. Galileo's experiment at the

198

leaning tower showed that all objects dropped from a height fall at the same rate regardless of the weights of the objects. Two different explanations follow. If you do not know physics, you might find the first discussion tough going. That's the point.

> *Formal Argument:* The force of gravity on an object of mass m near the surface of the earth is given by Newton's law of gravity as
>
> $$F = GMm/R^2$$
>
> where M and R are the mass and radius of the earth, respectively. Newton's second law of motion states that any force F on a body of mass m results in an acceleration a given by
>
> $$F = ma.$$
>
> Note that we have taken that the mass m that appears in these two equations to be the same quantity; that is, we have assumed the equality of gravitational and inertial mass. If we combine the two equations we find
>
> $$GMm/R^2 = ma.$$
>
> The mass m cancels out of this equation, which tells us that a is independent of the mass as Galileo realized.

The above is typical of textbook treatments. Next consider a nonmathematical explanation that tells in words what is going on in the mathematical discussion:

> *Intuitive Argument:* The force of gravity pulling an object toward earth depends on the mass of the object, that is, on the amount of material in the object. In other words, the larger the mass of the object the greater is its weight. However, when an object is given a push or a pull it has an inertia that resists the motion induced by that force. Moreover, for a given force the larger mass accelerates more slowly than a smaller mass; a Mack truck is harder to get going than a Volkswagen. If you were to drop two masses, one with twice the mass of the other, you would expect that gravity would pull the larger one down with twice the force. So at first thought you might expect, as Aristotle claimed, that the more massive object would fall faster. However, that larger one has twice the inertia of the smaller

one and so it is twice as hard for gravity to get it going. These two effects cancel out exactly and both objects fall at the same rate.

The second explanation is what goes on in the so-called Physics for Poets courses originated by N. H. March (1978) and P. G. Hewitt (1985). Indeed Hewitt's book contains an explanation much like the intuitive argument given above. In more advanced courses, good instructors supplement their own mathematical treatments with such discussions. Richard Feynman, one of the greatest teachers of physics, is noted for his use of intuitive arguments. Unfortunately most instructors don't often make adequate efforts to foster this kind of understanding by asking students to produce and use these kinds of arguments. Nevertheless, I frequently hear colleagues complaining that their students "know the formulas but don't really understand the 'physics' behind them." Is there a good way to get them to find this "real physics"?

The form of reasoning described above is also valuable to the professional physicist. Indeed, it is vital; it is the mode of reasoning most often used. The skilled physicist thinking about a research problem sets qualitative goals, works out an initial intuitive understanding — perhaps with a "back-of-the-envelope" calculation — looks for a more formal and rigorous development, searches for yet a deeper qualitative understanding, and then writes up and publishes the results in a very formal and rigorous manner. The qualitative steps in this process are necessary even though they often do not get into print because of their lack of rigor. Understanding goes far beyond just symbol manipulation.

An interesting example of this formal versus intuitive approach is given in a recent paper by two University of Massachusetts theoretical physicists (Donoghue & Holstein, 1987), published in the *European Journal of Physics*. This journal is meant for pedagogical articles but occasionally contains moderately technical material. The title of the article is, ironically, "Aristotle was right: heavier objects do fall faster." The article presents the calculation of an extremely small and experimentally undetectable effect that shows that the Galileo result is not exactly correct. Their initial derivation goes on for four and a half pages of relativistic quantum mechanics to come to this conclusion. The final section states, "We now summarize our results and will show how the curious conclusions derived via formal manipulations in the preceding sections can be understood in a more intuitive fashion." The new derivation, which is much simpler, and perhaps not so rigorous, gets precisely the same result in less than one page.

If these physicists were asked to discuss their results in a seminar, they would undoubtedly present the second, simpler method rather than the first. Physicists tend to use "quick and dirty" derivations when they do talk to one another. This point is made by physicists Gottfried and Weiskopf (1984) who say in the preface to their book on elementary particle physics:

> Like every intellectual pursuit, physics has both a written and an oral tradition. Intuitive modes of thought, inference by analogy, and other stratagems that are used in the effort to confront the unknown are transmitted from one generation of practitioners to the next by word of mouth. After the work of creation is over, the results are recorded for posterity in a logically impeccable form, but in a language that is often opaque. The beginner is expected to absorb this written tradition, and only the survivors of this trial-by-ordeal are admitted to circles where the oral tradition is current. . . . [W]e believe that this oral tradition plays an essential role not only in the creation of physics, but also in the search for a deeper understanding. A wider dissemination of the oral tradition is therefore in order. (p. i)

Let me give a couple of examples of how this oral tradition works, and then I will turn to the main point of how student writing can encourage our science students to use it. In a recent colloquium talk to the physics department a researcher described magnetism at low temperatures in liquid helium. He showed, with about four lines of discussion and a couple of figures, how the magnetism depended on essential quantities such as the magnetic field, temperature, density, and so forth. A precise numerical factor of 3/2 was absent in the qualitative argument. I looked up the rigorous derivation in a graduate physics book, one that gets the factor of 3/2 right; it takes more than 4 pages of detailed mathematics to produce the answer. The simpler four-line explanation is never mentioned. The poor student reader! The rigorous argument is absolutely necessary for completeness, but the short form is the one that produces understanding.

A prominent theoretical solid-state physicist visited us recently and gave a talk to faculty and graduate students in which he compared the electrons in an insulator to cars in a bumper-to-bumper traffic jam. Such a colorful simile is expected in our Conceptual Physics course, and its use in an advanced seminar is not particularly unusual. It made the seminar more interesting and ultimately led to a better idea of what the speaker was getting at.

Indeed, physics is largely based on analogy. For example, the ideas and mathematics of fluids are greatly similar to those in the theory of electromagnetic fields. In quantum mechanics we learn that electrons travel as waves in some ways similar to light. Current cosmology contends that the early universe underwent a phase transition analogous to that occurring when iron becomes magnetic. If you understand a bit about nature's right hand, you may already know something about its left hand.

Surely by now I have overloaded the discussion with examples of how physicists use qualitative insight. From observations of the way our students grope their way through the mazes of formulas we throw at them, looking for the right one to plug into, it should be equally clear that they are not so good at qualitative thinking. (Of course, you cannot hold down the very best physics students. They usually figure out the little tricks that are the efficient ways to understand the subject.) My claim is that writing can provide a mechanism that requires students to practice this vital skill.

USE OF WRITING ASSIGNMENTS

Students at the University of Massachusetts are required to take two writing courses. The first is a standard freshman-level course given by the English department, through the Writing Program. In addition, in 1983, the University's Faculty Senate instructed each department and program to propose to the University Writing Committee a course for its majors that would allow them to satisfy a junior-level writing requirement. These courses, finally implemented in 1984, are a rather innovative approach to teaching writing, for they mean that a departmental member who is a specialist in, say, zoology, may be teaching a course that, while it has considerable zoology content, also includes substantial amounts of writing. The Senate mandate specified that such "courses will be to enhance and reinforce the subject being studied, not to teach grammar and spelling at the expense of that subject." For the first three years of the new junior-year writing program I taught the course, Writing in Physics, for physics majors.

To support the claim that writing can help in teaching qualitative thinking, let me quote three advanced physics writing assignments that require heuristic and nonmathematical arguments (Mullin, in press). The first two are from Writing in Physics.

> *Assignment 1:* Write an essay explaining to a freshman Physics 141 student why an airplane flies. [Physics 141 is an introductory mechanics course without calculus.] Assume that the student already has seen the Bernoulli equation in his or her course and now wants to know why it works. Emphasize physical (qualitative) arguments — on the molecular scale — when possible. After all, the forces on the wing arise because air molecules hit it; does the faster horizontal motion of this air over the top of the wing somehow imply the molecules hit the wing with less vertical speed or less often or what? And why does the air move faster over the top of the wing? If you prefer you may

discuss the flight of a Frisbee, the operation of a sailboat, or some other analogous system.

The Bernoulli equation is a powerful tool that can be used to discuss air flow and the lift on an airplane wing. Derivations of it arise from very general principles. But what it is saying in terms of molecular activity is not clear in the derivation. Assignment 1 asks the student to go beyond the standard discussion found in textbooks and explain what is going on at a microscopic level. Writing this essay to the audience mentioned forces the student to examine the real physics involved and to view the phenomenon in a new light.

Assignment 2: Write a newspaper article for the *Science Times* (Tuesday science section of the *New York Times*) on the subject matter of Professor Eugene Golowich's talk (Strings or related matters in elementary particle theory). The audience can be assumed to be made up of college-educated nonscientists. The title of the essay should be a headline.

Science writing for newspapers is characterized by, among other things, concise explanations of complicated issues and by explanation by analogy. The traffic-jam explanation of an insulator is characteristic here. Since analogy is so prevalent in the very structure of physical descriptions of nature, an essay using analogies is itself a kind of metaphor for physical descriptions. A student who learns to see relationships between diverse elements in physical phenomena will have developed a powerful mode of inquiry. (For further assignments from Writing in Physics, see Appendix A.)

In recent years I have taught another junior-level course, Electricity and Magnetism. This is a quite theoretical and mathematical course that is strongly oriented toward problem solving. With each problem set I include an assignment to write a short essay. I instruct the students to follow a format that starts with a thesis sentence followed by one or two paragraphs of exposition addressed to a fellow student. Such a microtheme format has been used with success in an introductory physics course by Kirpatrick and Pittendrigh (1984). It seems to me that it has considerable value in advanced courses as well. The nonmathematical reader should ignore the very technical nature of this example and look for the feel of the assignment and sample essay.

Microtheme assignment: A fluid velocity field $\vec{v}(r) = y\,\hat{x}$ can be shown to have non-zero curl at the point (0, 1, 0). Explain the physical meaning of this result.

As I stated above there is a close relationship between fluid mechanics and electromagnetic theory. The assignment asks the writer to explain a highly technical result from vector calculus in terms of fluid flow. Once that understanding is clear to the student I will be able to better explain the more abstract points of electricity and magnetism by using fluid analogies in my lectures. One of my best students wrote the following essay in reply to the exercise.

An Answer: A non-zero curl at the point (0, 1, 0) means that the fluid at that point is "spinning" about some axis that passes through that point.

As we travel up the positive y axis, fluid in front of us is traveling across our path at a faster rate than the fluid behind us. We will get pushed more strongly across our front than we will across our back. If we allow the forces of the water to move us as they will, our front will rotate to the right. If we become very thin, thin as a point, we will experience the curl that exists at the point we are at.

As we feel no "tipping" sensation, we know that the axis we are spinning about must be perpendicular to the plane of the water.[1]

Note the qualitative character of the answer. No math is used and yet it is very evident that the author has a deep appreciation of how mathematics describes the physical world of fluids. (For further assignments from this course, see Appendix B.)

Macrothemes (like those required in Assignments 1 and 2) take a considerable amount of time to write and to grade. Despite their value the mechanics of essay writing may distract the student from the main task of learning physics. Such papers may not be appropriate for the average intensive physics course. Our course Writing in Physics is unusual as physics courses go; it is meant to incorporate such essays in order to use the physics to teach writing (while at the same time, of course, using writing to teach some physics). Still, I see no reason why a physics course at any level could not make use of microthemes without having the writing cause undue distraction.

Writing may be a present-day educational fad, but that does not

---

1. I would like to thank David Winston, a student in my electricity and magnetism course in spring 1987, for permission to use his brief essay.

automatically negate its value. My intuitive feeling is that microthemes are certainly useful. Macrothemes are also appropriate and valuable in a setting like our Writing in Physics course. More work needs to be done to establish rigorously the worth of various kinds of writing in mathematically oriented fields.

Do other science courses have the apparent need for writing components that physics courses seem to have? Since I know only one science well, I am not the person to answer this question. However, even the sciences that are not so mathematical as physics can be extremely technical. Giving the student practice in cutting through the precise stuff to the core qualitative meanings must be a good idea.

APPENDIX A
Additional Assignments from Writing in Physics

The assignments given in the text and those below are a selection from three offerings of the course.

1. This assignment is based on Professor Robert Hallock's talk on Superfluids and Superconductors. The physics department is attempting to upgrade the Advanced Laboratory course for senior physics majors. The Undergraduate Studies Committee (made up of Physics faculty members) is considering various possible experiments. Since funds, awarded by the NSF and the University, are limited, the cost of equipment is an important factor.

Write a proposal addressed to this committee, suggesting a particular low temperature experiment (or set of closely related experiments). The proposal should include a thorough discussion of the reasons low temperature physics should be an area studied, what the experiment is, the motivation for choosing the particular experiment, the equipment required, and the value and cost (insofar as you are able) relative to possible experiments in other areas of physics.

The committee is made up of faculty who do research in several areas of physics and who can be presumed to have only a vague knowledge of the field of low temperature physics. To make your case you must give sufficient information as well as convincing arguments.

2. This assignment is based on Professor William Irvine's talk on Halley's Comet. NASA was unable to send a probe to study Halley's comet because of budget restraints. What are one or two of the possible ways of studying this comet? What can be learned by each technique? What is the best way to do it? Did Congress make a good decision not to provide funds?

Don't make up information; support your discussion with hard facts or data on the comet.

Choose some knowledgeable audience; specify this audience on your paper.

3. Professor David Van Blerkom's talk is on the astronomy of the ancient Mayans. A paper based on this talk ought to be somewhere in the general area of the origins of mathematics, astronomy, or physics. This could be a paper on the history of science. A biography is a possibility, although biography is difficult to make interesting unless you have a very specific slant in mind. The specific topic, format, style, audience, etc. are up to you.

4. Professor Robert Guyer's talk is on fractals, mathematical entities that have received frequent application in studies of a wide range of physical phenomena. A paper based on this talk ought to be somewhere in the general area of the role of mathematics in describing nature. For example, you might write on fractals themselves. Or you might attempt to answer the very general philosophical question of why mathematics is successful in describing nature at all (see the essay on this subject by E. Wigner in the book *Symmetries and Reflections*). Or you might discuss the origins of mathematics. The specific topic, format, style, audience, etc. are up to you. Specify your audience on the title page of your paper.

5. Professor John Dubach's talk is entitled "Nuclear Physics." The assignment is to review the current status of some aspect of nuclear physics. Some of the possible areas that could be covered are an experimental facility, experimental devices, a current model of the nucleus, the relation between elementary-particle physics and nuclear physics, and some practical application of nuclear physics. Don't be limited to the above topics; be creative.

A review generally requires an exhaustive and up-to-date literature search. While I don't expect such an extensive library workout, I do expect that you will read and make reference to several recent sources besides the three on reserve.

I am the audience for this paper; I am interested in learning what is going on in this field.

6. Professor Ann Ferguson of the philosophy department, in her talk to us, will examine the claim that physics and many other sciences are sexist, just like many other human activities. Since most physicists do not closely examine the foundations of the scientific method, they often have a myth-like belief in its perfection and find such a declaration surprising.

Your essay for this assignment is to write about the scientific method, as it is applied to physics, with specific emphasis on its human aspects. The precise specification of the subject is up to you. You may, for example, want to respond to the question of sexism, or you may want to look at fundamental ethical issues involved in practicing physics. Identify your audience as well as your thesis.

Please do not write this essay off the top of your head; back up your discussion in true scholarly fashion with adequate reference to the literature on your subject. There are several items on reserve in the library that may help you. Included are the books *The Science Question in Feminism* by Sandra Harding, *Science and Gender* by Evelyn Fox Keller, and the very influential work of Thomas Kuhn, *The Structure of Scientific Revolutions*.

7. Professor Ted Harrison's talk is on the history of the discovery of aberration of light. You have freedom of choice to choose a topic and audience. However, the paper should relate to the history of astronomy or physics. It might be interesting for you to trace a topic back through to the original papers on the subject. For example, there are books containing the collected works of Maxwell, Faraday, Einstein, etc. in the library. Also, some of the journals date very far back.

APPENDIX B
Additional Assignments from Electricity and Magnetism Course

1. The divergence of the vector field $\overrightarrow{A} = \hat{r}/r^2$ is easily shown to be zero at any point except the origin. Explain why this is so.

2. Gauss's law relates the field at a Gaussian surface to the charge inside the surface. But surely the field at the surface is affected by the charges outside the surface. How do you resolve this difficulty?

3. Suppose experiments showed that the Coulomb law for point charges q_1 and q_2 were actually

$$F = \frac{q_1 q_2}{4\pi\epsilon_0 r^2} (1 + r/\lambda) \exp(-r/\lambda)$$

where λ is a new constant of nature that is extremely large. (It turns out that λ depends on the mass of the photon m_γ with $\lambda = \infty$ for $m_\gamma = 0$.) Superposition still holds. Describe qualitatively how you would go about reformulating electrostatics. Quote results if you are able to, but mainly just indicate what procedures you would follow. (See D. Griffiths, *Introduction to Electrodynamics*, p. 95, Problem 39, for some possible questions you might ask yourself.)

4. Suppose you want to determine the field at a point near a conducting sphere having a positive charge. You bring a small test charge to this

point and measure the force on it. Has this procedure given you what you want?

5. An electric dipole is placed above an infinitely conducting plane. Explain why the dipole does or does not feel a net force and/or a torque.

6. A point charge q is a large distance r from a neutral atom of polarizability α. The force between the two varies with r like r^{-n} where n is an integer. Explain what effect the charge has on the neutral atom and what effect there is on the charge. Establish the value of n. Is the force attractive or repulsive?

7. Explain the basics of the operation of the betatron. Make sure to relate your discussion to the principles of induction presented in the course.

REFERENCES

Donoghue, J., & Holstein, B. (1987). Aristotle was right: Heavier objects do fall faster. *European Journal of Physics, 8*, 105–113.

Gottfried, K., & Weiskopf, V. F. (1984). *Concepts of particle physics* (Vol. 1). New York: Oxford University Press.

Hewitt, P. G. (1985). *Conceptual physics* (5th ed.). Boston: Little, Brown.

Kirpatrick, L. D., & Pittendrigh, A. S. (1984). *Physics Teacher, 22*, 159–164.

March, N. H. (1978). *Physics for poets*. Boston: McGraw-Hill.

Mullin, W. J. (in press). Writing in Physics. *Physics Teacher*.

CHAPTER 17

What's an Assignment Like You Doing in a Course Like This? Writing to Learn Mathematics

George D. Gopen and David A. Smith

Dichotomies are neat. They require no contemplation of the complexities that result from intersections and subsets. There has been no more distinct dichotomy in the traditional American system of education than that between writing and mathematics. They are studied as separate "subjects" from early grammar school through the career of the undergraduate.

Surprisingly, then, when a two-hour session on the use of writing in mathematics courses was organized by Professor Andrew Sterrett for the 1988 Mathematical Association of America meeting, the length proved inadequate to satisfy the number of people wishing to present papers. The anticipated two-hour session (which initially would have accommodated four presentations) mushroomed into three separate sessions, totaling more than eight hours and accommodating 36 presentations. Those sessions were attended by an estimated 400 people. Why, seemingly out of nowhere, should there suddenly be such an interest in a previously inconceivable pairing of interests?

The 36 presenters of papers certainly found the pairing conceivable; many had been giving writing assignments to college mathematics students for years. The 1986 calculus conference at Tulane had already published its proceedings (Douglas, 1986), which strongly recommended writing assignments for calculus students. It may have been the stimulus that emboldened those already engaged in such clandestine practices to emerge from their closets. The question remains: Why now?

Over the past generation or two, many college mathematics professors

An earlier version of this paper was presented to the 71st annual meeting of the Mathematical Association of America in Atlanta, Georgia, 7 January 1988.

have been pressured to "service" an increasing number of poorly prepared students in courses such as calculus and statistics. In response, we have created memory-based courses, driven by efficient means of testing, in which "success" is defined in terms of calculational skill. We may rationalize that accuracy in computation implies a previous mastery of concepts, but we all know better.

Meanwhile, technological developments (calculators and computers) have rendered obsolete many of the very techniques we emphasize in our courses, especially for the students we "serve," the overwhelming majority of whom will not pursue careers in mathematics *per se*. Conceptual mastery may have been needed in the past to compute accurately, but that need has been significantly reduced by the sophistication of the technology now available to students.

Needing a new way to re-emphasize conceptualization in the mathematics curriculum, more of us have become willing to consider the pedagogical efficacy of writing assignments, which require students to (re)-articulate concepts before pushing the buttons. This new hope assumes that *thought* and *expression of thought* are so closely interrelated that to require the latter will engender the former.

At Duke University we have embarked on an experimental course that will lead to an experimental program. The ingredients are (1) a mathematics professor interested in investigating the possibilities; and (2) a methodology for analyzing and teaching writing, compact enough to be imported into the mathematics classroom and effective enough to make it worth the import. (Such a methodology is currently being adopted throughout the curriculum by Duke University's writing program.) In this chapter we share the problems we have had to face, the first results of our experiment, and selected principles of our methodology.

In our two-semester course, Introductory Calculus with Digital Computation, freshmen discover they are faced with the new and mysterious task of *writing mathematics*. The content of the course includes both the standard first-year calculus syllabus and a not-so-standard computer laboratory component. The computer-related material requires that the class meet an extra hour each week (the "lab period"), and that students do lab assignments in teams of two on their own time. They write weekly reports on their lab experiences to demonstrate their comprehension of the concepts involved and their process of achieving that comprehension.

These weekly lab reports typically include data, tabulations, graphs, and 1–3 pages of expository writing. We evaluate the students primarily by three open-book take-home tests per semester, each with three substantial problems whose solutions are written in essay form. The students are *ordered* to collaborate, to learn as much as they can from each other, and to write what they learn in their own words; thus, there is no opportunity to "cheat." In addition, we require regular homework (conventional exercises, no writing) and "mastery" tests of basic computational skills (open book, no writing, taken until a 95% score is achieved). The semester final examination takes place in a conventional setting (three hours in a classroom, no collaboration, open-book); it has two somewhat less substantial problems to be written out in full, plus an essay question on the meaning and importance of one of the major theorems.

THE DISSOCIATION OF WORDS AND NUMBERS

The very concept of writing in a mathematics course is foreign to most students. Witness the opening of one of the early student reports:

> Once upon a time, in an Engineering Building, far, far away, . . . there was a computer cluster. To this cluster journeyed two dutiful slaves of Calculus. These weary travelers had journeyed far, from the very reaches of East Campus, in order to ask their simple questions and calculations, of the Great MicroCalc Program. Sent on their quest by the High Wizard Smith, the only directions they were given were [instructor's directions follow].

The folkloric/gothic/Oz metaphor is maintained throughout the report, which represents a solution these two students reached to the befuddling command to introduce "writing" into their math homework. To them, "writing" was something learned in English classes, something Hemingway, Fitzgerald, and Hawthorne did. It has something to do with "style," but not necessarily with "thought." If "writing" has come to Math, that must mean that Math must now be done with imagination and "style." Hence the metaphor.

"Thought" (they believe) is the sort of thing encountered more often in classes devoted to the subject — philosophy, history, government, psychology, and the like. Math is in another category altogether. While it is clear to them that you have to "think" hard to solve the problems, you do not necessarily have to have "thoughts." You have to think in order to *do* things. Curiously, there is a connection between the misconceptions our students suffer about the relationships of thought to math and to writing: in both cases, thought seems to be something anterior to the other activity. You "think" first; then you do the math problem. You "think" first; then you "reduce your thought" to writing. In order for students to benefit more fully from their training in calculus, they must come to understand that they are engaging in a process of thought, in a new mode of thought.

Requiring them to *write* about what they are doing will in turn force them to *think*, to conceptualize what they are doing. At the same time, we need to demonstrate to them the inextricable intertwining of thought and writing — of thought and expression of thought.

We need not assign any blame to our students for their misconceptions. Why should they think otherwise, when throughout their former training the subjects mathematics and English have been so rigidly segregated? The subjects are taught by different teachers; the books have a different look to them; even the all-perceptive (they believe) college aptitude tests must be divided into "verbal" and "mathematical." Perhaps most convincing of all, a student is allowed to be good in one and relatively poor in the other and still remain in everyone's eyes a good student, intelligent, even stunningly brilliant. In fact, it is a relative rarity to find the student who is a genuine double threat, outstanding with both words and numbers.

Our students reasonably infer from all this that numbers and words signify differently. (We use "numbers" generically to represent arbitrary mathematical objects, symbols, and constructs.) Numbers always imply truth; words more often produce mere concepts. Numbers not only *have* boundaries; essentially they *are* boundaries. Words might individually seem to have boundaries (or what's a dictionary for?); but individual words often have several different definitions, and the combination of words (into sentences, paragraphs, essays) is so essentially boundary-less that it becomes one of the major objectives of certain kinds of writing to establish boundaries.

> Words strain,
> Crack and sometimes break, under the burden
> Under the tension, slip, slide, perish,
> Decay with imprecision, will not stay in place,
> Will not stay still.
> (Eliot, 1936, p. 121)

In many senses, numbers "stay still." They were evolved to obviate the difficulty of multiple interpretation that is inherent in verbal texts. As recent literary theory argues, a verbal text has as many interpretations as there are readers of the text; the text does not exist by itself, as an indelible expression of authorial intent, but only as a product of the intersection of text and perceiver of text (Fish, 1980). Without entering into the debate, we simply note that no one is arguing analogously for numbers. Virtually the entire community of number users and perceivers, acting like one collective author, agrees on the meaning and function of mathematical symbols. By having writing assigned in their calculus courses, then, students may indeed be puzzled as to how to apply slippery, sliding, constantly re-interpretable words to a subject previously infused with the truth and unchanging exactitude of numbers. The numbers and the formulae have become for them the thought itself, no longer the symbol of thought. We are asking them to abandon that dissociation.

The model of good mathematical prose most available to students would seem to be their textbook; however, the writing found there is often less than effective, and the students often avoid reading it. We trace the blame for this to generations of combined efforts from two quarters: On the one hand, authors and publishers produce textbooks that do not have to be read before doing the exercises; on the other hand, teachers acquiesce by agreeing that this is the way mathematics ought to be taught. What prose there is has tended to be introductory, apologetic, and self-justifying. It implies that the real importance lies not in the students' ability to conceptualize, but rather in their ability to function. Teachers tend to underscore this by their rapt attention to correctness, completeness, and procedure. Students comply with the grand scheme by establishing as their local goal the correct completion of a given assignment and as their global goal receiving an A in the course. For most, once it's over, it's over.

A SOURCE OF HELP: DUKE'S WRITING ACROSS THE CURRICULUM PROGRAM

Confronted with a requirement to write in English what they are doing in mathematics, students experience a range of problems, including

1. Difficulty in finding conceptual rather than factual content: "What is there to write?"
2. Failure to connect narrative with data or to support conclusions with evidence.
3. Inability to make the sensed connection explicit: "I see it, but I can't say it."
4. Denial, suppression, or minimization of mistakes.

Mathematics instructors who give writing assignments experience their own set of problems:

1. What techniques should they use to help students with their writing?

2. Are they to add to their already substantial burden the unaccustomed task of teaching and grading writing?
3. Will the new requirements conflict with the main task at hand, that of teaching mathematics?

Duke University is building a Writing Across the Curriculum Program that not only teaches students to write but also supplies faculty the kind of help a mathematics teacher might need. The major difference between the Duke program and others is its reliance on a new methodology for teaching and analyzing writing. Its concepts are briskly learned by faculty (in 12–15–hour workshops) and have proved universally applicable across the curriculum.

The methodology differs from other strategies in the way it forsakes the more traditional perspective of "writer strategy" for the newer perspective of "reader expectation." "Writer strategy" asks "What can the writer think of to say next?" Such an approach probably grew out of the more immediate problem that afflicted the writing course instructor — how to fill several weeks with assignments engaging enough for students to be motivated to write anything at all. "Reader expectation" asks the more pertinent and lasting question, "Is the reader likely to come away from this prose with the precise thought(s) I intended to communicate?"

Reader expectation methodology is taught at Duke to all freshmen in their required University Writing Course. In small sections of 10–13 students, they are taught its principles and are given opportunities to teach them to each other through a series of peer evaluation experiences. Now in the fourth year of the program, we have an entire undergraduate body able to talk the same language about language. Moreover, well over half of our faculty have attended two-day workshops on the methodology. As a result, teachers and students in every department are now able to communicate directly, concisely, and effectively about the strengths and problems of students' prose.

Reader Expectation Theory

Reader expectation theory was born of the linguistic recognition that readers expect certain components of the *substance* of prose (especially context, action, and emphatic material) to appear in certain well-defined places in the *structure* of prose. Once consciously aware of these structural locations, a writer can know how to make rhetorical choices that maximize the probabilities that a reader will find in the prose precisely what the writer intended the reader to find. The creators of this theory of reader expectation are Professors Joseph Williams (University of Chicago), Gregory Colomb (Georgia Institute of Technology), and George Gopen (Duke University). (For many of its main principles, see Gopen, 1984, 1987; Williams, 1985.)

Readers have what we call "reader energy" for the task of reading each different unit of discourse. (A unit of discourse is anything in prose that has a beginning and an end: a phrase, clause, sentence, paragraph, argument, article, book, etc.) Those energies function in a complex simultaneity: one reads a clause while reading its sentence, which is also part of the chapter. . . . Each of those energies is available for two major tasks: (1) perceiving structure (how the unit of discourse hangs together); and (2) perceiving substance (what the unit of discourse was intended to communicate). For the most part, the distribution of this energy is a zero-sum game: Whatever energy is devoted to one of these tasks is thereby not available for the other. For most expository prose, one almost could define bad writing as that which demands a disproportionate amount of reader energy for discovering structure. If a reader is spending most of the available reader energy trying to find out where the syntax of a sentence resolves itself or how this sentence is connected to the sentence that preceded it, that reader can have precious little left for considering what ideas the writer is trying to communicate. Conversely, if the resolutions and connections appear exactly where the reader expects them to appear, then the reader can devote most of the available reader energy to perceiving the nature of the substantive thought.

Placing information in one structural location instead of another results in subtle but remarkably significant effects, as the following extended example demonstrates. Compare these two sentences:

   a. What would be the employee reception accorded the introduction of such an agreement?
   b. How would the employees receive such an agreement?

Putting aside questions of "better" and "worse," we can probably agree that (b) is *easier* to read than (a). What makes that so? At first we might suggest that (b) is shorter than (a); it turns out, however, that the reduced length is a manifestation of the improvement, not its cause. Instead, we would do better to investigate exactly what is going on in the two sentences, what *actions* are taking place. When we seek out the possible action words of the first sentence, we find several candidates: "Reception" seems a likely action (because it sounds potentially significant that employees are receiving something); "accorded" sounds for all the world like an action here, but turns out not to be (since it is not important that anyone is "according" anything here as opposed to "receiving" something); "introduction" may or may not be a significant action (since introduction may only be equivalent to existence here, a piece of grammatical mortar to shore up the sentence structure). What about "be"? What about "agreement"? In any event, we cannot be sure exactly which words the writer intended us to perceive as actions. When we turn to the (b) sentence, our task is significantly simplified. It is clear to a significant majority of readers that "receive" is the one and only action happening in this sentence.

Why the great difference? Because readers *expect* to find the action of a sentence in the sentence's verb. (Most of us were taught in high school that a verb was "an action word." That was not quite accurate. We should have been taught, instead, that the verb "ought to be an action word.") Since we expect the action to be located in the verb, we perceive action in the verb slot unless that perception makes no sense. In (a) above, "accorded" sounded like action but made no sense as action. When that expectation is foiled, we have to look elsewhere in the sentence to find the action. Unfortunately, readers have no expectations concerning a secondary structural clue. All that remains are highly interpretable semantic clues: "accorded"? "reception"? "introduction"? Perhaps some concept not actually named by a word on the page? We are using our reader energy for hunting through the structure to find something that the writer could have pointed out to us easily by depositing it in the verb slot. Fulfilling the reader expectation (that the action will appear in the verb) greatly increases the probability that the reader will perceive what the writer intended the reader to perceive.

When something is badly written, more than cosmetic grace is at stake; communication itself may falter. The solution just offered for the interpretation problem posed by this example may be a false one. For example: The author of sentence (a) might well complain that (b) is an inaccurate revision of (a), since it omits the concept of "introduction," which she had intended as a significant action. After defending our previous decision on the basis of our not being able to perceive that intention from her sentence structure, we could then suggest a different revision that would accomplish her objective. If "reception" and "introduction" are both actions, make them both into verbs. One possibility: "How would the employees receive such a proposal if we introduced it at this time?" Note that this revision has forced an articulation of *who* is doing the introducing ("we") as well as a qualification of that action that makes the action worth considering here ("at this time"). If these communications were indeed the ones the author had intended, then the problem of the prose was not merely a lack of grace, but rather a lack of clarity. We would argue that the two cannot be separated. Reader expectation theory allows readers to identify a lack of clarity by perceiving a difficulty in structure. We may not know what is missing from the thought, but we can learn how to ask the right structural questions ("What *did* you intend the action of this to be?") that will eventually turn up the answers if the author is present.

The same kinds of discoveries concerning reader expectations have been made on the sentence level for the locations of context ("where am I coming from?") and of emphasis ("what is new and important here?"). Yet others have been discovered for the linking material between sentences, for the placement of points in paragraphs, and for the placement and development of thesis statements in complete essays. None of this material is strikingly new in and of itself; good writers, upon hearing the principles, will nod and say they "knew" that, although they had never heard it put quite that way before. The newness lies in its having achieved two things:

1. Principles that have been mostly intuitive to this point are now objectified and made conscious for the writer, the better to be controlled and used;
2. There is now a systematized language with which to speak of reader expectations, no matter what the nature or the field of the substantive material.

These principles allow an instructor to comment not simply on what a student has done "wrong" in a given paper, but rather on what ineffective rhetorical choices a student tends to make with great consistency. The student who puts the action elsewhere than in the verb in one paragraph is highly likely to do so in other paragraphs. Teaching such a student about verb/action reader expectations will aid that student not only to revise the present paper effectively, but also to avoid that structural pitfall in all future writing tasks.

As the product of such revision is by no means merely cosmetic, so the process of that revision is by no means merely mechanical. In order to "fix" a sentence whose action does not appear in the verb slot, a writer has to ask the salient and substantive question, "What is going on in this sentence?" The writing process, including this kind of revision process, does not merely lead back into the thinking process; it *is* a thinking process. Eventually the methodology transforms itself from a set of revision tactics to a set of invention procedures. Knowing how structures need to be built eventually leads the writer to recognize logical progressions while still engaged in the original writing process. The result is sometimes a quicker pace of writing, usually a greatly reduced need for revision, and almost always a clearer, more forceful product.

A note about what this methodology does *not* do: It does not propose a new set of rules that must be slavishly followed. It only sets before the

writer the expectations that most readers have most of the time; the writer
can then choose to fulfill those expectations or to foil them. Every one of
these reader expectations can be violated to good effect. In fact, the greatest of stylists turn out to be the best violators. (This can only be done if the
reader expectations are regularly fulfilled, so that the violation comes as a
surprising exception.)

The Methodology at Work

We turn now to examples from the first graded writing assignment
(Lab Report 1) in our experimental course. The mathematical content of
Lab 1 was modest: Tabulate and graph three functions, answer some questions about approximate locations of their zeros, and describe the relationships among the functions and their zeros. We noticed in these early efforts
that certain kinds of rhetorical problems surfaced frequently. Each can be
resolved briskly and effectively by the methodology.

The List-of-Facts Paragraph.

Perhaps the single most common writ-
ing problem in the lab reports resulted from students merely listing their
observations, in pseudo-paragraph form. That is, they would indent the
first line (therefore "paragraph"), but fail to construct the connections
between sentences that would create a coherent unit of discourse (therefore
"pseudo").

Reader expectation theory offers several ways of combatting this problem. One can begin by checking the verbs in each sentence. If they consistently fail to state the action of the sentence, it is highly probable that the
burden of making the decisions concerning cohesion and coherence will be
shifted from the writer to the reader.

In the following example we have underscored each of the verbs.

> We <u>observed</u> that the function h <u>is</u> the derivative of the function g, which, in
> turn, <u>is</u> the derivative of the function f, therefore the function h <u>is</u> the second
> derivative of the function f. MicroCalc <u>confirms</u> these observations in the
> Derivatives unit of Quarter 1. Our second observation, concerning the f-g-h
> relation, <u>was</u> that the relative maxima and minima of an equation <u>are</u> equal
> to the x-values of the point where the derivative of that equation <u>crosses</u> the x-
> axis. MicroCalc <u>confirmed</u> this observation also, in the Extrema unit of Quar-
> ter 1. The final observation <u>reveals</u> the connection between the f-g-h relation-
> ships and questions 3, 4, 5 and 6 answered below.

With one exception, all the verbs are of observing (on our part), existence
(on the part of our observations), or confirmation (on the part of Micro-
Calc). What does this paragraph tell us? Only that the students observed

certain things which MicroCalc confirmed. It does not convince us that the students have *conceptualized* anything that they have managed to observe.

The purpose of assigning writing in this course was to force students to think about that which they might otherwise perform in a mechanical way only. The constant presence of weak verbs allows the mechanization to continue, the prose acting solely as narrative. Requiring the student to articulate the action of the sentence in the meaning of the verb will force the student to consider what actually is happening during the mechanized process. That, in turn, transforms what was merely narrative prose into expository prose.

The Overpacked Sentence with Incredible Connections. "We made a table of values for x of [0, 20] and narrowed down the interval to [15, 20] as well as observing, from Table 1, that at $x=0$, $f(x)$ also equals 0." In Lab 1, the function f was a polynomial with non-zero constant term; thus, the final assertion in this example is false. However, the connections in the sentence are deceptive, not actual, and thereby distract the reader from noticing that the conclusion is incorrect.

The author of this example could just as easily have continued to add phrases and clauses. No need to stop there: "$f(x)$ also equals 0, as well as . . . , after which we . . . , which resulted in. . . . " It all would make perfect sense to the writer, who was proceeding linearly through time. However, it would become an increasingly annoying and confusing burden to the reader. How can we tell our students that they have packed too much into one sentence?

Readers expect the single most important thing in the sentence — the thing that the writer intends the reader to emphasize — to appear at the end. We call this location the "stress position." Stress positions are created by syntactic closure. Hence, every sentence has a stress position at its end, as the period brings it to a close. Colons and semicolons are strong enough acts of closure to create secondary stress positions in the middle of sentences. A sentence is too long when there is more than one viable candidate for the stress position.

In the above example, it is unclear just how many things the writer wishes us to emphasize. As a result of that, we also do not know precisely the relative weights and the explicit connections we should be observing. Do either of the following express more accurately the authorial intent?

In making a table of values for x of [0, 20], we narrowed the interval to [15, 20]. [Reader's thought: What's the connection?] From this table we observed that at $x=0$, $f(x)$ also equals 0.

> We chose to limit the table of values for x to [0, 20] because. . . . Similarly, we narrowed the interval to [15, 20] because. . . . [What's the connection?] We observed from the first table that at $x=0$, $f(x)$ also equals 0.

Given the author's prose, we now see that we are unable to perceive the authorial intent. Notice how much thought and information we lack to make the proper balances and connections. Insisting on one emphatic point per stress position will unearth (or stimulate) a great deal of student thought.

Lack of agency.   Nobody did anything; things just happen; things just are. "The function g is the derivative of the function f. The function h is a derivative of the function g. This is displayed on the table marked c. . . . " Nobody *does* anything here. Students were asked to report what *they* saw and did, and yet they are nowhere to be found in the prose. Some will complain that they were carefully taught in high school not to write in the first person. We argue that it matters not whether one ought or ought not to use the first person; it matters only whose story is being told. Readers firmly expect the story of a clause or sentence to be about whoever appears at its beginning. If a lab report must tell what students observed, then students ought to appear quite often at the beginning of clauses and sentences.

> We discovered that the function g is the derivative of the function f, because. . . . Using the same principle, we also perceived that the function h is a derivative of the function g. (See Table C.)

Combining the principles of action-in-verb and whose-story-up-front, students can lead themselves to discovering the emptiness of their own statements. We were surprised, for example, by the frequency with which students wrote that they "received" answers. That formula — "We received the answer of 3.742 for x" — reveals and sums up for us the central pedagogical problem in calculus courses.

In sentences written in the active mode, the person whose story it is also turns out to be the agent of the action. Students find they can avoid some of the consequences of making mistakes if they substitute other agencies for their own at the beginnings of sentences. For example (from Lab 2, devoted to turning points): "The complexities of the graph of $f(x) = (x^4+x-1)/(x^3+2x^2-1)$ resulted in us not being able to correctly determine any turning points on the graph of that function." Whose fault? "The complexities'." Another example:

> Any difficulties in the lab occurred because some numbers were not quite accurate. The computer only carried out the figures to the sixth decimal

place, and the students tried to make the results as accurate as possible by narrowing the range, *a* and *b* on the table of values while at the same time increasing the number of intervals, *N*, to up to 500.

In the first sentence, "difficulties" occurred. In the second, "the computer" fails badly to do its job, but "the students" come to the rescue ingeniously. If the students had been around earlier in the prose, they might have come to understand that for the approximate results required, a much shorter table (20 numbers) would have sufficed. By escaping responsibility here, they landed themselves with several times the labor.

The Multi-Topic Paragraph.   Here is yet another fact-filled, chronologically linear paragraph:

> From our previous study of calculus, we determined that $G(x)$ is a first derivative of $F(x)$, and $H(x)$ is a second derivative of $F(x)$ and a first derivative of $G(x)$. We confirmed our assumption by using the "Derivative" command from MicroCalc. We took the first two derivatives of $F(x)$, and they were the same as $G(x)$ and $H(x)$, respectively. Next, we found the first derivative of $G(x)$, which resulted in the function $H(x)$. We also observed that each time $F(x)$ would reach an extreme point $G(x)$ would be equal to zero. This held true for $G(x)$ and $H(x)$. When $G(x)$ reached an extreme, $H(x)$ also equalled zero. We confirmed this by using the "Extrema" command on MicroCalc. Using this command we found out the extreme values for $F(x)$. Then, we plugged those x-values into $G(x)$, and $G(x)$ was found to be zero.

In addition to all the revision tactics suggested above, we can approach this example in terms of reader expectations of paragraph structure, which are amongst the most important for students to understand in responding to the kinds of tasks we required. Readers expect an expository or argumentative paragraph to be about one main point. That point should normally be expressed in a single sentence, from which or to which all other sentences flow. This paragraph violates reader expectations significantly:

1. There are too many points being made for the number of stress positions available;
2. No one sentence articulates the point that gives shape to the rest of the paragraph.

We have found, however, that students tend to have few problems with the concept of the *unity* of the paragraph. Indeed, they seem delighted to bring their momentary labors to closure by ending the topic and indenting the next line. How, then, can the above example of prose have been written as a paragraph? The answer we suggest to our own question we find most disturbing. To the student, the entire paragraph was indeed on one topic, to them, the most important topic of all: "How much can I say about this problem so that I can get full credit for the answer?" All the sentences in the paragraph connect to that unstated and inappropriate point sentence.

We need to move our students away from being centrally concerned with producing enough material and direct them towards grasping and developing concepts. We can help accomplish this by getting them to understand the reader expectations of paragraph structure. They will be hard-pressed to fulfill those expectations without entering into the kind of conceptualizing thought process that we wish them to experience.

Two Before-and-After Samples

We provide here two samples from the first lab reports that display several of the rhetorical problems described above. Each sample (a) is followed by responses from the instructor to the team of authors (b) and by the second submission of the equivalent text (c). In the section that follows we will describe a "peer response" exercise conducted in class and as homework. This exercise used these same lab reports, so each team had both peer and instructor comments to use in their revision.

1a. First Draft

> Due to brief misinterpretation of questions two and three, only one x value was sought and found. Only after leaving the computer facility was it discovered that two or three values were required. Hence, some of the value tables were constructed using a simple "home-grown" program on an Apple II and do not contain as accurate a scale as the tables printed with Microcalc.

This team has just barely admitted that they had made a mistake; they counterbalance that with an overly apologetic explanation of its repair. The authors actually had been most creative in repairing their error but were not confident enough to take appropriate credit. But they were also hiding the problem of having started the lab too close to the deadline to permit a second try.

1b. Instructor's Comments

> Whose story is this? (Nobody actually did anything.)
> Check the verbs. Do they express the action? (For example, the action "to misinterpret" appears in the nominalization "misinterpretation.")

The second version still has problems, but the improvement is evident. The deadline-crowding problem remains hidden; but the students have identified themselves as agents, and their actions are now expressed in the verbs. In particular, they have found that they *can* say "we solved our problem."

1c. Revised Version

> As we proceeded through the lab, we encountered one small problem: we misinterpreted questions two and three. To be exact, we sought and found only one *x* value as an answer. Only after leaving the computer facility did we discover that two or three values, and not simply one, existed. Hence, we solved our problem by constructing some of the value tables using a simple "home-grown" program on an Apple II.

Our second example is a typical list-of-facts paragraph, featuring weak verbs, missing agencies, and absent logical developments or reasons.

2a. First Draft

> The relationship among the functions f, g, and h is one in which $g(x)$ and $h(x)$ are the first and second derivatives of $f(x)$, respectively. This means that $g(x)$ is the slope of the tangent line to $f(x)$ and $h(x)$ is the slope of the tangent line to $g(x)$. Therefore, whenever there is a turning point in $f(x)$, the graph of the derivative of $f(x)$, $g(x)$, will cross the x-axis. Likewise, whenever there is a turning point in $g(x)$, the graph of the derivative of $g(x)$, $h(x)$, will cross the x-axis.

2b. Instructor's Comments

> Whose story is this?
> Check the verbs. Do they express the action?
> What is this about? Which is the point sentence? Is there more than one?
> What have you emphasized in each stress position?
> How are the sentences connected? Where is the logical development?

Again, many of the problems are attended to by the revision. Note especially that the authors have discovered that they had really been discussing two topics; as a result, they revised the one paragraph into two. The revision also contains a correct embedding of simple equations in a complete sentence, a difficult concept for most students.

2c. Revised Version

Observing that the exponents of the first terms of the functions decrease by one between $f(x)$ and $g(x)$, and between $g(x)$ and $h(x)$, we took the derivatives of the functions. We discovered that $f'(x)=g(x)$ and $g'(x)=h(x)$. We concluded that $g(x)$ is the first derivative of $f(x)$ and $h(x)$ is the second derivative of $f(x)$. We confirmed this by using the Derivatives unit of MicroCalc.

We noticed that, as a result of this relationship between the functions, whenever $f(x)$ changes direction, the graph of $g(x)$ crosses the x-axis. Likewise, whenever $g(x)$ has a turning point, the graph of $h(x)$ crosses the x-axis. This observation led us to be even more certain that $g(x)$ is the slope of the tangent to $f(x)$, and $h(x)$ is the slope of the tangent to $g(x)$.

EFFECTIVE PROCEDURES

Peer Response

Early in the calculus course we conducted some short writing exercises in class. For one, we instructed the students to write a paragraph on the relationship between lines in the plane and linear equations. The papers were then circulated among the students, and some were read aloud by people other than the authors. We devoted 15 to 20 minutes to discussion of structure and content of the paragraphs that had been read, starting with whether the reader or anyone else understood what the author had attempted to say.

This peer response exercise is a modification of the peer evaluation process used in the University Writing Courses. There it is used to teach students both what to look for when they attempt improvements of their own writing and to relieve the instructor of the burden of being the sole responder to the writer's prose. Peer response was used formally in the calculus course for a short time only. After that, students were expected to have at least one other person read their work and offer comments, which might then be incorporated into the draft submitted to the instructor.

Shortly after the first lab reports were turned in, we devoted an entire class period to a peer response exercise. We copied all of the reports and distributed them to each of the students. We then directed attention to particular sentences, paragraphs, or sections of the reports and raised questions similar to those raised in the Writing Course, for example:

- What's *happening* here? How many of the verbs in this paragraph announce the action of their sentence? If they do not, what does?

> Can you turn it into a verb and restructure the sentence according-ly?
> - Whose story is this? Who is the agent?
> - What seems to require emphasis within a given sentence? Is it in the stress position? Is there more than one emphasizable point in the sentence? Is there less than one?
> - What is this paragraph about? Underline the point sentence. What does it mean if we can't agree on the point sentence?

Prior to this session, our attempts to tie the writing requirements to the standards of the Writing Course meant almost nothing to the students, mostly because they had completed only two weeks in both courses. However, we could see the lights go on as they got into a spirited discussion of each other's writing, both good and bad. Every member of the class was able to see that somebody else had found a better way to express something, and their attention was riveted on ways to improve their own writing.

The assignment for the next class was to mark up the copies of all the lab reports with their suggestions for improvements. These marked copies were then distributed to the authors for use in preparing the second submission of the assignment.

Double Submission

Another especially effective technique for coaxing good written work out of students is double submission. The students rewrite their papers after the first response from the instructor, with only the second version being assigned a grade. This effectively conveys the idea that rewriting is a *normal* activity for a writer. Moreover, it provides a built-in "second chance," a very popular feature with students.

Late in the semester, when the time frame no longer permitted double submission, we told the students to do their own evaluations on what they had considered their final draft and to revise it accordingly before turning it in. Most of them were so successful in incorporating these new revision techniques into their initial writing process that the quality of these late-term first drafts equalled the quality of early-term second drafts. We believe this was due to the students' having experienced, perhaps for the first time, *real* revision. Prior to this experience, their so-called second drafts of papers had mostly been limited to cosmetic firming up and smoothings over — a word in here and out of there, a misspelling respelled, a grammatical error corrected. They had learned to replace *correction* with *re-vision*.

Efficacious Instructor Responses

To get substantial improvement on the second draft, instructors must attend not only to the correctness of the written product but also to the nature of the process by which it was written. They must focus their comments less on factual correctness and more on whether the student's prose style is capable of producing reasoned and cohesive thought. Mathematical errors must be indicated, of course, and mistakes in grammar, punctuation, and spelling may be; but the student should not be allowed the impression that correction of these mistakes is all that is needed for the second submission. In particular, the mathematical errors are often intimately related to the meaning the student attempted to convey or to essential gaps in that meaning. The most helpful comments for the student are those that highlight the connections between structure and content. The reader expectation methodology is perfectly geared to attend to that.

To make effective use of the methodology, an instructor need not read every sentence or every paragraph of a submission. Selective reading of a paragraph from the beginning, middle, and end of the paper will be sufficient to discover whether this particular student is one who consistently foils a particular reader expectation. Once that is discovered, one returns the paper to the student, explains how to go about restructuring the prose through revising the style, and waits for a greatly improved second submission to appear. Thus, the double submission procedure actually takes *less* time than single submission. It will take more time and energy to read the entirety of a poorly written first draft than it will to critique only two or three paragraphs of it and then glide through a second, greatly improved draft.

Students are quick to learn that if their first submissions are not riddled with structural problems, the instructor will quickly ascertain *what* it was they were trying to say and can then attend to the *substance* of that clearly articulated thought. This in turn allows students to produce a second draft that does not merely *clarify* the earlier draft, but rather goes *beyond* it. They quickly perceive that it is in their best interest to make the paper readable on the first pass.

To illustrate how much good these procedures seem to have done in our first attempt at this, we give an example from a final examination paper. (We are therefore dealing with an in-class written response to a question not previously encountered.) The problem was to determine the temperature at which the density of water is greatest, given a cubic polynomial formula from the *Handbook of Chemistry and Physics* for the *volume* of water as a function of temperature between 0 and 30 degrees Celsius. The student has correctly explained that density will be maximized when volume is minimized. She has also calculated the derivative of the volume function and used the quadratic formula to find its roots at $T=3.9597$ and $T=79.5946$. She continues:

> Immediately, we can disregard $T=79.5946$ because it doesn't lie in the domain. $T=3.9597$ is the value for T when $V'(T)=0$ in [0, 30].
>
> However, maximums also occur when $V'(T)=0$. A minimum will occur when the slope changes from negative to positive. To verify that $T=3.9597$ is a minimum, we must find the slopes at two points on either side of this point. [Calculation of $V'(3)=-1.5\times10-5$ and $V'(4)=6.2\times10-7$ follows.] Since the slope changes from negative to positive at $T=3.9597$, we can conclude that $T=3.9597$ is a minimum.
>
> Therefore, the maximum density of water occurs at 3.9597 degrees Celsius. This answer is consistent with what I have learned about water's density in the past—that its maximum density occurs at approximately 4 degrees Celsius.

We can still see room for improvement both in the writing and in strategy for solving the problem; but for a first-semester freshman with no prior exposure to calculus, this is quite a sophisticated statement about differential calculus and its connections to the real world.

CONCLUSIONS

It would not be accurate to say there were no further problems with writing in this course, but the overnight transformation in what the students found they could do was really remarkable. In our responses to their subsequent first drafts, we needed to spend less time on matters of structure, thereby freeing us to concentrate more on substance. For example, they still had to come to grips with the nature of a laboratory experiment and of a report on that experiment, even though these should have been familiar to them from some lab science course. Since their mathematical training, not surprisingly, emphasized reporting only "answers" that had to be "correct," they found it difficult to record and report "data" and to draw inferences from those data. Some of the content problems revealed fundamental misunderstandings of mathematical matters, which they found painful to reveal. Their past experience had enabled them to finesse lack of understanding by patterning a computation after some example in the text, which would usually lead to a "correct" answer, except for careless "math" errors, which were often treated lightly, resulting in the mathematical grace known as "partial credit."

But all the qualifications notwithstanding, we feel that this initial experiment has proved an exciting success. Several things are clear to us:

1. Mathematics teachers can incorporate writing assignments into their courses, with significant success and without unduly burdensome extra effort.
2. Thought and expression of thought are so inextricably intertwined that one cannot be good unless the other is as well.
3. Reader expectation theory succeeds in making not only better written products, but better writers.
4. Writing assignments can actually help students understand calculus.

Perhaps most remarkable of all, the students, by their course evaluations, graded us A for having added this writing component to their calculus course. Quoth one: "Putting theory into words often was — and still is — a challenge; but this helped me really *learn*, not just memorize, the concepts." Quoth another (an electrical engineering major): "One day I might actually have to *use* these writing skills."

REFERENCES

Douglas, R. (Ed.). (1986). *Toward a lean and lively calculus: Report of the Conference/Workshop to Develop Curriculum and Teaching Methods for Calculus at the College Level* (MAA Notes No. 6). Washington, DC: Mathematical Association of America.

Eliot, T. S. (1936). "Burnt Norton," V, *Four Quartets*. London: Faber & Faber.

Fish, S. (1980). *Is there a text in this class?* Cambridge, MA: Harvard University Press.

Gopen, G. (1984). Perceiving structure. *Harvard Law School Bulletin, 35*(3), 27–29.

Gopen, G. (1987). Let the buyer in ordinary course of business beware: Suggestions for revising the prose of the uniform commercial code. *University of Chicago Law Review, 54,* 1178–1214.

Williams, J. (1985). *Style: Ten lessons in clarity and grace* (2nd ed.). Chicago: Scott, Foresman.

Part V

THE CONTEXT OF LEARNING

"The problem remained open-ended," Erika Duncan quotes a student in a math-writing course she taught with Anneli Lax. Open-ended may mean incomplete, unfinished, the student goes on to explain. "But open-endedness can also mean that there is space left for further questioning and stimulation of thought."

The next four essays describe the general context in which open-ended learning occurs, and describe how writing, so foreign at first to the math or science class, seems particularly to invite "questioning and stimulation of thought." These essays focus less on teaching activities and techniques than on how students' abundant use of their own language enhances the environment for learning. Hassler Whitney, himself a distinguished mathematician at the Institute for Advanced Study, Princeton, tries to let children speak for themselves in his essay, so that we hear "how children *can* explore, think, and talk, if allowed." Dale Worsley argues that the *dignity* students gain from being heard, from being allowed to form their own understanding in their own words, enables them to succeed in learning where previously they had failed. "To become a responsible learner," Anneli Lax says in her essay, "a student must develop his or her own criteria for being 'right.' Writing will help him do this."

All four essayists in this section deplore how little time is allowed for reflective, integrative learning; how little teachers know what is going on in students' minds; how much is driven by testing and the "basics to be covered." All four — successful writers or mathematicians themselves — urge that education support risk, invite experiment, allow error, so that more students may succeed.

There is an ecology in each classroom, a relationship of organisms and their environment. The essays in this concluding section point to a stagnant ecology that often exists, but they also affirm the value of students' own language in revitalizing the learning environment.

229

CHAPTER 18

On Preserving the Union
of Numbers and Words:
The Story of an Experiment

Erika Duncan

"There are 16 dogs having to go to the bathroom. There are 4 fire hidrents. How many dogs will go on each fire Hidrents?" a fifth grader wrote when given the instructions: "Make up a story problem that uses $16 \div 4$. Use your imagination and make the story as outrageous as you would like." Through a series of stages which will become clear in the course of this article, Anneli Lax and I had gone from designing a special course combining writing and mathematical thinking for New York University freshmen whose placement tests scores indicated that they might have trouble tackling our required first-year mathematics classes, to running workshops involving both language arts and mathematics teachers working with at-risk student populations in several Brooklyn high schools. Our project had been funded by the Ford Foundation,* with the hope that we might be able to develop a model adaptable to a variety of different milieus. Now in our second year of working under the auspices of the foundation, we had extended our weekly hands-on seminars into the lower schools, into a Brooklyn junior high school, and into P.S. 230, where we found ourselves working with teachers of gifted as well as "slow" and average students.

Over and over, as we met various obstacles posed by the multiplicity of pressures experienced by teachers in the public schools, and by our own very often radical disagreements as to how directive we ought to be — from moment to moment, from week to week, we had to continually remind ourselves of the common goals that had spurred the unlikely collaboration between a fiction writer and a mathematician. Although each time I tell

*Special thanks to Barbara Nelson of the Ford Foundation's Urban Poverty Division for the active role she took in helping us to conceptualize the implementation of our program in the public schools.

the story of how we first came together, Anneli Lax protests that she cannot see herself in it, I will retell for the record what remains with me—my memories of that encounter, sifted over time (for often it is only in our own necessarily distorted reprocessing that we are able to take out of an encounter what ignites our own imaginative interaction—that driving force, half fictionalized, half distilled to an essence unseen by the other). At a Language Across the Curriculum Committee meeting, I remember quite distinctly being startled to hear an extraordinarily moving speech about the language of mathematics, with its symbols and its symmetries; I remember hearing Anneli speak about the difficulties that arise in trying to impose on thinking that might not have occurred in a sequential fashion, the sequential form that recording requires. I suggested we have lunch; and we talked for many hours about the problems that writers and mathematicians share in carrying intuitive concepts to their manifest conclusions, and in feeling that as they arrive at a product, they must eliminate all traces of process. We spoke of the sense of hopelessness that students feel when they are allowed to see only the finished products of those who have met success—while they themselves feel so stuck in the process—unable to see the paths that the "greats" who have gone before have taken, unable to see even the faltering paths of their fellow students, who, in conventional classes only perform when they already have the answer, right or wrong though it may be.

We decided to work together because we wanted to convey to our students our shared belief that, as different as our disciplines might appear on the surface, in both, one must not think of fixed methods for finding the solutions to a given problem, but rather one must learn to conceptualize a wide variety of converging and diverging possibilities, forever being refined as each student let her or his own beginnings shape and set up logical boundaries for each new forward-reaching step. We were eager to help students realize that in mathematics, as well as in writing, the imagination plays a crucial role. Whatever the age group we worked with, whatever the circumstances, disciplinary problems, and unwieldly class size, we determined a great deal of our work would be oral: students would be required to read to one another attempted solutions to problems which left them unsure; they would be encouraged to pursue their thinking out loud—and to free-associate on possible directions that another student's searching stirred.

ELEMENTARY SCHOOL: WHERE THE PROCESS BEGINS

Now as we sat with the dozen or so teachers who joined us weekly, in a cozy circle on child-sized chairs in the sunny library of P.S. 230, while Paul

Feder read to us stories of snowmen holding cookies, sleepovers in which two, three or four children had been excluded due to petty jealousy, partying "punkrockers," procreating kittens and peeing dogs, we felt lucky to be let into that moment in small children's lives when the split between imaging real situations and mathematical play has not fully occurred.

"What if four dogs pee at the first hydrant, two at the next, then four, and then six? Wouldn't that also work out?" Paul reported on a suggestion made when the fire hydrant problem was presented, telling us how studious and serious his fifth graders had seemed as they worked to come up with a wording of the story that would let the reader know that the author intended the dogs to distribute themselves in equal number at the four available peeing posts. Although rumor has it that children hate word problems, clearly these children were able to sustain a very lively — even heated discussion of the rather subtle mathematical and linguistic nuances that the problem raised. Clearly this problem was very real to Toby Shandy who invented it.

So often we tend to draw dichotomies between creativity and realistic thinking, forgetting to let our beginning students learn about the role of the imagination in science and mathematics, forgetting to let them know how much even the fictional forms cry out for grounding in reality. Although the children we see in the elementary schools will be soon asked to cope with textbook mathematics problems shorn of all descriptive flourishes and adjectives, it is heartening to note their freedom to include emotional and descriptive nuances in mathematics problems of their own invention.

"One day Kate went to the park with eight kittens. She played, running in the grass. Then to her surprise she had lost five kittens! How many kittens did she have left?" wrote Laura Six-Pattay, a third grader who had been assigned an invention centering around 8-5. The assignment of translating a specific subtraction problem into a real-life situation allows us to see exactly how Laura conceptualizes subtraction at this stage. The posing of an identical task using 6×6 as a base shows that at the same age although Elena has mastered the operational aspects of multiplication (even before beginning to write she had scribbled the number 36 on the top left hand corner of her paper), she has not yet assimilated the underlying concepts. Hers was the most charming among many mathematically similar papers that opened our participating teachers' eyes to the fact that without such written assignments there is no way to know whether students able to solve simple problems are developing the understanding that will come into play when problems grow more complicated. As long as the right answer is given by a majority of students, the teacher feels ready to move on.

"I had 6 insects. 7 of my insects died because there had been a baby born," Elena Masquer's rendition begins. Already, with the addition of numbers — perhaps, I will argue, *because* of the addition of numbers — her sense of chronology and cause and effect has gone awry. "But then I found 6 insects. five were on my shoe and 12 were in the bathroom. But all of them died. Then I found 6 insects in a field, each insect had 1 baby. All of the addits [adults] and babies died. How many insects do I have now?"

It would be an oversimplification to venture that mathematical confusion alone created this delightful tale of dying and re-emerging insects, or to decide that Elena was so interested in the flow of her narrative that she let the mathematical content "fend for itself." For both the emotional flow and the structure of her story are determined by certain magical powers that she seems to attribute to the act of multiplication, powers that never would have become clear to us, if we had not helped her to write down her own, very personal interpretation. When I stop for a moment to compare her work to that of a high school girl given the task of inventing a story around the equation $3x + 5 = 1,025$, who wanted it all to be the result of '4 matrimonies" (who later, when I questioned her figure, substituted 9 matrimonies for 4), I wonder about the almost demonic procreative power of the multiplicative process in so many students' minds. I think of the many bright students in high school and college who, when asked to multiply somewhat complicated numbers, seem merely to shut their eyes, pulling any old number out of a hat, and hoping against hope that by some miracle their answer will be right.

And of course our system feeds into this tendency, by asking for simpler and simpler single-word or single-number answers that machines can check. In keeping with our college students' observations that they either lost interest in math or lost their sense of being in control of the material around third grade, Sylvia Oberferst, the principal of P.S. 230, observed that her students' test scores begin to drop at exactly this point. A mother attending one of our parent workshops observed that while her first grader loved math, her fourth grader was beginning to lose interest. Although her fourth grader continued to do well on her math tests, all of her early enthusiasm had diminished. Why should this be? And is this necessary?

In the earliest grades there is very little sense of separation between the disciplines. Teachers make no formal movements from English to mathematics to history. Whatever comes up, whatever feels relevant, becomes a valid basis for a lesson. While our preschool and kindergarten teachers had not shown any particular interest in mathematics before our project came into their school, as their awareness was stimulated by our group discussions, they were amazed to report the number of spontaneous mathematical discussions occurring among their students. They were able to slow down and make more conscious use of those discussions, and to report some of the difficulties that students had when they tried to shift from adding, subtracting, or dividing sets of concrete objects, which they did spontaneously when a real-life situation caught their imaginations, to working out operations involving numbers where concrete representation was not involved.

As one primary school teacher after another described the struggle that their children had to undergo in order to eliminate conceptual structures based on actual imaging of dying insects, disappearing cats, and dogs having to go to the bathroom, to clear their minds for the bald abstractions that symbolic representation seemed to require, I tried to imagine how they would feel nearly ten years later — after all vestiges of mathematical playfulness had been suppressed — upon discovering that in order to earn a high school diploma one must know how to handle such stilted word problems as: "Shirts cost $7, pants cost $12, and jackets cost $25. Fred has $100 to buy 1 jacket, 2 pairs of pants, and some shirts. What is the greatest number of shirts he can buy?"

HIGH SCHOOL: OLD HABITS DIE SLOWLY

By way of experiment, in an effort to belatedly heal the gap, we brought the above word problem from the standardized New York Regents Competency Test into a remedial English class at Sarah J. Hale High School in Brooklyn. Myron Antenoff, the math teacher who worked with this particular group of students, had told us that he was irked at the wording, which, he felt, did not fully allow the young people in his class to demonstrate even their very sadly limited mathematical abilities. He was irked by the phrase "some shirts," he said. He was irked by the fact that the problem was presented "out of order," so that the students would not be able to set it up step by step as they read it.

The first response among those seated at the table in the math and science office where we have been meeting for over a year was indignation that students troubled not only in mathematics but in reading and writing as well should have to be subjected to reading that might prove tricky while they were trying to illustrate their mathematical competency. And yet, I knew, a great deal of students' inabilities to handle word problems came from reading with an eye towards the quick solution — the inherent set-up — instead of an intuitive search for the sense out of which a reasonable method of finding the right answer might grow. I thought once again of Paul Feder, the teacher who had assigned the word problems at P.S. 230, and remembered his tale of the student who insisted that while he could think of a problem involving the operation 6+8, he couldn't think of anything for 8+6. I thought of that wonderful sense of realism that must have motivated that child — and mourned the way that it has been systematically beaten out of our older students who think nothing of the sort of logical reversals that allow them to divide gallons of gas by miles traveled in order to arrive at a number that seems to having nothing to do with either miles or gas.

Because our project advocated as its stated goal the re-integration of language and mathematical thought, I was able to make a reasonable argument for allowing the possibly confusing wording to stand untouched. I was able to ask Richard Salvin, the inventor of many fine exercises for our project, if we might present the problem during his students' language tutorial time in order to have them evaluate it from a linguistic point of view, rewrite it however they liked, and then solve it.

Already we had been discussing issues of taste in mathematics in our weekly workshops; we had been encouraging teachers to help their students identify and verbalize what they liked and disliked about the discipline. We had played the taste game several times among ourselves and were greatly amused to find that Shirley Hopkins, who taught some of the advanced mathematics classes, hated puzzles and games, while Myron Antenoff, who had expressed his distaste for the problem presented above, adored such things. Shirley loved geometry, because of the orderly fashion of its logic — and hated trigonometry. Juliana Rogers, the chair of the math department, loved trigonometry because she found it orderly and predictable; she hated geometry because she found its particular constructs did not appeal to her. Richard Salvin, who loved all sorts of puzzles, also liked geometry because he felt that he could use his imagination to figure it out.

What would happen if we could share those discussions of mathematical tastes with our students? We had done this already, in our orderly small workshop settings in the university. But could we bring this important ingredient of our approach into the far larger, more chaotic classrooms of the New York City public high schools?

A group of students were doing their homework in the mathematics office during this particular meeting. We interrupted them, quickly explained what we were doing, and collected a collage of responses of the order: "I like multiplication because it's easy to check," so that Shirley might have something tangible to share with her students. The next week she reported that immediately following the class discussions of mathematical tastes she was able to see a dramatic rise in risk-taking among her students. For the remainder of the semester, within the groups where the taste discussions had taken place, she reported that students continued to bring even imperfectly conceptualized solutions before the class for discussion. They appeared far less concerned about being proven wrong.

As a natural follow-up, carrying our discussion of taste into an area where mathematical and linguistic preferences might overlap, we asked the students in Richard's English class to respond from a "taste" point of view to the wording of the problem that had so upset their math teacher. Although on other occasions students in English classes have seemed resentful when we threw them problems out of mathematics, here they were immediately intrigued at the idea of being asked to evaluate and rewrite a question that they had encountered on the Regents Competency Test that so many had failed. Although there was one student in the class who argued vehemently that there was nothing wrong with the wording of the problem, and although many—in the more relaxed context of this English class—were easily able to solve it, most of the students shared Myron's discomfort around the word "some." While they worked to reword the problem—each student adding a slight variation, some arguing that the only way to make it easier would be to give an extra hint, others playing with ways to make it a bit more complicated and interesting—I talked a bit about the discomfort that so many students feel with the unknown thing, and about the relationship between the word "some" and the letter x, or a, or b. I spoke of the fact that often in our writing or our speech we overuse the word "some," because we are unwilling or unable to identify more specifically just what we mean. From that moment on, there was laughter anytime someone used the word "some." Later on, when the students tried to translate a mathematical expression into a story—following Paul Feder's model—I would find many instances of "something-or-other number" substituting for x in their early drafts.

As the students were working out their revisions of the clothing problem, a girl in the back of the room raised her hand rather urgently. "This doesn't have to do with math," she said. "But tell me what kind of a jacket can he buy for twenty-five dollars?" Already the exercise was taking on a kind of realism for the students. There was a high level of laughter; but there was an astoundingly high level of concentration as one by one the students read their rewritten versions of the problem to one another. The attention was such that when I picked up in one oral reading the phrase "two pairs of pants for twelve dollars" and asked what was missing, a student on the other side of the room immediately called out "each," inserting the missing word into her own revised version of the problem at hand.

Inspired by Paul Feder's good work, we now gave the students the equation $3x + 5 = 1,025$ as a basis for working out their own story problems. In order to illustrate what we wanted the students to do, we told a few of the tales that had emerged from Paul Feder's experiment, thus quickly conveying the idea of inventing outrageous stories and sticking to numerical facts. It had been our observation over time that without accompanying stories and examples, students told to invent interesting word problems more often than not simply get stuck. Perhaps more interesting, in light of our wish to help others replicate our experiment, is Paul Feder's lifting from Family Math* the notion of providing a specific number operation around which the students must focus whatever they later invent. Although I had often asked students to invent creative word problems out of real or imagined situations, and although I had often watched Anneli work with direct translation of specific formulas supplied by science teachers, until I saw Paul's work I had not thought of combining literal translation of a "closed-choice" mathematical situation with imaginative invention.

Lynne Impina, a visiting mathematician from Wyoming who was working with us for the semester, had designed the problem $3x+5=1,025$ with numbers adequately large and awkward so that these often underutilized and underchallenged high school students would have to strain to conceptualize what was being conveyed. When the student who changed her original "4 matrimonies" to nine still found herself in a state of confusion, I tried to help her return to a tangible vision of what $3x$ might represent. Eileen Fernandez, a graduate intern who works with Richard Salvin and me every Wednesday designing mathematical materials to be brought into English classes, had noticed that one student worked out the equation before beginning to invent her "story" and suggested that others might want to do this as well, so that they might have some idea of the quantities involved, in order to have their tales make sense. Having located x in the region of the middle three hundreds, what kind of a tale might be developed? In order to provide a starting point, I suggested that the student have her various matrimonies take place in three separate buildings — then she might be able to resolve some of her logical inconsistencies, increasing her numbers if need be, reorganizing her information. (Here I feel that we must play an active role in helping our students begin to image; the entire procedure is so new to them that, if we leave them too much to their own devices, they will never fully grasp the skill that we are trying to impart. If at first we ourselves must do a great deal of work for them, they will return our efforts in their own attempts to follow the workings of our minds — and bring our burgeoning associations, called forth by their faltering attempts, to fruition.) Our student returned to her seat to try to incorporate three buildings holding 340 people each into her matrimonial scheme.

Another student came rushing up to me. In answer to the same equation, she had invented a school where 1,025 oranges were given out to all of

*Workbook available from Family Math, Lawrence Hall of Science, University of California, Berkeley, CA 94720.

the students and five teachers. Did she have the correct idea? she asked. I noticed immediately that although conceptually the quantities and objects she had invented were sensible, she too had neglected the tricky $3x$. I pointed this out to her, and received the not-too-unexpected blank look of confusion. "What if you give your school three floors?" I asked. (I had already done my own conceptualizing in the inventing of three buildings, so that the shift to three floors was now easy.) "Oh," she said, and suddenly a smile crossed her face. A few minutes later she came back to me with the problem completely rewritten: her first version, "The teacher gave the students, 1020 oranges and added five more for the teachers. how many oranges will each child get," had been changed to "The principal gave students on three floors a certain amount of oranges. All together there was 1,025 and only 5 for the teachers. How many oranges were given to each floor." In concentrating on helping her to conceptualize a spot for $3x$, I had not even mentioned the fact that her final question in the first version was conceptually absurd. Notice that in her second version, without any intervention on my part, she has corrected this. Not only are her mathematical structures more sensible; in addition, we note a marked increase in the use of punctuation, in differentiation between sentences, and structural coherence. We notice that the far more evocative and precise "The principal gave students on three floors . . . " has taken the place of the conceptually amorphous "The teacher gave the students. . . . "

What does this mean in the context of schools where increasingly math teachers complain that children are either unwilling or unable to check their own work, where English teachers insist that one is lucky if students write at all, so that to ask for rewriting would be an act of sheer folly, in schools where more often than not students tear up their corrected papers without even looking at the notations that their teachers labored long into the night to add? What are the ways that we might learn to listen to our students on the spot, to make the work of rethinking, refiguring and rewriting a shared experience that can go on even during those appallingly chopped-up forty-minute class periods, in order to prepare for that time when our disheartened young people will once again be able to engage in the solitary figuring-things-out so familiar to every undamaged young child, working to learn and grow?

The students in Richard Salvin's English class would need many weeks and months before they would master the skill of reading given word problems and inventing word problems of their own; they would need a great deal of experience moving between the thoughtful analysis of test questions and listening to the flaws and possibilities in one another's first faltering attempts. But already the process had begun; their interest had been sparked; they were listening, rewriting — and perhaps most important — they were questioning. We agreed to repeat on a weekly basis, continuing throughout the semester, the two-pronged format we had accidentally discovered — presenting a different Regents Competency Test problem to the students every week for rewriting and analysis, followed by a chance to invent their own problems out of a given expression. We agreed that no time would be lost for these students from a language arts point of view; on the contrary, precisely because this work was in mathematics — and therefore nonthreatening to those who feared they could not write — certain issues of logical sequencing and clarity, previously threatening, could now with safety be addressed. Certain hierarchies between the "good" writers and the bad were automatically eliminated by this meshing of the disciplines.

THE UNIVERSITY: THE UNDOING BECOMES A MUTUAL EFFORT

Indeed, it was this elimination of hierarchy that had first become apparent as a serendipitous side-product when we began our experimental workshops combining writing and mathematical thinking at New York University. While within a single discipline some formal or informal ranking of students was inevitable, with the combining of the disciplines, the whole concept of ranking became extraneous and students were suddenly forced to work together to pursue a common goal. The returning student who worked as an editorial assistant at Random House would suddenly find herself having to borrow structures from the eighteen-year-old sitting next to her, who had trouble pronouncing three-syllable words. The philosophically oriented dreamer who worked so quickly that all thoughts became a bit of a jumble, needing to be sorted out, would suddenly find herself learning from students she might previously have dismissed as too dull or slow to capture her interest. She would find herself listening to their work intently — to see just how they had done this or that — and they in turn would gather confidence through the surprising seriousness of her listening.

"In my writing I float. A vivid mental picture of my body, held aloft by fluffy white clouds, taunts me. I have always enjoyed going off on tangents, and not connecting topics; however I feel a pressing need to be organized at the same time," Tye Smith had written in the mathematical autobiography which she read to our workshop members during the second "English" meeting of our experimental class. We had asked if we might take for a term fifteen incoming freshmen, who might work with us simultaneously in mathematics and expository writing. They would meet with us four mornings a week, in intensive sessions with alternating emphases.

They would not only do mathematics with Anneli; they would be required to put their mathematical thoughts into writing. My work would not end abruptly with my own area. Whether the students were writing about the Platonic notion of reality or about the demonstrable properties of triangular numbers, I would help them to structure their essays so that their individual processes were effectively presented. Which students did better starting with a single question? Which preferred to outline possible results before even beginning? I would show our students how, whatever the subject at hand, each began with his or her own personal "Let x equal . . . " after which the choices could no longer be arbitrary. I worked hard to devise assignments in which the distinctions between solving a mathematics problem and writing an essay would be blurred.

Our first shared assignment, "the mathematical autobiography," simultaneously satisfied the English department's requirement that the first student writings be personal and the Mathematical Thinking Program's need for mathematical profiles. Because of the specificity of its focus, we found the results more focused and more satisfying than the usual, more general autobiographical writings which come into freshman composition classes, in which students rightfully withhold the deeper confessional layer without knowing what to provide instead. Because of our focus on creation of aesthetically pleasing forms to house specific mathematical information, we received compositions in which negative attitudes towards mathematics were revealed with a clarity missing from the conventional profiles in which students understandably feel the need to prove themselves.

As we attempt to distinguish between the very public and technique-oriented nature of our approach and the relative inwardness of approaches relying on the private learning log or dialogue journal, it is important to note that from the moment of its conception, through all of its many stages, even this first very personal piece of writing was meant to be shared with every other member of the class. In order for our students to get as much as possible from observing one another's ways of working, it was critical to establish from the onset an atmosphere in which our students would be able to watch each other work — alert to the quirks and the differences, able to analyze without reproach or judgement. In order to accomplish this, we found ourselves — sometimes consciously, more often unconsciously — reversing many of their previous expectations as to usual class procedure. The following provides a case in point.

In the conventional mathematics class, the teacher demonstrates the "proper" way to solve a problem before assigning the students examples of applications, while in the usual writing class, students are given an assignment and left on their own as to the specifics of how to fulfill it. In our classes, there were numerous instances when mathematics problems were given out for homework devoid of any particular instructions as to how to construct solutions (with the exception of the one standing instruction that all solutions must be written), while before pursuing assignments in literary analysis or creating extended narratives, our students were asked to image aloud their first instincts as to how they might go about the actual execution. As we circled the room, each student was asked to image a specific opening, and to explain why he or she chose that particular course.

In our mathematics classes, when the written homework was shared with the group, often one student would read out the prose explaining his or her process, while another student stationed at the blackboard would attempt to schematize the outlined steps. In English and math alike, oral sharings of the works of individuals were performed in the context of tracing the evolution from the moment of the first spoken conception to the present stage. Class members were expected to maintain an up-to-date picture of every piece of student work that was discussed. Our students took very seriously our requirement that they catch up via peer reports on any oral presentations that they missed. They worked quite hard to hone their listening skills.

Although the assignment of the mathematical autobiography had come from both of us, we decided that after working together with this first shared assignment it would be more productive if each of us used our own day to work out of our discipline without forcing connections. In this way, we decided, we would remain more open to the natural connections that might arise. The first connections that we were able to make came from observations of how individual students carried certain habits of performance from one discipline to another. These observations were enormously fruitful in shaping the direction of our future class work. Remembering how Tye described in her autobiography her fear of disorganization and floating, we watched with interest the parallel ways that her tendency to go off on tangents caused problems in math, which prior to our work together she could only identify as "a dislike of paying close attention." We noticed that whenever Tye would write, she would create elaborate syntactical structures with abounding parentheses within parentheses — multiple insertions that alternated with frequent series of dots for supposed deletions. Whenever she would read her work out loud, she would stop herself mid-parenthesis, to further explain what she was trying to articulate. On occasions when she was working out a mathematical proof, just as she was beginning to move forward, she would suddenly stop herself for a clarification, completely losing the momentum that she had been building up. Because of the day-to-day alternation between working with math and writing, and because so much of our work was oral, it was easy for all of us to see these patterns.

As I tried to describe my observations to the class — asking the question, why? — I kept returning in my mind to the time when I was first learning to ride a bicycle. If I rode too slowly, inevitably I would lose my balance — and yet whenever I attained the speed which would have allowed me to ride forward smoothly, had I maintained it, a terrible fear of falling would overtake me. The fear would grow and grow until at last in my anxiety I would create the fall I feared, so that at least it would be mine. I shared this image with Tye and with the rest of the class.

Simultaneously we had begun to notice a slightly quirky twist in the quality of Tye's listening. When a complicated verbal explanation was given, when a question was put to the class, or when an assignment was read out loud, Tye would panic and ask for a clarification long before the presentation was complete. While others were willing to let the whole wash over them before deciding whether they had caught its gist, giving themselves the space of their own silence to re-hear what had been said and to mentally re-organize the echoes, Tye's anxiety over fully grasping every part invariably interfered with her holistic understanding. Yet clearly Tye did not shun complicated thinking. Clearly she enjoyed challenges.

In a less process-oriented atmosphere, Tye's tendency to speak up the moment she thought of something could have become the source of considerable embarrassment. It is my suspicion that in the past she often had been teased for doing so much of her thinking out loud. But now, even as we worked with her on developing skills of waiting and relaxation, we were able to assure her honestly that the transparency with which she showed her process was a gift to all of us. We were able to use what she expressed so openly in unearthing what was going on inside other students who were more reticent to show their vulnerabilities.

I will never forget the day that Susan Buttenwieser brought in a "completed" essay that was barely three lines long — not unexpectedly Tye had just read us a twelve-page "beginning" which included every digression imaginable, in answer to the same assignment. The only work that Susan brought to class to share was skeletal. In English, her essays would merely reiterate the question, and then stop. Despite Anneli's insistence that all math assignments show the links between steps in complete prose sentences, her mathematics papers were dotted with seemingly random numbers and words, the final entry in each section serving as "the answer." It was during a discussion of Tye's fear of leaving the right things out (which led to such unmanageable volume and such agonizing repetition) that, acting on a hunch, I suggested that Susan's inhibitions might come from a fear of putting the wrong things in. (If we had not been dealing in such detail with Tye's anxieties and the technical troubles that they brought about, and if we had not been spanning two disciplines at once, I suspect we might never have come to the source of Susan's difficulties.)

Once Susan and Tye began to talk, other students quickly joined the conversation, trying to locate their own fears in terms of the polar points that Susan and Tye had articulated. A vocabulary of event had been established, to which we could return in subsequent class discussions, whenever anxieties caused repetitions or deletions that disturbed the flow of the recording. As the group began to work on allowing a freer, more fluid exploration to replace the old obsessions with instantaneous correctness, through the very specific examples of Susan and Tye each student was able to articulate equally specific needs in this area, and to set up an individual agenda to begin to meet them.

THE SPECIAL BENEFITS OF COMBINING MATH AND WRITING

What was it about the combining of the disciplines that allowed for this kind of interchange? We often asked ourselves this question during the first two years of our experiment. For much that I have just described takes place in any well-run writing workshop. A great deal of revelation of sources of fear also takes place in the "mathematics anxiety" workshops pioneered by Sheila Tobias. And yet, something was happening through the combination course that neither of us had observed to this extent in those settings or when we taught our own subjects individually. Because there was such a merging between the emotional work and the technical forays into two separate disciplines, our students were making faster progress in both areas than their counterparts who were studying each area separately. Because they were revealing their vulnerabilities so early in the semester, we were able to use our analyses of their patterns in our planning. In addition — and perhaps this is the most important factor! — there was something about combining the two subjects that seemed to take the onus off the individual student, even as it opened the way for particularized, potentially quite vulnerable discussions of personalities of work. From the beginning there was a great deal of good-humored laughing over shared and individual tendencies, as they carried over from one subject to the other, from one day to the next.

There were ways that each person's approach to our work shed a special light on the content we were trying to cover together. We learned a great deal from Addiss Clark, who had written that she wished for a time when her words and her thoughts would become one, who had great trouble with ordering cause and effect, reversing them frequently in her efforts to tackle mathematical proofs, who one day, in the middle of an essay about birth and death, came up with the sentence "Unless you have the courage to live life to the fullest, you might as well commit suicide." In helping her find the thoughts from which this startlingly strong, misplaced statement had derived, and in linking our discussion to *showing* "the path from here to there" in a mathematical proof, we were helping our other students understand how to present their own proofs in a meaningful fashion. In laughingly helping Ann Marie Letteiri to recognize the connection between her "slight" misuse of words in her sentence praising "freedom of inquisition" and her use of memorized formulas in which xs were only "slightly" misplaced, we were working to convince the entire class that derivations tended to be more reliable than memorizations. A single jumbled sentence in which it was unclear where the author's references to one thing ended and where her references to the next began provided a wonderful opportunity for Anneli to jump up in the middle of a writing lesson and exclaim: "Look, it's like factoring!"—improvising a short mini-lesson on the use of parentheses in stating the distributive property of multiplication with respect to addition that was sure to be remembered during the next day's math lesson. Daily the students read their homework solutions aloud; daily we would find that when the mathematical thinking was clear, the writing would also be clear. As our students became more used to writing mathematical solutions, they learned to see within the jumbled moments in their prose helpful markers that something in their thought had gone awry.

There is so much more that one could say about our experiment—each school that has given us a temporary home for our workshops, each group of entering New York University freshmen, has generated an endless array of observations and tales. In speaking for a moment to the many who are working with students who may never learn to love math, I wish to quote from an essay by John Paul Layedra, a boy who spent a year in our experimental class, who entered feeling very shaky in both English and mathematics, and who left feeling ever so much more sure of his own intellectual prowess. If he never touches mathematics again, if he never writes again, I will still rejoice in the ground he has gained; I will still thank him for what he gave back to us all, at the moment in time when our paths came together.

Anneli had begun to work on a problem in class, to which the solution remained unclear. (It is not true, as John Paul suggests, that no mathematician knew the answer. Anneli had merely shared with the class her confession that although the question can be explored and resolved with the tools developed in an elementary calculus class, she herself had not yet pursued its solution.) Because I noticed that my own tendency to image a result both inspired my curiosity and adversely affected my openness, I shared my observations with the class, and asked the students to use the lesson as a jumping-off point for a composition about the virtues and drawbacks of open-endedness and imaging in math and writing.

Here is John Paul Layedra's composition:

> Does anything ever reach an end? Is there anything after an ending? These
> questions arose from a classroom mathematics inquiry concerning whether or
> not a series of ever-lengthening lines, formed from the longest sides of right
> triangles with a constant outer side of 1, lying next to each other, radiating
> from a single point would ever come around in a full circle to reach the first
> drawn line. The truth was that no mathematician knew the answer or could
> prove that the lines did or didn't reach the beginning. The problem remained
> open-ended.

Would John Paul have dared to stretch his language so far, to take so
many risks, if he had not been writing about mathematics? I do not believe
so. As I read his words, and remember the diagram that had inspired them
(see Figure 18.1), I am struck over and over again by the bravery of his
attempt to use language to replicate something so simultaneously complex
and precise. I remember how one day he came into my office, both smiling
and sighing, bearing a gigantic stack of "cut and paste" revisions, in which
he had painstakingly re-ordered his week's work, inserting missed transi-
tions into his English essays, inserting explanations of process work that
might have been taken for granted into his math. "I'm not used to this," he
had said to me. "Here we have to revise everything, even our math."
"Would you have preferred it another way?" I asked. And he shook his
head, smiled, and walked away.

His essay continues:

> Open-endedness has the connotation of something being incomplete and
> therefore not finished. But open-endedness can also mean that there is space
> left for further questioning and stimulation of thought. In writing, open-
> endedness should promote some questioning, but not to the extent that it
> creates gaping holes in the writing and creates confusion. When something
> isn't open-ended there is a finality about it, a feeling that all has been said and
> answered. There is no room for further inquiry or speculation. This close-
> endedness creates an accept-but-don't-think mentality that dissuades inquiry
> and results in knowledge without purpose. Images can be placed in people's
> minds, but will they incite a person to search for or create other images?

My mind wanders once again forward in time, to another image. In
the interest of exploring "replication," we have taken our two-part experiment around analyzing and inventing word problems out of Richard
Salvin's high school English class, into Catherine Albergo's. Here the energy level is high, as students vie with one another, projecting the problems

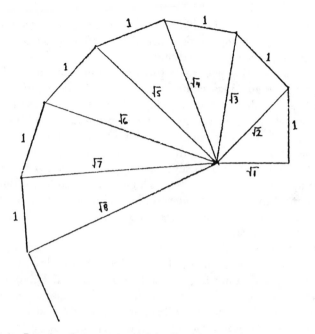

Figure 18.1   Drawing that prompted John Paul Layedra's composition

into ever-expanding levels of absurdity, as Lynne, Eileen, and Catherine and I circle the room trying to unravel such first attempts (again for the problem $3x+5=1,025$) as "Three sports cars times large cars were in the parking lots. There were also 5 ugly cars. . . . There were 1,025 cars in the parking lot. How many large cars were there?" — enjoying the element of parody even as Lynne tries to explain why the statements wind us up with "cars squared" — deliberately running the workshop like a Quaker meeting where students are encouraged to call out and read out even very partial solutions, so that the attention and inventiveness of each other student in the class will be stirred, so that many, many possibilities will be modeled.

"Look at Ramu!" Catherine calls out. "This is the first time he has put pen to paper!" At first I felt more than a bit uncomfortable with the back-and-forth teasing that gives a sort of slapstick, "I will never quite take you seriously," texture to so many of Catherine's interchanges with her students. But over the year and a half we have worked together, I have come to respect the spontaneity and warmth that allows these young people, thrown into a cold and violent alien world, to play around because they cannot yet dare to take themselves seriously, that allows them to come to their teacher for a moment of lightness or laughter, a joke or a hug. "Come on, Ramu. Let's see what you're writing," Catherine calls out again, playfully snatching the paper from his hands.

"There were 5 dog pounds in town and 5 dog catchers. There were 1,025 dogs how many dogs would be put into each pound," she reads. The other students are all listening, thinking. Clearly they like his example. But the five is somehow misplaced, given an inappropriate role. I try to explain this in a way that will help them see, without giving it all away. "What if the dog catcher caught five squirrels by accident, and then turned them loose?" a boy several rows back suggests. Ramu does not take the suggestion about the squirrels, although he lets its logic color his solution. But perhaps more important to our deeper purpose, he is able to show to his classmates his very real delight in being taken so seriously, in having his example played with in that way.

Now the closing bell rings. The other students have already gathered their books. But Ramu is sitting, his head bent to the desk, still writing, "There were 3 dog pounds in town and 5 dog catchers. There were 1,025 dogs 5 got away. Out of the dogs that are left. how many dogs would go into each pound." Had the period been longer, a second discussion might have taken place about whether one had to keep the 5 dog catchers. Ramu might have been asked to reread his paper, in order to punctuate it more properly. But already a major breakthrough had been made.

Catherine had told us that because of Ramu's refusal to write, they were considering him for special education classes. Now perhaps she can persuade them to wait and to watch a while longer. She mentioned that despite repeated notes she has written to his parents, he refuses to carry a notebook. He spends most of his class periods alone in the corner, refusing to listen, refusing to participate. Now suddenly, after our appearance in his English class, he has acquired a notebook. Although he has not done any new writing, still he carries it everywhere with him. Is Ramu also waiting? For us to return? For more mathematical sorts of writing assignments?

"I can see that he seems to need to have his problem-solving skills challenged," Catherine Albergo says to us. "I will have to think of some English assignments that do this for him." And there beneath the mural of half-colored-in textile workers begun in the era of the WPA and never completed, which covers three of the four walls of the Sarah Hale teachers' cafeteria, together we put our heads back to the planning board, knowing that there is an essence about our combination, too often intangible — and yet, during those moments when we can catch it and convey it, worth those long times of waiting and of struggle to break through.

CHAPTER 19

They Think, Therefore We Are

Anneli Lax

Demands for clarity and precision are made in all fields where people express ideas. Language teachers show students how syntax and structure give clues to meanings. Mathematics teachers, however, although aware of their students' linguistic deficiencies, generally feel that language instruction is not in their domain. I would urge them to insist that students speak and write in mathematics class; for when we examine what our students say or write, we discover some linguistic habits that get in the way of communication and that sometimes reveal incorrect mathematical preconceptions. Students need to learn different ways of saying the same thing, for example "twelve divided by three is four" and "three goes into twelve four times." Prepositions can be tricky, as was demonstrated by the carefully recorded observations of Eleanor Wilson Orr (1987).

Although mathematicians are precise in their thought, they can be a bit sloppy in their language. For example, when they want their students to prove that the square of every odd integer is odd, they may say "show that the square of an odd integer is odd" and be dismayed when a student says "3 is odd, its square, 9, is also odd, so I have picked an odd integer with an odd square." In the insider's jargon, "an odd integer" means any arbitrary odd integer rather than a particular odd integer. Spelling everything out precisely seems too pedantic and may offend our aesthetic sense, so we use abbreviations. When those of us who are used to speaking in mathematical idioms now add mathematical vocabulary and notation to our discourse, our language becomes quite incomprehensible, and we should not be surprised when our students feel excluded from our dialogue. How often do we indict our students' reasoning power when perhaps the problem has to do with their interpretation of our questions asked in our language? We expect them to understand us, but we rarely meet them halfway by trying to understand their language.

We and our students need feedback to strike the right balance, and time to learn how to use the common language. When students talk to each other and to us about their attempts at solutions, when they try to convince one another of their mathematical deductions, find fallacies, and repair them; and when they write down their findings, they feel more and more at home with our linguistic and notational conventions. Most important, they see that this is just what these are—conventions or tacit agreements, not mathematical rules or magic mantras. The lecture format leaves no room for any of that.

MATH ANXIETY—SOME AVOIDABLE, SOME INEVITABLE

Many seemingly trivial linguistic problems unite to confuse students who are generally weak in English. Erika Duncan and I had some inspired help from English teachers who allowed their classes to play with mathematical "word problems," the most widely feared items on mathematics tests (see Chapter 18). Students have read, interpreted, paraphrased, and criticized word problems. They were asked to make up their own word problems on a given mathematical theme, such as $7-4$, and to solve those invented by their peers. Such exercises sharpen linguistic and mathematical skills simultaneously. Above all, they contribute to the feeling, "I can pore over this problem until I understand it thoroughly, and, given enough time, I can explain clearly how I plan to solve it. If I get stuck, I can explain where I got stuck and ask the kid in the seat next to mine or my teacher, and I can argue about the problem until I understand it."

The student who speaks and writes, is listened to and read, gains self-confidence and a sense of belonging to a group that is exploring a mathematical matter. She is not likely to succumb to learning-impeding attitudes and emotions, usually called "math anxiety," at least not for any protracted period of time.

We must realize, however, that some anxieties are built into any challenging learning process. There is some frustration at not being able to do something or understand something. The cause of the tension may be a physical task like carrying something too heavy for us, or a mental task, like "getting" the joke in a cartoon, or sorting out the steps for solving a hard problem. This frustration can be observed in very young children. It is exacerbated in a setting where almost everybody else seems to have no difficulty. The child begins to feel isolated, to doubt his ability, and to fear future situations fraught with similar frustrations. The grown-up version of this feeling of localized inadequacy and being left out is akin to the "insider-outsider" phenomenon Sheila Tobias (1985) describes. I suspect these frustrations are quite natural and unavoidable (the other side of the coin of feeling elated at having understood), even in the absence of inadvertent cruelties by thoughtless peers, awkward parents, impatient teachers. The question is how to handle such frustrations. Those that are related to mathematics are best handled in the context of learning mathematics. If they loom so large that whenever we are confronted with a mathematics problem, we worry about whether or not we can do it, then we cannot concentrate. And if we feel in addition that our failure might disappoint people who believed in us, or that we shall be judged or even humiliated by others, our anxiety gets worse. There are people who, in the face of such anxieties, say to themselves "I'll show them a thing or two!" and who manage to channel their efforts into a successful performance. But for most people the best chance of overcoming such self-doubts and anxieties is to get so absorbed in the task as to displace self-conscious thoughts. The act of writing about the mathematical task and about one's feelings concerning the context of that task has helped many a self-conscious writer-learner overcome frustration and get back into mathematics.

Some anxieties — for example, those due to time pressure — have nothing to do with mathematics; the simple fact is that one needs time to think. While in some instances our survival may depend on our ability to make quick decisions, it does not seem reasonable to treat education as training in short-term survival skills. Our schools, especially those in large cities, do not provide enough time, nor a sufficiently relaxed atmosphere for any kind of contemplative work. Not only are students rushed through recitations, exercises, and tests, but also teachers lack the time to think about their teaching and their students and to talk to one another about their ideas and their work. To increase one's speed in thinking, one needs lots of practice. By imposing unreasonable time constraints, we encourage shoddy work, "getting by" with a minimum of thinking, frantic memorization. I suspect that the time pressure is largely responsible for students' poor handling of mathematical word problems. Solving problems takes time; only practice in figuring things out, in exploring connections, will increase the problem solver's speed. Writing serves as a kind of pacer. It takes time to write; one has to think about what one wants to say, to whom, what words to choose, what images to create, what connections to make.

WAYS OF REPRESENTING CONCEPTS

When we talk to students about mathematical concepts and techniques, we tend to make unwarranted assumptions not only about the degree to which our listeners master our technical jargon, but about the context in which they might understand new material and about their mastery of everyday language. We are not in the habit of giving precise descriptions; we become aware of their importance mainly when we are at the receiving end, for example, when we try to learn how to use a new gadget by reading a poorly written manual.

It seems particularly difficult and tedious to explain in words familiar procedures that we "know by feel." We should rather show the students than tell them, and they often would rather imitate than hear lengthy explanations. Yet having to put something into words forces us to look closely at each step while keeping in mind the totality of steps and subprocedures in relation to the whole picture. As teachers, we want to give clear descriptions that make sense to our students. We work hard at figuring out just how to present a topic. Although the material is not new to us, we learn a great deal more about it in this process, and this may be one of the reasons we assume that our students will understand. In fact, most students will not really understand, unless they too struggle with ways of representing the material for themselves.

In our mathematics workshops Erika and I give students many opportunities to understand material by working out among themselves representations of it that are meaningful to them. I have written some pseudo-verbatim reports of such class discussions; I call them mathematical "vignettes" or "fables." They reveal the diverse ways in which students image a mathematical problem and various valid attempts at solutions. They demonstrate how different people select different parts of a problem to think about, and the open-endedness of mathematical explorations. They describe typical learning processes. In my opinion, these accounts strengthen the argument of those researchers who do not believe that the human brain is hard-wired, like a computer, but that its enormously many cells are activated in overlapping groups by our mental activity, form connections that are strengthened while others are weakened as we categorize and process what we perceive, and that it is an extremely flexible, adaptive system, constantly being modified as we re-categorize, recognize, and think (Reeke & Edelman, 1988). This theory seems in harmony with what perceptive teachers observe about how and what their students retain. They do not retrieve inert information from memory locations in their brains, but recall by association things they experienced in various contexts. Even one's memory of a particular event changes with time. Unfortunately, so does a memorized formula in many a student's mind.

I do not want to give the impression that every mathematical exploration we suggested to a class has "taken off" into fruitful directions; but even the failures have been instructive.

EXPLORING A SCHOOL MATHEMATICS PROBLEM

We assume that the people whose explorations we are observing will be led to certain conclusions. Suppose we are teachers under pressure to "cover" a given syllabus. We shall then be disappointed if our students do not reach the conclusions to which we tried to lead them. We complain that they have not learned or understood the material. We do not take time to investigate what directions our students' thoughts have taken instead. If these students are not good at verbalizing and explaining, they can neither defend the validity of, nor discover faults in, their reasoning. But to become responsible learners, students must develop their own criteria for being "right." Writing will help them do this. It will also help them convince their teachers or peers or collaborators that their thinking is valid. I would advise teachers to listen patiently and without preconceptions to the often confused, awkward student utterances. The time spent in helping students explain clearly what they mean and to subsequently examine the stated ideas will lead to major savings in instructional time later on.

A long story will illustrate how we use language and notation as a speculative tool for exploration, and why it takes so long to follow divergent paths some of which converge again to lead us on. During one of my visits to a school, I heard a teacher say: "The syllabus requires that I finish consecutive integer problems tomorrow, then do one-step equations, then two-step equations." I had learned by then which class activities usually go with these mandates. On one occasion, I visited a class where several students had had trouble with homework problems on consecutive integers. It turned out that several did not understand what "consecutive integers" were. When the problem was "gone over" in class (which usually means that either a student or the teacher puts it on the board), the meaning of "consecutive integer" was not elaborated. Yet after many such problems are "done," the phrase triggers a response: students write n, $n+1$, $n+2$, and some can actually "solve" such problems (i.e., arrive at the right answer) without knowing what consecutive integers are. The teacher is relieved at the thought that students are now prepared to answer test questions on consecutive integers, at least for the next few days. Deep in his heart, he knows something is amiss, but feels that there is no time to get to the bottom of the trouble, let alone to fix it.

Here is a "consecutive integer" problem, its solution as usually presented, followed by a leisurely treatment that would take up a whole period or more (and may therefore be rejected by the teacher or his supervisors). My aim here is to convert people to the belief that, in the long run, the leisurely treatment pays off and even saves time.

Problem and Short Solution

The first of three consecutive integers, squared, exceeds the sum of all three by 7. What are the three integers?

The integers are n, $n+1$, $n+2$. The first squared is n^2. The sum of all three is $3n+3$. The problem says $n^2=3n+3+7$, so $n^2=3n+10$,

$$n^2-3n-10=0$$
$$(n+2)(n-5)=0,$$
$$n+2=0 \quad \text{or} \quad n-5=0,$$
$$n=-2 \quad \text{or} \quad n=5.$$

The three integers are 5, 6, 7. Check: $5^2=25$ indeed exceeds $5+6+7=18$ by 7.

How about -2, -1, 0? $(-2)^2=4$, $(-2)+(-1)+0=-3$; since $4=-3+7$, the integers -2, -1, 0 also work.

Even this short solution contains more words and explanations than one customarily sees in a classroom.

Leisurely Version

Rephrasing the Question. Does everybody know what the problem is asking? "Yeah, for 3 consecutive integers." What are consecutive integers? Silence. Then, "You know, numbers like 3, 4, 5, or 10, 11, 12."

Are $3^1/_2$, $4^1/_2$, $5^1/_2$ consecutive integers? Divided opinions. Eventually, the definition of integer has to be reviewed. We need numbers that are integers *and* consecutive.

What does *consecutive* mean? Cognates such as *sequence* and *consequence* may be discussed. Some ordering principle is involved. Are 10, 9, 8 consecutive? Must we assume that the author of the problem had in mind an ordering according to increasing size when he wrote, "The first of three consecutive integers?" If so, why didn't he write "the smallest of . . . ?" Such in-context speculations about what an author had in mind are important steps in critical reading and thinking. They also help writers see how to revise their writing.

At this point students make various attempts at paraphrasing the question in writing, then read and debate until they feel they have clearly expressed the question.

Trial and Error. To actually find the three numbers, some students might first try out a few triples: Try 2, 3, 4. The square of 2 is 4, so that's no good since 4 doesn't exceed the third number, let alone the sum of all three. How about 10, 11, 12? $10^2 = 100$ exceeds 33 by much more than 7, so that's no good. Probably something in between might work. A written record of these initial guesses is extremely useful.

It is very likely that some students will hit upon a triple that does the trick by such a trial-and-error method. All who play around with it will get some practice in squaring and summing numbers, and at least a vague feeling of how quickly n^2 increases with n, compared to how slowly $3n$ increases with n. This will come in handy.

Translating into Symbols.   Even if a solution is quickly found by trial and error, the question "Are there other solutions?" comes up; students want to know if there isn't a systematic way of going about it, perhaps with the help of algebra they have learned. At this point, a translation process begins leading to an equation, that is, to a statement that two numbers constructed from the conditions of the problem are the same. This can be done in many ways; a good way to begin is to represent the numbers to be found by symbols. Since three numbers are to be found, a commonly heard suggestion is "call them x, y, z."

Are these whole numbers? Must they be positive? Which is the "first" mentioned in the problem? The first two questions are based on the meaning of *integer* and lead to the answers yes and no, respectively. The third reminds the class to consider a consecutive ordering and leads to "if x is the 'first,' i.e., the smallest, and y is the next, then y is bigger than x by one:

$$y = x+1, \qquad z = y+1 = (x+1)+1 = x+2."$$

Then, there might be a discussion of various conventions for naming things. It is customary, but by no means necessary, to assign letters from the middle of the alphabet (such as n, m) to whole numbers. Suppose we name the smallest number of our desired triple n. Then the next must be $n+1$, and the largest $n+2$. We see that the definition of *consecutive* leaves us no choice, once we have assigned the name n to the smallest.

Varying the Notation

But why give a name to the smallest? Why not to the biggest, or to the one in the middle? This would lead to three notational variants:

1. Let n be the smallest of three consecutive integers n, $n+1$, $n+2$.
2. Let ℓ be the largest of three consecutive integers. Listed in order of decreasing size, they would be ℓ, $\ell-1$, $\ell-2$.

3. Let m be the middle integer of the three. Then, in increasing order, we seek the numbers $m-1$, m, $m+1$.

At this point, we would ask one group of students to translate the conditions of the problems into symbols, using the n, $n+1$, $n+2$ notation, another group using the second notation, and a third group using the third notation. They would work simultaneously in their seats, discussing this translation and producing written versions of it. We would hope that before the period ends, at least one of these groups would be ready to present its translation to the whole class.

A student of the group working on the first notation would, with feedback from peers and teachers, eventually come up with a fairly polished written version:

The three numbers we are looking for shall be named n, $n+1$, $n+2$. The problem says that the first number squared (n^2) exceeds by 7 (is 7 more than) the sum of all three. That sum is $n+n+1+n+2=3n+3$. $3n+3$ is smaller (by 7) than n^2; to make the numbers the same, we can either add 7 to the smaller to make it as big as n^2:

$$n^2=3n+3+7 \qquad (=3n+10),$$

or we can subtract 7 from the bigger, n^2, to cut it down to the size of the sum $3n+3$:

$$n^2-7=3n+3.$$

Now that we have arrived at two equations,* let us talk about their equivalence in both, English and symbols. To say that $3n+3$, increased by 7, is the same as n^2 is equivalent (means the same) to saying that n^2, decreased by 7, is the same as $3n+3$. The words "exceed," "increase," "decrease," "the same as" become familiar and easy to relate to the operational symbols $+$, $-$, $=$; if a number is smaller than some other number, you have to add something to the smaller to make it as big as the second number.

I would assign as written homework, the technical matter of finding solutions to the equations derived under the three notational schemes.

---

*Special attention needs to be paid to the phrases "is the same as" and "is equal to." They translate into the symbol $=$, and a symbolic expression containing the symbol $=$ is called an "equation," i.e., an assertion (not necessarily true) that the thing on its left is the same as the thing on its right. I have heard several educated nonmathematicians refer to symbolic expressions as "equations" when no equals symbol was in sight.

During the following class meeting, representatives of each group would discuss their findings, giving detailed explanations of their solution attempts. These discussions may well take up another period and should end with a comparison of the three notational schemes and with a list of additional results and questions.

   Again, I summarize each of the three approaches. Something along the lines given here would be the outcome of another writing assignment, with revisions.

   First Notational Scheme.   Let n, $n+1$, $n+2$ be the desired consecutive integers, satisfying the condition $n^2 = 3n + 10$ of the problem, as we saw in class. Which number, squared, is the same as three times that number plus 10?

   If the class has studied quadratic equations, the student would subtract $3n+10$ from both of the allegedly same numbers and proceed to solve $n^2 - 3n - 10 = 0$ by finding two linear factors, $n-5$ and $n+2$, of the left side and arguing that their product can be zero only if at least one of the factors is zero. If $n-5=0$,

$$n=5, \quad n+1=6 \quad n+2=7;$$

and if $n+2=0$,

$$n=-2, \quad n+1=-1, \quad n+2=0.$$

Both would be checked. Both pass the tests of being consecutive integers and satisfying the conditions of the original problem. If the student has no experience with quadratic equations, he might make the table:

n	1	2	3	4	5	6
n^2	1	4	9	16	25	36
$3n+10$	13	16	19	22	25	28

and ask: for which n are the numbers in the second and third rows the same? He would not have to look long, but perhaps long enough to discover that entries in the last row go up by 3 for every increase of n by 1, while entries in the previous row go up by 3, 5, 7, 9, . . . No wonder the n^2 row catches up with the $3n+10$ row, although it is behind for $n=1$. (Note that the explanation of the table itself constitutes a writing exercise.)

   At this point, students might wonder if their observed patterns would continue to hold if they extended the table in both directions:

n	-4	-3	-2	-1	0	...	7	8	9
n^2	16	9	4	1	0	...	49	64	81
$3n+10$	-2	1	4	7	10	...	31	34	37

They would find more evidence for the validity of both patterns and discover the second solution, $n=-2$, of the problem at hand.

If the class has played around with computer graphics, a student might graph n^2 and $3n+10$ and be led to suspect two solutions. A more careful graph would lead him to good approximations, eventually to the exact result.

Later, one can distinguish the functions

$$\ell(x)=3x+10, \qquad q(x)=x^2$$

defined for all real x from the sequences

$$L(n)=3n+10, \qquad Q(n)=n^2,$$

and view the latter as functions defined only on the integers.

Second Notational Scheme. Let ℓ, $\ell-1$, $\ell-2$ denote the three desired numbers, ℓ standing for the largest. Then the smallest is $\ell-2$, its square is $(\ell-2)^2$, and the sum of all three is $\ell+\ell-1+\ell-2=3\ell-3$. The problem says $(\ell-2)^2$ exceeds $3\ell-3$ by 7, so

$$(\ell-2)^2=3\ell-3+7=3\ell+4$$

or

$$\ell^2-4\ell+4=3\ell+4.$$

Decreasing each of these equal numbers by 4, we find that

$$\ell^2-4\ell=3\ell,$$

and subtracting 3ℓ from each of these, that

$$\ell^2-7\ell=0.$$

The number on the left can be written as the product of ℓ and $\ell-7$, and can be zero only if at least one of the factors is zero. If $\ell=0$, we have $\ell-2=-2$, $\ell-1=-1$, $\ell=0$ as one solution of our problem; and if $\ell-7=$

0, we have $\ell-2=5$, $\ell-1=6$, $\ell=7$ as another solution. Both triples satisfy the conditions of the problem.

Third Notational Scheme. Denote the middle integer by m; then the smallest of the three is $m-1$ and the largest is $m+1$. The square of the first is $(m-1)^2$, the sum of all three is $m-1 + m + m+1 = 3m$. The problem says that

$$(m-1)^2 = 3m+7 \quad \text{or} \quad m^2-2m+1 = 3m+7.$$

If these are equal, so are the numbers obtained by subtracting $3m+7$ from each. We get

$$m^2-5m-6=0,$$

and write the number on the left as the product

$$(m+1)(m-6)=0.$$

It can vanish only if one of the factors vanishes. If $m+1=0$, we get $m=-1$, and if $m-6=0$, we get $m=6$ as our middle integer. In the first case, our triple is $m-1=-2$, $m=-1$, $m+1=0$; and in the second case, it is $m-1=5$, $m=6$, $m+1=7$. We have seen that both triples solve the given problem.

Which Notation Do You Like Best, and Why? Probably two class periods have by now been spent on one measly problem, not particularly fascinating to begin with. Remember, I did not pick the problem; it typifies a class of mandated problems. Is it better to have students work through one such problem in three different notations (we shall compare the three below, using up yet a third class period), than having students *do* about ten different "consecutive integer" problems without fancy explanations, let alone revised write-ups? Before answering this question, let us look at what we (and our students) can gain by the work of two periods and lots of verbalizing, written and oral.

What do the three notations have in common? What is different about them? Which do you like best and why?

This "compare and contrast" exercise will lead to such observations as: All three ways gave us the same two correct answers to the question posed. In all three cases, the symbolic representation of the condition stated in the problem led to a quadratic equation.

So far, no surprises. After all, what is in a name? Once you choose which of the three integers you like to name, you are stuck with names for all three and just have to use their names consistently when you write down what the problem tells you. How do you know that there are no other triples with the required properties besides the two you have found? Because, if a triple has all the properties specified by the problem, then it satisfies the equation we concocted for one of its members, and this equation has only two solutions. Some students may question this last assertion and initiate another exploration.

What is different about the three schemes? The equations look different. Some people like the first scheme best because the problem refers to the "first" of the three numbers, and so it seems natural to them to name the first. Others like the second scheme best because it leads to the easy-to-factor equation $\ell^2 - 7\ell = 0$, and they are not good at factoring quadratic trinomials. Still others like the third scheme best because it leads to such a simple expression for the sum of the three numbers; their sum is just three times the middle number! This is not so easy to spot in the other notations, but just as true since $3n + 3 = 3(n + 1)$ and $3\ell - 3 = 3(\ell - 1)$, where $n + 1$, $\ell - 1$ stand for the middle numbers in the first and second scheme, respectively. Who likes which notation is best discovered via a writing assignment: "Explain why you chose your notational scheme." This deepens the student's understanding of the meaning behind the notation and permits him to make a personal choice. It shows the reader how the learner-author connects the task at hand with her or his previous experience, taste, curiosity.

Posing Related Problems

> Suppose we had 5 consecutive integers, would their sum be just 5 times the middle integer? What about 7 consecutive integers, or any odd number of consecutive integers?

> Suppose the three integers were evenly spaced but not consecutive — say, 2 apart, like $m - 2$, m, $m + 2$; or k apart, like $m - k$, m, $m + k$? Is their sum still 3 times the middle one?

The next experiment might be a formal name change of the following kind. The group who called the smallest number n might see what happens if in any of their quadratic equations for n, they substituted $m - 1$ for n. Would they end up with one of the equations that the group who used the third notational scheme had found? What would happen if the second and third groups used tables and graphs as suggested earlier for the first? Also, what is wrong with using such graphs when the inputs (and outputs) of the function considered are integers? How do graphs of n^2 and $3n+10$ compare to those of $(\ell-2)^2$ and $3\ell+4$, or $(m-1)^2$ and $3m+7$?

Finally, what would happen if we changed the problem a little bit? What if the problem had asked for three consecutive *natural* numbers (i.e., positive whole numbers) fulfilling the other conditions? Then we would have been forced to add the requirement that the smallest member of the triple be at least 1, and this would have eliminated the non-positive solution -2, -1, 0 in all three notational schemes.

Or, suppose we had asked for three consecutive *odd* integers such that the square of the first exceeds the sum of all three by 7. If the first is odd, then its square is also odd; the sum of three odd numbers is also odd. Two odd numbers differ by an even number, so could never differ by 7, which is odd. Clearly our new problem has no solution! Suppose we tried to set it up algebraically; where would the trouble show up?

Suppose you asked for *even* consecutive integers. The square of the least is even, the sum of all three is even; again, one cannot exceed the other by the odd number 7. Conclusion: If the integers we seek differ by two (i.e., are of the form x, $x+2$, $x+4$), and the square of the smallest is required to exceed the sum of all three by 7 (or by any odd number), then the problem has no solution in integers. Can it be modified so that it has solutions which are not integers? How could you tell?

SCHOOL PROBLEMS AND MORE NATURAL PROBLEMS

If students can become involved in solving this not very interesting problem — and I have seen that they can if their oral and written contributions to its discussion are taken seriously — how much more involved might they become in tackling less artificial problems? Consecutive integers actually come up, for example, when we ask in how many ways we can select a committee of three from members of a group of fourteen people. Such combinatorial problems occur in every school curriculum, especially with the recent mandates that probability be treated early on. The expression

$$\frac{14\times13\times12}{1\times2\times3}$$

is eventually derived, and its evaluation (a good exercise in fraction reduction) yields the *integer* 364. That this is an integer is no great surprise, since you hardly expect a fractional number of differently composed committees; the *context* of the derivation furnishes the proof. Next you can answer the more general question: "Is the product of three consecutive integers always divisible by 6?" If you picture

$$\frac{n(n-1)(n-2)}{6}$$

as the number of 3-person committees that can be selected from n people, then you know the answer. But if you have never heard of combinations nor of binomial coefficients or such, you can reach the same answer to this question by entirely different means. And you can go one step further and ask if the product of any four consecutive integers is divisible by 24. These kinds of "consecutive integer" problems lead to practice in prime factorizations, and as far into elementary number theory as one wishes to go.

There are other desirable by-products. When students are asked to guess at the number of differently composed committees of 3 that can be formed from 14 people, they rarely guess so large a number as 364. There is an element of surprise, and surprise is well known to be a large factor in making us remember the surprising result. As we wonder why our guess was so far off the mark, why our intuition failed us, we rethink, revise, recategorize and see the use of mathematical principles when our intuition fails. We also begin to learn when not to trust our intuition. This, in turn, motivates us to seek convincing arguments, eventually formal mathematical proofs, in contrast to students' customary lack of motivation when introduced to proofs of assertions that are obvious to them.

ENCOURAGING, NOT MANDATING NEW APPROACHES

During the past two years, I have written about a number of interesting problems my students and I have played with. Some of my mathematical friends and colleagues like them and encourage me to use them as "curriculum materials." So why do I use the rather tedious school problem in this paper?

The reason is simple. In the schools I visit, the teachers, students, and administrators seem to be judged by the scores students get on mandated objective multiple-choice tests. Teachers work under chaotic conditions and conflicting pressures from Albany, New York City's Board of Education, their principals, their union, and so on. They feel forced to devise strict lesson plans to cover the material students will be tested on. When we talk about some alternative, perhaps less fragmented or more intuitive, approach to a lesson, they listen politely, sometimes are tempted to try something out, but then retreat to their standard lesson plans. They say: "This is enrichment material; my students can't handle it" or "my students will work only on material they are tested on." This attitude on the part of teachers is easily understandable by anybody acquainted with the conflicting pressures on teachers in our chaotic urban schools. Fortunately, there are now encouraging steps toward enhancing teacher autonomy and improving the teaching and learning atmosphere in the schools. In the meantime, I try to reach teachers in the only way I can; and that is by offering to help with what concerns them most, getting kids to perform well on tests. Since I — and many of them — believe that the important thing is getting the students to think about and explore the main topics of the syllabus, it doesn't matter so much where one begins. If it is easier to engage them in test items than in questions I consider more useful and interesting, so be it, at least for now. And this is why my tale was about a standard school problem on somebody's lesson plan. Moreover, it was useful in illustrating the role of language in eliciting the many directions this little problem initiated.

My reason for not making curriculum pieces out of my stories is that curriculum pieces get imposed on teachers, often with instructions on when and how to teach them. I fear that as curriculum pieces, my vignettes would inhibit spontaneity and teachers' imagination, whereas I wrote them to show what can sometimes happen in a class if one lets it happen and connects it with important topics to be learned.

CONCLUSIONS

What does it mean, in practice, to "let things happen?" Here, we must ask ourselves to what extent our instructional strategies are based on how children "naturally" learn by exploring in a safe and friendly environment with caring help and feedback when they need it, and to what extent our strategies, like those of most reformers, are geared to curing educational ills. Erika Duncan and I are seeing, in an elementary school with a friendly atmosphere where teachers encourage their students' exploration and build their class activities on these, that interesting things, many of them with considerable mathematical depth, happen every day. In contrast, older students in a typical mathematics class spend a period performing prescribed exercises according to somebody else's rules. Math class is disconnected from other parts of their lives. They are given little opportunity for exploring and know little about their peers except who is good at getting right answers and who is not. We have found that even in such a class, it is not difficult to engage students by asking them to play with a mathematical concept or problem, for example, to illustrate it in a meaningful context, or to rephrase a problem in a clearer or more interesting way. The words of students — spoken or written — lead to responses from their peers, sometimes to arguments. The class comes to life, mathematical debates begin and often continue even after the bell announces the formal end of the period. Homework becomes a meaningful extension of classwork and generates questions for the next class discussion.

We have also found, especially in high school and college mathematics classes full of students who view mathematics as an alien, inhuman body of formulas and techniques, that they initially resent an instructional approach that requires them to participate responsibly. Accustomed to being told what to do and how to do it, they find it difficult to suddenly accommodate freedom and muster the responsibility that such freedom necessitates, to chart their own mathematical paths. The transition from "what do you want me to do?" to "what do I need to know in order to proceed in the direction I want to pursue?" is difficult. It involves a weaning process into greater maturity, often a change in one's self-image as well as in one's view of the nature of mathematics. It is in such classes that a learning community is hard to build and, once begun, remains fragile. Even when such students become involved and are beginning to explore and ask questions, their mathematical activity may not survive the next mental challenge, or the next external stress. It is in such classes also that teachers are most often frustrated and tempted to abandon a new approach that seems to be failing, for the traditional approach that is known to have failed with respect to our serious educational goals, but that had the virtue that the teacher could be "accountable" for teaching what he was told to teach and how and when to teach it. When the student gives up responsibility for his own learning and growth in favor of external incentives — a high test score or a passing grade — then it is easy for the teacher to give up the responsibility of doing what he or she believes in, in favor of external incentives such as job security or good test scores on the part of the students.

I would like to persuade teachers (including myself) that in educational, as in mathematical, problem solving, one needs to explore the difficulties, formulate them, suggest strategies for coping with them, discuss them with colleagues, try them out and refine them. A new approach to learning mathematics may work beautifully in one class and fail dismally in another. This is no reason to give up the new approach; rather, it is a reason to try it again and look at why it worked in some settings and not in others as we study approaches to learning. By "look at" I mean finding out who our students are, how they learn, and why. Getting students to speak and write will make our challenging task easier, just as speaking and writing will make the challenging task of learning mathematics a bit easier for students. This is hard work, full of struggles and challenges, full also of deep reward and triumphs; in short, a worthwhile activity.

Acknowledgments

I gratefully acknowledge the opportunities afforded me by New York University to experiment with unorthodox instructional formats and to make possible my collaboration with Erika Duncan. Our contacts with New York City schools were established by New York University's SEHNAP under the guidance of Professor John Devine, the wise administrator of our Ford Foundation grant. I am greatly indebted to Barbara Nelson of the Ford Foundation for her deep understanding and encouragement of Language-Linked Approaches to Mathematics Instruction.

Finally, I thank my NYU "Mathink" students and the teachers, students, and administrators in the schools for what they have taught me.

REFERENCES

Orr, E. W. (1987). *Twice as less*. New York: W. W. Norton.
Reeke, G. N., & Edelman, G. (1988). Real brains and artificial intelligence. *Daedalus*, 143–174.
Tobias, S. (1985). Math anxiety and physics: Some thoughts on learning "difficult" subjects. *Physics Today, 38*(6), 60–66.

CHAPTER 20

Writing and Reading for Growth in Mathematical Reasoning

Hassler Whitney

A century ago, arithmetic was a study of the four operations taught by rote, with applications largely to agriculture and commerce. The texts gave many problems, often with numbers with four to six digits, mostly in the form of "word problems" (as we would now call them). This served the needed purposes in that period.

With the present growth of science and technology, far more complex mathematical reasoning is needed in nearly all fields, so we ask for good education in basic mathematics for all students. Unfortunately, we are too eager to embrace simplistic solutions. In particular, we want immediate learning of "math skills," assessed through standardized tests. For this, the skills are broken into tiny bites (since "the children cannot think"), taught with a myriad of objectives. Such fragmentation renders the children helpless, "proving" that they cannot think. Thus, the normal growth of children in school is largely suppressed.

How can we do better? It would be wise to start by defining the basic goals of schooling. In this complex world, the most fundamental need is surely sane decision making; for instance, to choose and work for high ideals rather than lapse into drugs and crime. Faced with an important problem, one needs to examine the situation as a whole and in all its parts and interrelations; grasp the important features as an entity, keeping full control through going back and rethinking; consider various aspects of proposed actions; and have true and open communication with others on the work. The basics for schooling are then much learning and experiencing in all phases of the process. And the needs of the students are, in brief, a full and rich self-identity allowing deep commitment, a desire to use their full powers, the use of critical thinking and flexibility to reexamine the parts and the whole, the freedom to let creative powers lead to better solutions, acceptance and respect of others and self, and a sense of responsibility for actions.

In the remarkable growth and learning of preschoolers, in complex and subtle situations impossible to teach, we see the natural powers of humans blossoming. Our primary responsibility to the children and to the world is to give students support and nourishment, to let this blossoming continue through the long span of years to adulthood. This chapter illustrates such growth at a halfway point, in junior high school. The four children working in a group are a composite of my twenty years of experience with children of all ages. The mixture of little progress and spurts with new ideas that I describe occur naturally in all real learning situations. The great blocks to improvement in the schools are also discussed briefly.

INVESTIGATING AND COMMUNICATING

The following scenario is about Mrs. Mullin's junior high class. She is learning how to present material less and let the children explore situations more. Increasingly, the class breaks up into groups; the groups share with each other when there are interesting findings.

As the children came in from the playground, one asked "How fast do you bike?" This started a series of questions for the groups. We follow a group of four children through six or eight sessions, picking out those sessions in which real advances were made; some sessions seemed to get nowhere, but in fact gave basic clues for later work. Soon the group makes the question more specific. Alex and Carla think, a car has a speedometer; can we find a bike with one? Betty and Dan ask, "*What is* speed?" and come out with, "If you go faster, you get there sooner." Then they all remember Mrs. Mullin's advice: "*Make it real; act the story!*" So Carla and Alex walk together, Carla pretending to pedal with her hands, while Alex, in a "car," looks at the speedometer. Betty and Dan pick up the words "get there;" Betty walks from one chair to another, while Dan checks her time.

Each suggestion becomes a project. They have become involved, and tell Mrs. Mullin their plans. "That was quick work!" responds Mrs. Mullin. "Write out just what each said, and how you got the ideas. Then you can look back at it. You are learning how to learn!" The projects were not easy to organize. But in a couple of weeks they reported to the whole class as follows:

Story I. Alex and Carla walk together, Carla "pedaling" with her hands, Alex talking. They draw the picture in Figure 20.1. Alex

Figure 20.1   Alex and Carla's drawing

explains, "Carla is biking, my friend is driving, I am watching the speedometer. It says 15 miles per hour."

Story II. Betty and Dan act their story as Betty talks, "With a 50-foot tape, we are measuring 200 feet. Now I get ready to start. Dan, at that end, calls 'One, two, three, go!' and I bike. When I reach him, it was just over ten seconds." (See Figure 20.2.)

Mrs. Mullin asks the group to write an account of all this. Also, she wants them to make careful drawings, working together so they are clear. Then they discuss all the happenings, particularly to see not only *what* they learned, but *how* they found out, how they got their ideas. At the next session, they comment in various ways.

DAN: In the first picture [Figure 20.1], I can't see what is happening.
CARLA: In the second picture [Figure 20.2], did Dan bike too? There is a watch at both ends.
DAN: Why is there only one bike in the first picture but two in the second? The car and the bike look as though they were just sitting there.
BETTY: How can one show that the car is *moving*?
CARLA: I saw a photo of a car moving so fast that it was blurred at both ends.
ALEX: I'll put little lines in front and in back of the car to show this.

By now they are talking animatedly, several at once, and Mrs. Mullin comes over.

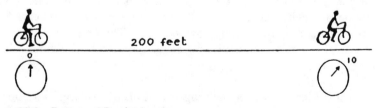

Figure 20.2   Betty and Dan's drawing

MRS. M.: PAUSE! You're talking but *not listening* enough. Pauses enable you to collect thoughts. Write down everything you can that was said. I hear fine ideas coming out.

At the next session, they are more subdued and more deeply involved.

BETTY: I realized that if I think more carefully, I can say it shorter and more simply, and perhaps you can hear me better.

DAN (also speaking more slowly): In the second picture, I see *both* 200 feet *and* 10 seconds; in the first, I see *only* 15 miles an hour without my knowing how it did that.

ALEX: But *you* have to believe *two* figures, 200 and 10, and *I* only have to believe *one*, 15.

They decide on a short summary:

1. See 15 miles per hour.
2. See 200 feet *and* 10 seconds.

Suddenly they realize that they do not yet know which is the faster! But they are now much more interested in the whole process and how they are learning than in that one little question. They are truly involved in their growth in learning.

CARLA: What *is* "miles per hour"?

The group is quiet. They are thinking: Teachers explain things, "concepts," like speed, but we never understand.

BETTY: When you drive, your speed changes; you don't do 15 miles an hour for an hour.

CARLA: But 200 feet and 10 seconds are real things; how can you make *miles an hour* real?

DAN: What is *fifteen* miles an hour; does that make it more real?

Suddenly it is all clear. "200 feet in 10 seconds" is like "15 miles in one hour." And if you want your speed *at a moment*, if your speed is changing, you must take a short time (or distance), and find the corresponding distance (or time).

They now feel ready to ask "Which is faster?" And they quickly agree on turning "15 miles per hour" into a short distance and time. Dan draws a picture (Figure 20.3).

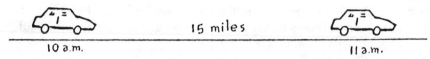

Figure 20.3   Dan's new drawing

ALEX: It's awfully slow. I'm sure they stopped for a drink.
CARLA: Divide that into three equal parts. That's five miles in twenty
  minutes.
DAN: And that's one mile in four minutes!
BETTY: How many feet in a mile?
ALEX: 5,280. What is a fourth of that?

So they quickly get 1,320 feet in one minute; that is, 60 seconds, or
220 feet in 10 seconds. So Carla was biking just a bit faster than Betty —
that is, if those figures 15, 200, and 10 were correct.

In the next meeting, Mrs. Mullin says she has never seen "changing
units" for velocity done in that way. Why do they think it is correct? Do
they *believe* they have it right? They express certainty about this; it is all so
simple and clear!

MRS. M.: Can you write this up in a simplified form, so others can see
  what you did, and understand and believe it?
BETTY: What we did is just like fractions! If we think of, divide the top and
  the bottom by 3, we get:

$$\frac{15 \text{ miles}}{60 \text{ minutes}} = \frac{3 \times 5 \text{ miles}}{3 \times 20 \text{ minutes}} = \frac{5 \text{ miles}}{20 \text{ minutes}} = \frac{1 \text{ mile}}{4 \text{ minutes}}$$

ALEX: But how about that change from 1 hour to 60 minutes?
DAN: Can you write 1 hour = 60 minutes?
CARLA: Certainly one hour is the same as 60 minutes. Cook the roast for
  one hour, or for 60 minutes, it's the same.
BETTY: So whether you can write = or not; it's merely convention. You can
  choose to write 1 hour = 60 minutes, or choose not to. But the meanings are the same.

In one more session, they discuss what "speed at a certain moment"
means. They quickly agree: Just take how far it goes in a very short time;
and the shorter a time you take, the more accurate the speed will be. Then
they add, this supposes that the speed does not suddenly jump, like the
speed of a bullet when you fire a gun. Yet even then, say when the bullet is

halfway out, if you take a millionth of a second, you will probably get an accurate speed. In the fancy language used in calculus, the children have defined the "derivative," and used it not with numbers but with physical quantities. See Whitney (1968) for a full description.

So far, we have seen how a math classroom may, as part of its functioning, break into groups that explore situations with mathematical content and how, through taking responsibility for and control over their work, the members may grow in power and learning in the finest way. A basic part of the process was the constant recording of what has been happening, followed by reading the record and continuing further explorations with greater control and a broader view of the parts in the whole.

TAKING CONTROL

Next, we give an example of testing "problem solving" in a school-like setting. The National Assessment of Educational Progress gave 9-year-olds with calculators a variant of the following problem:

A class of 26 children is making a trip to a museum; cars will be available. If each car can take four children, how many cars are needed?

First, think about children you know; can they find the answer? Next, try the problem on different children in different circumstances. Can they use any materials they please? Can they work with other children? Do they feel pressure to come quickly to an answer? Personally, I believe any children who have an understanding of numbers to 30 will be quite capable of finding the answer — and being sure of it.

On the assessment, 3 percent gave the right answer. Why this near-total failure? Did they guess "it is division" and push buttons, copying what they saw? If so, what are their *attitudes* about school math and about finding out about numbers? Incidentally, 12 percent chose 6.5 and 7 percent chose 65 as the answer. We hear a great deal about "using technology to help teach problem solving." Does it always help?

My point is that working for a certain objective without considering the whole situation may be futile; the children are most commonly only trying to learn the rules of the day, and direct attempts to get them "achieving" through giving correct answers will leave the basic cause of failure untouched. Children must learn to adapt meanings to their own purposes. I illustrate this with an example.

A recent publication speaks of teaching a group of children how to find the year of their birth, using a certain type of calculator. It can be paraphrased as follows:

> Ask the children to enter into their calculators, first, the year of their last birthday. Then press [−] and 1. Now press [=] once for each year of their age. Finally, read the answer in the display.

This can be deciphered. But it is pure rote. Does it help your growth?

But suppose a child with joy in life and growing reads this, and he or she has had some practice in the symbols used. The child may wonder, "This looks funny; why does it work?" but find the task of studying it laborious. Next may come "It must be simple, I will work it out myself." Some possible further thoughts are as follows:

"I was born long ago, I am nine; I can't see how to find the year." And later: "What is time? How can I act it out? Well, it keeps moving ahead, like this" (walking, or sweeping an arm). This may give a further idea: Record, or picture it: Draw a line. Suddenly a tool is at hand (and the thought "*I* have found the tool!"). So the moment of birth is marked on the line, and "now" is marked to the right. Next may come, "Here I was one year old," marking that part of the line. From here on, there is little difficulty (if the child is happy to make several trials). This child has made a great advance in power.

MATH ANXIETY OR POWERFUL REASONING?

Most students get math anxiety to varying extents, in elementary school or junior high; and algebra brings it on more strongly yet. A basic reason for the latter is that those terms "variable" and "equation" are a mystery; furthermore, students never *use* algebra for *their* purposes, so they have no way of *looking for meanings*. Let us pose the following as a more natural question for our students to explore:

You have heard that if a square has side length s, then the length of a diagonal is $\sqrt{2}$ times s. What sort of number is $\sqrt{2}$?

You try decimals, and find that $(1.4)^2$ (which means 1.4×1.4) is 1.96, and $(1.5)^2 = 2.25$. So $\sqrt{2}$ is a bit more than 1.4. You could continue guessing, getting more accurate values.

But since you have learned that exploration is easy, fun, and very educational, you want to find a good process for finding $\sqrt{2}$. Instead of 1.4, *about* how much more is needed? Would a picture help?

Draw that square of side 1.4; its area is 1.96. Now we want to add a little, an *extra* amount, to 1.4, to give a square of area 2 (see Figure 20.4).

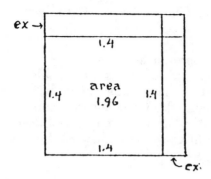

Figure 20.4   Drawing to clarify the calculation of √2

We can *see* that extra area; two rectangles and a little square, of total area that must be .04. Using "ex" to mean extra, each rectangle has area 1.4×ex, and the little square, area ex×ex. These three areas must add up to .04, so we must have:

2.8×ex plus ex×ex is .04.

Do we dare write + for plus and = for is? Perhaps yes, provided we remember what we mean by them! Then why not write x for "ex," too? This now gives:

$2.8x + x^2 = .04$.

Looking at *this*, our anxiety may arise again; it looks like algebra! Worse yet, we see that we have written a quadratic equation, and we *ought* to solve it! (To the reader: Do this, see what you get.)

So we hastily put this aside, and look at the picture again. We have made that ex much too large; so really the little square is very tiny. Oh, then we can forget it, and find (using a calculator if desired):

$$x = \frac{.04}{2.8} = .014,$$

and √2 is 1.4+x=1.414, approximately.

But we dropped that tiny square; what difference does it make? Oh, we know its area! It is $(.014)^2 = .000196$. So the rectangles need only add up to .04 minus this, which is .039804. What fun! Now:

$$x = \frac{.039804}{2.8} = .014215$$

and $\sqrt{2} = 1.414215$, approximately.

We may be *told* that we have used a *variable*, x, and *equations*. We needn't be bothered, *we* know what *we* meant, so we do not have to understand their strange definitions and explanations. Moreover, we have found a way to *write* what we are doing, and then *read* it to get fuller understanding. And that was how we succeeded so admirably!

FACING BASIC ISSUES

We have seen the great contrast between what could be and what is. Note that the aforementioned 3 percent success on the problem of the 26 children implies at most 15 percent success among the top 20 percent of students; and the failing ones certainly have no real control over their work, have math anxiety, and are probably lost to future math and science applications.

There is an increasing crisis in the poor, especially urban, school districts. The public is demanding improvements, and state departments of education commonly call for more monitoring and testing, and raising test scores. They put pressure on districts and schools, and the teachers are forced to focus strongly on tests, with more drill and insistence on lots of right answers. No freedom for students to look for meanings or use results is left; they guess what to do, and thus are learning rituals, not math. Seeing subtraction, for instance, as one process is now impossible, the mass of rules for this cannot be fathomed, and scores are apt to go down rather than up. Hence the departments add to the pressure, and the destructive cycle is firmly in place. So the students become still more apathetic, and start dropping out sooner. Here is the real tragedy in the urban districts.

We seem to be blind to the direct contradiction in the "accountability": "They *must* learn basic skills!" But a *skill* must be controlled, and an answer found by guessing is not controlled. The joker is that test *scores* mean counting answers only, where the count should be zero when there is no meaningful question visible to the test taker. Answers without questions have no value. So the accountability is essentially a misnomer, and the whole process is a sham. In trying to avert tragedy, we push students further into it.

We have understood the essence of this process for decades if not centuries. As long as we hide from it, the crisis will grow. We need to require from the groups in power full communication and cooperation and a resolute facing of the issues. We need to require sane decision making, including evaluation of all actions planned or taken, using true goals, including state goals, as the basis.

And badly missing is full communication with the students, finding from them their attitudes and all that is happening with them. Of course teachers must be included here. The dynamics of the failure are studied in Whitney (1985, 1987); we need to extend this.

We can regain faith in the children and teachers if we study carefully Benezet (1935, 1936); his extraordinary account of change to high-level growth is a model we cannot afford to forget. I have seen what those children are capable of in all sorts of situations. So I close with this challenge.

REFERENCES

Benezet, L. P. (1935, 1936). The story of an experiment. *Journal of the National Education Association, 24,* 241–244 and 301–303; *25,* 7–8.

Whitney, H. (1968). The mathematics of physical quantities, Part II. *American Mathematical Monthly, 75*(3), 227–256.

Whitney, H. (1985). Taking responsibility in school mathematics education. *Journal of Mathematical Behavior, 4,* 219–235.

Whitney, H. (1987). Coming alive in school math and beyond. *Educational Studies in Mathematics, 18,* 229–242.

CHAPTER 21

The Dignity Quotient

Dale Worsley

The world is a remarkable place, filled with curiosities and mysteries. As Claude Monet, the French Impressionist, said, "By expanding our vision of the world, we enlarge our knowledge of self." Beginning with themselves, high school students ought to be able to grasp a considerable amount of interesting and pertinent information about the world. The information is at their fingertips, in the newspapers, in the library, in the classroom, and in the evidence of their senses. They ought to be able to develop it along any number of different lines, moving from hypothesis to proposition to theory to proof and back, inductively and deductively, mingling fact, opinion, speculation, example, and observation as needs be. They would be most motivated to do this if allowed to follow the line of development that interests them most. They are young, full of vitality and intelligence. With encouragement from teachers, they should be able to overcome their fear of mysteries and explore them with open minds. They should be able to experience deep satisfaction in the discoveries they make, and the contemplation and ordering of these discoveries should be a pleasure. Learning that others have made similar discoveries before them should be an inspiration. The quality of their writing should reflect their satisfaction, pleasure, and inspiration. Its accuracy and thoroughness should be a sign of their experience.

So I theorized in 1986 when I began a series of science writing workshops at a New York City public high school for select, primarily minority students. The school had been in existence four years. The academic goal was to "provide for the technological needs of the nation," as one of the founders put it. It was a matter of record that the school was successful. Every student in the first class to go through grades 9–12 graduated and went to college. An indication of the strength of purpose of the administrators, teachers, and students alike was that they decided together to adopt an extra period over the schoolday's standard eight.

Along with my theory that these, or, for that matter, *any* students ought to enjoy science writing, I brought a full complement of experience and tools to my workshops: I was a writer of novels and plays that often explored scientific subjects. I had been conducting creative writing workshops in public schools for years through Teachers & Writers Collaborative (see Worsley, 1987; Mayer and Worsley, 1988). And I had learned how to use dialectical notebooks, directed freewriting, summary writing and many other techniques at the Institute for Writing and Thinking's Math and Science Writing workshops.

In two years of work on the science-writing project I saw dismal failures, shining successes, and everything in between. I discerned a correlation between the success rate of the students' writing and the presence of a quality that, to my knowledge, has never been measured scientifically, but that probably should be: dignity.

In the class of a teacher who respected the students enough to listen to their ideas, nearly every student produced a well-developed essay. In the class of another teacher, who merely sat sourly in front of the class and wrote an assignment on the board in what appeared to be an act of self-defense, every student talked throughout the period. Not even shouting got their attention. When I asked the teacher to do something about it, she said, "I can't give them *all* zeros." Not one essay was produced in her class.

Many classrooms in the school had broken windows, dingy walls, and desks with no tops. With effort these irritations could be ignored, but it was impossible for students to write in the classroom where they had to sit on one another's laps for lack of enough chairs. Did the custodians' union, the party most responsible for these conditions, consider maintaining dignified learning environments a priority item for its next contract negotiations? If not, why not?

When I was setting up my classes, I discovered that ninth-grade physical science classes and a couple of senior classes were open to me but none of the Regents classes were scheduled to have a writer in residence. (The school subscribes to New York's Regents system, which provides a rigorous curriculum and standardized tests to guarantee the quality of the education of those students who intend to go to college.) When I asked to see examples of the Regents students' writing I was handed a stack of lab reports, apparently the only writing they did in Regents classes. A science teacher lamented, "The communication skills of the students are very low." I had to agree. Many of the reports were incomprehensible. The best were grammatically passable but still contained only spit-back information. In fact, the lab reports did not constitute writing; they were simply notations. The situation called for drastic measures not only to improve the students' literacy, but to provide opportunities for deeper thinking about the subject matter. "There's no way I can be squeezed into *any* of the Regents classes?" I asked administrators. "Absolutely not," was the response. "We agree with you that the students need work with their writing, but the time is too tight. We have to be sure to cover all the material in the syllabus."

Joe Ciparick, a chemistry teacher, said, "I want to teach *science*. I want to give my students a vision of what true science is all about, and invoke a sense of wonder and enthusiasm. I want to introduce them to the rigors of science, and try to get them to appreciate the sweat and hard work that scientific research demands. But I can't. In order to cover the 11 or 12 units of the New York State Regents syllabus, I must move on whenever there is an opportunity to treat an interesting topic in depth. Someone has decided that the students must learn all the 'basics' in their one-year course. More and more after teaching these 'basics,' I wonder, 'Why?'"

One of the students who had been admitted to an elite group called "General Electric scholars" said, "I'm frustrated both ways. If the teacher is teaching for the Regents, it's not interesting, and if he isn't, I still have to take the Regents tests."

Another G.E. scholar said, "You could be a 98 student and they say 'Regents' and your thoughts go all to pieces."

Where is the dignity of administrators when they are not given enough authority to alter the curriculum to address a terrible deficiency among their students? Where is the dignity of teachers when they are not allowed to treat interesting topics in depth? Where is the dignity of students when their thoughts can be shattered by a single word?

The tail that wags the dog of curriculum is testing. Administrators in my school, as in many schools ruled by centralized testing, commonly advise teachers to "teach for the test." If all the students who graduated from the first senior class in my school went to college, chances are they performed well on their Regents tests. Those who follow will probably also perform well, but are they being equipped to become good scientists? On the contrary, "teaching for the test" sets them up to fail when confronted with the problem-solving situations faced by advanced students and professional scientists. Speaking at the Institute for Writing and Thinking's 1987 conference on "The Role of Writing in Learning Math and Science" at Bard College, astrophysicist David Layzer (see Chapter 10) said, "Students have to relearn their whole experience very quickly. Even the brightest have trouble doing it. Going from plugging numbers into formulas to understanding *real* math and physics can be fatal." Such a death cannot be a dignified one.

I was working in a tenth-grade English class where there was time to write science essays and we had just concluded a discussion of evolution. The topic was pertinent in part because the students were learning about meiosis and mitosis in their biology class, where, once again, there was no *time* to put their learning into this larger context. A student's summary writing read, in part: "Maybe humans derived from apes and monkeys, but then again, they are very different in culture, appearance and intelligence. They are somewhat intelligent but still have not reached the brain's ability to suck in more and more information. . . . " Note that she said "*suck in* more and more information" instead of *think*. Surely "sucking in information," a mechanical act, isn't so dignified as thinking, a human one. Do we consider young people to be no more than data-processing machines?

I developed, inspired, thoroughly researched, and revised essays with students in a general physics class that wasn't part of the Regents curriculum. Comparing the students' interest in and respect for my efforts with the dullness and disrespect he often saw for their usual curriculum, their teacher said to me, "We have failed these students in science education." While I was personally pleased at both the success of my workshop and his praise of it, I attribute it to the application of ideas that were the same or similar to those expressed in speeches by other participants in the Bard conference.

Sheila Tobias (see Chapter 4) indicated that time pressures and stage-fright might lie at the root of math anxiety, making us realize that patience and calmness, two qualities associated with dignity, need to be incorporated into our teaching methods. (Taking the political measures necessary to incorporate them would clearly benefit society: creative thinkers currently excluded from science and math professions would be permitted to make their contributions.)

Educational policy throughout the country seems to swing back and forth between competitive, quantitative standards and cooperative, qualitative ones. What if we stepped away from that grandfather's clock of a dialectic into the world Hassler Whitney (see Chapter 20) described, where the cooperation of all concerned in helping children grow toward their futures is achieved? Imagine the dignity of that.

Erika Duncan (see Chapter 18) spoke of the need to foster a greater tolerance for ambiguity among both teachers and students. It's more dignified to ask questions than to live in fear of being discovered ignorant. To make a mistake entails no loss of dignity, but to be expected not to make mistakes certainly does.

Marcia Birken (see Chapter 3) mentioned the difficulty of persuading colleagues too distrustful or fearful of using writing as a learning tool in their classes. It is a difficulty worth overcoming. I once persuaded a chemistry teacher to have his students use directed freewriting and summary writing to design their own lab experiments. He reported that the students got excited and learned the concepts better than when they had used prescribed designs, because the risk that the experiments might fail forced them to make their observations more objectively. When experiments did fail, students revised their designs after discussions with groups whose experiments had succeeded. Altogether the writing techniques were a success. A math teacher working with underachievers reported a similar success. He said it was remarkable how much easier grasping difficult concepts was when the students wrote narrative definitions of them. Nonetheless, when I asked the teachers if they were going to continue using writing as a learning tool in their classes, they both said no. There wouldn't be enough *time* to cover the rest of the work. There was no dignity in the expressions of defeat on their faces.

Anneli Lax (see Chapter 19) noted the importance of pace, of feeling free to interrupt professors to ask them questions. A professor who is no easier to stop than a talking head on television is not according his students respect.

William Mullin (see Chapter 16) expressed concern that learning be open enough to allow students' intuition to function. I share this concern: In one of my novels an artist finds his way to meaningful work via his intuition. (I am glad two men are concerned with the issue, because it relieves women of the undignified old husband's tale that intuition operates only in their province.) James Gleick (1988), writing Richard Feynman's obituary in the *New York Times*, recounted the story of how Feynman and fellow Cal Tech physicist Murray Gell-Mann explained interactions of the weak force in terms of such particle properties as spin, but their theory ran counter to specific laboratory evidence. Thinking that their theory was too simple, straightforward, and beautiful to be wrong— sticking to their intuition—they did not give it up, however, and errors were subsequently discovered in the evidence. Truth perceived by intuition must ultimately stand the test of reason, of course, but it is a key to learning and discovery because it validates the authority of the student and the scientist. Is there dignity in an environment where intuition is irrelevant?

My workshops were based on the idea that students could write science essays best if they began with their own preoccupations before directing their attention to the subjects of their science classes. Judging by the excellence of the essays they produced in dignified classrooms, the idea was sound.

Encouraging students to begin their projects by writing about themselves validated their world view. When they realized their whole nature was being recognized, they were in turn willing to approach the whole nature of their subjects. One of the more salient aspects of students' natures, often ignored by the syllabus, is their idealism. Ignoring it is regrettable, because besides being an unlimited source of motivation, idealism is the cable that binds science to real-life situations and invests it with personal meaning — and isn't science without meaning the hubris of our age?

Writing narratively about topics of interest not only makes study more relevant, it increases the accuracy and systematic thoroughness of the students' work. It does so because narration uses metaphor and simile, powerful tools of visualization and discernment, which are two central goals of scientific study.

Narrative in the science classroom has another power. It is by hearing accounts of those who have made scientific discoveries before us, the Galileos, Newtons, and Curies, that students appreciate them for the life they have breathed into history rather than resent them for the monumental immutability of their theories and formulas. Young scientists need the liberation of myths, not the oppression of authority, if they are to acquire the dignity of thinkers.

While ingesting and regurgitating dry facts may not hurt a machine, it is painful for human beings, who need their facts "wet," if you will, in order to digest them. It is painful for those who dry them out, those who eat them, and those who catch them for analysis when they are vomited back. Digesting dry facts is painful, but to think and write one's thoughts is a pleasure, albeit often a demanding one. Given an informed choice, students prefer this pleasure.

In 1880, in an address delivered at the opening of Sir Josiah Mason's Science College, in Birmingham, England (Gardner, 1984), Thomas Henry Huxley said, "A pleasure-loving character will have pleasure of some sort; but, if you give him the choice, he may prefer pleasures which do not degrade him to those who do" (p. 146). While Huxley was referring specifically to the few worthy consumer goods being created by industry more than a century ago, his comment applies equally to teaching methods today. The *raison d'être* for the creation of the school I worked in, as stated by one of its founders, was to "provide for the technological needs of the nation." I wonder, like Huxley, "if the increasing perfection of manufacturing processes [read: technology] is to be accompanied by an increasing debasement of those who carry them on" (p. 146). Debasement is indignity. Have we structured it into our educational systems?

If a device (a "respectograph?") were invented to measure dignity, and the results indicated that a correlation existed between the presence of dignity and the quality of learning, would we restructure our systems accordingly? A good way to begin would be to permit meaningful writing in the study of science and mathematics.

REFERENCES

Gardner, M. (ed.). (1984). Science and culture. In *The Sacred Beetle and Other Great Essays in Science* (pp. 130–148). Buffalo, NY: Prometheus Books.

Gleick, J. (1988, February 17). Richard Feynman dead at 69: Leading theoretical physicist. *New York Times*, p. 1.

Mayer, B., & Worsley, D. (1988). *Science writing*. New York: Teachers & Writers Collaborative.

Worsley, D. (1987, May–June). Writing at the races: Science essays in a public high school. *Teachers & Writers Magazine*, pp. 1–9.

Part VI

RESPONSES

The proposal that more written language will improve students' learning of mathematics and science, and suggestions in the twenty-one prior essays as to how this be done, are still novel. Reflection and experimentation must continue. In the closing section of this book, Professors Vera John-Steiner and Reuben Hersh were invited to begin that reflection by reviewing the other essays in the collection and by responding freely to them in a "meta-essay" that looked for patterns and polarities and commented on issues relevant to their own teaching experience.

Vera John-Steiner, a distinguished psycholinguist, examines the connections between this movement and other contemporary educational innovations, and highlights the influence of Bruner, Freire, Polya, and Vygotsky. She notes that the influence of these four innovative thinkers become clearly apparent when one compares their approaches to more traditional education. In discussing the "writing-to-learn" approach to mathematics, Reuben Hersh, co-author of the award winning book, *The Mathematical Experience* (Boston: Birkhauser, 1980), concentrates on writing-to-learn's implication for college teaching and the mathematics professsion.

CHAPTER 22

Is Mathematics a Language?

Vera John-Steiner

Starting in the late 1950s, the documentation of the processes of thought has shifted from an exclusive reliance on laboratory studies to work conducted in naturalistic settings. Central to such development has been the work of Jerome Bruner, whose book *A Study of Thinking* (1956/1986) was instrumental in defining the "cognitive revolution": "Flying in the face of established behaviorist methodology, the subjects were treated as active, constructive problem solvers, rather than simple reactors to the stimuli presented to them. Their introspections actually mattered" (Gardner, 1987, p. 94). While some of these early studies focused upon categorization and classification tasks, there is now interest in an examination of long-term cognitive strategies and their relevance to real-life settings. The most effective way of conducting such studies is through the collaborative efforts of cognitive psychologists and specialists in diverse domains of learning, for instance, mathematics.

The effectiveness of such collaboration has been enhanced by parallel developments in a number of fields where learning is explored from a process point of view rather than through a focus upon its products. Indeed, the most striking commonality in these varied essays on the role of writing in learning mathematics and science is that all the authors focus on process approaches to their subjects. In describing her approach to teaching mathematics through writing, Barbara Rose in Chapter 2 states: "Unlike the more traditional view, which defined writing as a product, newer theories of composition understand writing as a unique learning strategy in which process is at least as important as product."

This strong emphasis on process approaches is not only part of the rapid development of cognitive science in the last three decades; it also is a reflection of the impact of the social theorists of thought. While Jean Piaget laid the foundations for the contemporary study of cognitive development, L. S. Vygotsky's role in emphasizing the social aspects of the transmission of knowledge from one generation to the next has greatly affected our understanding of the impact of history and culture in shaping cognitive patterns of language use. Vygotsky's influence is particularly striking in the examination of the role of language in thought. Paul Connolly, writing within the Vygotskian tradition in his introductory essay to this book, emphasizes the functions of language as a communicative as well as a reflective instrument

> through which we think, alone or with others, about what we are doing. Our natural language, operating as the "metadiscourse" of all our other symbol systems, from math through money, from dance to drawing, enables us to distance ourselves from, for example, our own mathematical problem solving, and reflect on our procedure, thereby making knowledge of it.

In this description Connolly expands on the Vygotskian notion that speech is the bridge between social and individual behavior; it is the way in which knowledge is internalized and transformed to best suit the individual speaker's need to know, remember, and create. Is mathematics, then, another form of knowledge elaborated by a language system? The authors of these chapters assume that an important core exists common to human language and mathematics. That commonality is most striking at the conceptual rather than the communicative level. In Chapter 13 Powell and López quote Jerome Bruner (1968), who "advised that both writing and mathematics were 'devices for ordering thoughts about things and thoughts about thoughts.'"

While the construction of systems of thought is a potential of all varieties of human symbolic exchanges, the ways in which symbols are constructed in language differ from their use in mathematics. As Sheila Tobias suggests in Chapter 4,

> [In books on other subjects], clarity is achieved through repetition, using different words to restate a single idea, slowing the pace, using a spiral kind of organization that keeps coming back to the same idea at different levels, using topic and summary sentences to nail down what the paragraph contains, and always foreshadowing the points to be made later on. . . . [But] in mathematical writing clarification is achieved by constructing very precise sentences without any extra words.

The precision of mathematical symbols requires sustained effort at constructing meaning that provides a concrete equivalent to symbolic representation. Frequently students, when confronted with precise symbols that have a given meaning and that are embedded in a large set of presuppositions, resort to memorization. In this way, they fail to engage in the demanding endeavor of mastering the essential meaning of these symbols. In spoken language, we rely on varied forms of negotiation with other speakers that are external to the language system. Rephrasing, question asking, the redundancy of many utterances all contribute to achieving comprehension through successive approximations. The authors represented in this book are exploring ways students of mathematics can also be given opportunities to talk to themselves as well as to their peers as they do problems. As Russel W. Kenyon suggests in Chapter 6, the use of writing enhances cognitive learning in mathematics:

> As an example, . . . consider that solving an equation is undoing what has been done to a variable. . . . A similar technique is to ask students to write the steps to a problem solution. Nonmathematical problems work as well as mathematical ones here. For example, ask students to describe how to build a tower using blocks of different sizes and colors. Then have the students exchange their solutions and attempt to rebuild the tower using only the given instructions. Finally, have the students evaluate their solution by discussing the results of the tower construction. The same procedure can be used with a mathematical solution.

The varied techniques suggested in this book encourage reliance upon writing in order to achieve the following results: the clarification of mathematical concepts, the construction of connections across different units of learning, and even more importantly, the internalization of mathematical concepts and thus their appropriation into the learner's own words and thought processes. Some of the techniques are aimed at helping students use the resources of human speech as tools of reflection about mathematics as part of their personal experience; e.g., keeping journals in which they record the application of mathematics in their daily experience, writing personal letters in which they offer advice concerning the solution of a mathematical problem. Some writing exercises are meant to extend the students' communicative use of language while deepening their perspective of the scholarly discipline of mathematics, as when writing a report on the history of the origins of a particular measurement or an evaluative essay on a biography of a famous mathematician.

Of no less importance are writing exercises that encourage students to explore areas of anxiety and confusion in their study of mathematics. In Chapter 4 Sheila Tobias describes, in her treatment of comfort/non-comfort zones of experience, how students, through written self-expression, learn to monitor themselves in the non-comfort zone of mathematics. She suggests in addition another form of writing, the "Divided Page Exercise," which also encourages students to confront and so cope with their anxiety thresholds while learning mathematics. Here students express their negative feelings and confusions while in the process of laying out mathematical problems and calculations.

Such exercises can be as significant to instructors as to students. As Anneli Lax suggests in Chapter 19:

> We and our students need feedback to strike the right balance, and time to learn how to use the common language. When students talk to each other and to us about their attempts at solutions, when they try to convince one another of their mathematical deductions, find fallacies, and repair them; and when they write down their findings, they feel more and more at home with our linguistic and notational conventions. Most important, they see that this is just what these are — conventions or tacit agreements, not mathematical rules or magic mantras.

In exploring the utility of language approaches to the study of mathematics, one cannot ignore David Layzer's admonition in Chapter 10 when he suggests that

> Mathematics, by contrast, is an unnatural language. It is the medium in which one thinks and speaks of worlds that impinge on but don't coincide with the world of ordinary experience — the world of ideal geometric figures or the world of numbers, for example. Mathematical terms derive their meanings not from experience but from axioms. Axioms are, in a sense, definitions (they are sometimes called implicit definitions), but they differ in a crucial respect from the definitions one finds in a dictionary: they don't refer, directly or indirectly, to ordinary experience.

Ordinary language and the language of mathematics have many features in common, even though as symbol structures they are not identical. Writing can scaffold the acquisition of the more abstract system by linking it to the experiences it regularly mediates. The drive to achieve precision in words or symbols can be empowered by using these two symbol systems in interaction with each other; such strengthened accuracy in the communication of mathematics is what the writing techniques described by the authors of this anthology attempt to facilitate, directly or indirectly. Conversely, the clarity of mathematical expression has entered into ordinary discourse, particularly at a time when mathematics is increasingly needed for the understanding of contemporary science. As Layzer suggests, "Mathematics is the language in which the book of nature is written. To read the book, we must learn the language; no adequate translation exists."

But the teaching of so important a language does not depend upon a single approach, nor does it imply a sole reliance upon deductive methods. Indeed, in the spirit of George Polya's classic essay on mathematical problem solving entitled *How to Solve It*, more and more gifted teachers of mathematics rely upon inductive, inferential approaches, making connections through many means, building on past knowledge and acts of intuitive cognition, many of which are effectively described in this stimulating volume. The writing-to-learn movement in mathematics and science, however, has a unifying purpose, that of attaining more reasonable, realistic means of communication in the realm of higher education in those fields. This book describes very clearly ways of achieving such communication.

REFERENCES

Bruner, J. S. (1986). *A study of thinking*. New Brunswick, NJ: Transaction Books. (Original work published 1956)
Bruner, J. S. (1968). *Toward a theory of instruction*. New York: W. W. Norton.
Gardner, H. (1987). *The mind's new science: A history of the cognitive revolution*. New York: Basic Books.
Polya, G. (1945). *How to solve it*. Princeton, NJ: Princeton University Press.

CHAPTER 23

A Mathematician's Perspective

Reuben Hersh

I am a math teacher in a large state university in the Southwest. I have been teaching here for over 20 years, with interludes visiting at other schools. I am a liberal-minded, progressive teacher. I use and propagate the teaching ideas of Georg Polya (1945) as much as I can. I have friends in colleges of education and in my city's public school system.

I have as well a second vocation: writing. I have studied literature, I have written books. Yet I have never used writing in any of my "main line" math courses. (I do teach a "Philosophy of Math" course, which uses term papers and essay questions.) Indeed, until last year's Atlanta meeting of the Mathematics Association of America, I had never heard of "writing to learn mathematics" (at least, so far as I can recall). To my knowledge, none of the teachers in my department is using "writing to learn"; I suspect that almost none have heard of it.

Therefore, it is as a well-meaning ignoramus that I respond to this book. Since I have no experience with "writing to learn math," I can't pretend to evaluate or correct or improve any ideas about it. I can, however, offer a few thoughts on related matters. Here are some questions worth posing:

1. Why are math teachers reluctant to introduce writing in their classes?
2. Are there any real drawbacks or dangers associated with this movement?
3. Since many math courses are "service courses," preparing students for work in engineering and other departments, how should we expect these other departments to respond to writing in "their" math courses?
4. How can math teachers who feel uncomfortable with writing be assisted in mastering this teaching method?

5. And finally, the crux of the conversation, when will *I* start to use writing to teach calculus?

For a long time there has been a distinction, taken seriously in educational and psychological circles, between "word people" and "number people." This was glorified by C. P. Snow in his "Two Cultures" thesis.

Part of the significance of the writing-to-learn movement is smashing this distinction. Certainly one can give many examples of literate mathematicians, or number-minded litterateurs. Nevertheless, one readily finds in math classes, not only students but also professors, who dread the requirement to write something, especially something nontechnical, personal, self-revealing. Even easier is to find in an English class people who recoil at the sight of a long-division sign. Yet some of these people do find themselves in a math class at times.

Now, when we require *writing* as a way to learn math, we are shooting at two sparrows at once. Some students have bad feelings about math; others have bad feelings about writing. These are two *different* problems, and they call for different helping strategies. If we consider the writing-to-learn movement as a method to be used *both* in a pre-calculus "developmental" class and a post-calculus "engineering math" class, the students' problems in doing these assignments are bound to be quite different.

And what about the professor's problems in assignments and grading? The first time I assigned essays in my philosophy class, I felt odd about it. What about your run-of-the-mill mathematician who would feel totally at sea with a "freewriting" assignment? In Chapter 3 Marcia Birken grants to all of us the free right to take or leave writing to learn. This is a good approach right now, while the movement is still in its infancy. But the day will come, I believe, when the value of writing to learn will be universally acknowledged. More people will have to provide re-training workshops for ordinary math teachers, to unblock them for freestyle writing and teaching.

If the writing-to-learn math movement achieves the total effect I expect it to have, it will yield an unexpected benefit on the practice of mathematics, by professional mathematicians: that of communicating their field to laymen.

Several disgruntled nonmathematicians have complained that mathematicians seem to believe in a small elite of the mathematically talented; the rest of the race falls outside their charmed circle. Believe it or not, this exclusivity of my profession is not a matter of snobbery or malice. It is a matter of *inability*. Many of my colleagues have great difficulty, or no ability at all, to talk about high-level (advanced professional) mathematics, except in a specialized technical lingo known to a few.

But what if these mathematicians had been trained, as an essential part of their education, to write comprehensibly in English? I believe their styles, attitudes, and values would be permanently affected, making them more willing and able to speak and write comprehensibly. This would be a great benefit to the whole mathematics profession, which is often handicapped by the difficulty of professional mathematics practitioners to read (or hear) with understanding the communication of other professional mathematics practitioners.

I now return to the five questions I proposed earlier.

1. *Why are math teachers reluctant to introduce writing in their classes?* Because they feel nervous and incompetent to do it. They need help with the course syllabi and teaching materials. (Of course, some of the chapters in this book *are* such "materials.")
2. *Drawbacks and dangers?* Yes, writing to learn contains the same drawbacks and dangers found in any innovative, interdisciplinary movement. It is possible for people who write badly, know hardly any math, and have doubtful credentials or experience in math teaching to become active in this movement. This is possible because new movements don't have established standards and criteria. I would suggest anyone establishing writing-to-learn programs by hiring new, unknown people should remember the age-old slogan of Roman commerce, "Caveat emptor."
3. *Writing in "service courses"?* At first thought, service courses would seem to be an ideal opportunity to teach writing. In the course Ordinary Differential Equations for Engineers, for example, let the writing assignments start from an engineering problem — even better than in ordinary math classes. But the truth is, if your problem has to do, say, with structures (civil engineering), then the electrical and chemical people will be even less interested than they would be in the math. Service courses usually serve several different clients, who are not much interested in each other. This problem cannot be solved. On the other hand, it is not essentially different from the same problem faced before writing is introduced. The teacher has to muddle through somehow.
4. *How can math teachers be assisted?* I now notice that the answer to this question is the same as for 1.
5. *When am I going to do it?* As soon as I can, probably next year.

REFERENCES

Polya, G. (1945). *How to solve it.* Princeton, NJ: Princeton University Press.
Snow, C. P. (1959). *The two cultures and the scientific revolution.* New York: Cambridge University Press.

About the Editors and Contributors

MARY BAHNS is assistant professor of education at Texas Christian University, where she teaches courses on science and mathematics in the elementary school. She has published numerous articles in the field of biology, her primary research interest.

WILLIAM P. BERLINGHOFF is visiting professor of mathematics at Colby College, and was previously a professor of mathematics at Southern Connecticut State University.

MARCIA BIRKEN is assistant professor of mathematics at the College of Science, Rochester Institute of Technology, where she teaches a sequence in honors calculus, in addition to other math courses. She is the author of "Teaching Students How to Study Mathematics, A Classroom Approach," *The Mathematics Teacher* (September 1986).

PAUL CONNOLLY is John D. & Catherine T. MacArthur Professor of English and director of the Institute for Writing and Thinking at Bard College. He is the author of *Building Family: An Act of Faith* (Abbey Press, 1982) and editor of *On Essays: A Reader for Writers* (Harper & Row, 1981) and *New Methods in College Writing Programs: Theories in Practice* (Modern Language Association, 1986).

ERIKA DUNCAN conducts writing workshops and has taught expository writing at New York University. Since 1986 she has been co-director, with Anneli Lax, of a project funded by The Ford Foundation to bring a language-linked approach to mathematics into several Brooklyn schools. She is the author of two novels, *A Wreath of Pale White Roses* (1977) and *Those Giants: Let Them Rise* (Schocken Books, 1986).

KATHRYN BLACKBURN DUNN is associate professor of mathematics education, Department of Curriculum and Instruction, at East Tennessee State University, where she is also director of the Mathematics Consortium for

Applications and Problem Solving, funded by the National Science Foundation.

GEORGE GOPEN is director of the Writing Program at Duke University. In addition to a Ph.D. in comparative literature, he has a law degree and consults with law firms on improving writing.

REUBEN HERSH has taught at Stanford and as a visiting scholar at the Center for Research and Advanced Studies in Mexico City. He is now professor of mathematics at the University of New Mexico. He is co-author with Philip J. Davis of *The Mathematical Experience* (Birkhauser, 1980) and *Descartes' Dream* (Harcourt, Brace, Jovanovich, 1986). He has won the Chauvenet Prize of the Mathematics Association of America and is especially interested in partial differential equations and related areas in analysis.

VERA JOHN-STEINER is professor of linguistics at the University of New Mexico in Albuquerque; in spring 1988 she was visiting professor of psychology at the University of California, Berkeley. She is an editor of Lev Vygotsky's essays, *Mind in Society*, (Harvard University Press, 1978) and has written about the use of natural language and other symbol systems by gifted creative thinkers (*Notebooks of the Mind*, University of New Mexico Press, 1985).

SANDRA KEITH is assistant professor of mathematics at St. Cloud State University, and has written for *The Mathematics Teacher* on writing to learn mathematics.

RUSSEL KENYON has taught mathematics at Lenox Memorial High School in Massachusetts, where he introduced computer programming to the school. He has also taught at Berkshire Community College in Pittsfield and at Mohawk Valley Community College in Utica, New York.

ANNELI LAX is professor of mathematics at New York University, where she developed a course of study called Mathematical Thinking, which serves mainly non-science students whose mathematical performance is insufficient to meet NYU's liberal arts requirements. Since 1958 she has been the editor of the *New Mathematical Library*, a series of monographs written by eminent mathematicians for high school students.

DAVID LAYZER is a theoretical astrophysicist at the Harvard–Smithsonian Center for Astrophysics, specializing in the origin and evolution of astronomical systems. He is professor of astronomy at Harvard University, and teaches a course on "Space, Time and Motion," alternating with another on "Chance Necessity, and Order." He is the author of *Cosmogenesis* (Oxford, 1988).

RICHARD J. LESNAK is professor of quantitative and natural science at Robert Morris College in Pittsburgh, specializing in remedial math and algebra for college students.

JOSÉ A. LÓPEZ was a student in Arthur Powell's course in Developmental Mathematics at Rutgers University, Newark College of Arts and Science.

ALAN MARWINE is professor of psychology and chair of the Social Science Department, Green Mountain College. He was visiting tutor, Graduate Institute in Liberal Education, St. John's College, Santa Fe, 1986–87. He has been a faculty member in Bard's Workshop in Language & Thinking since 1985.

KATHRYN H. MARTIN is professor of biology at the State University of New York at Oswego and coordinator of advisement for 450 biology students there.

WILLIAM J. MULLIN is professor of physics, director of undergraduate studies in the Department of Physics and Astronomy, and associate director of the Writing Program at the University of Massachusetts at Amherst. He is the author of numerous scholarly articles and co-author, with J. Brehm, of *Introduction to the Structure of Matter*, a modern physics text to be published by Harper and Row.

ARTHUR POWELL is associate professor of mathematics at Rutgers University. He teaches in the Academic Foundations Department at Rutgers and is director of the Learning Center there.

BARBARA ROSE teaches mathematics at Roberts Wesleyan University in Rochester, New York.

DAVID A. SMITH is professor of mathematics at Duke University.

JOANNE SNOW is assistant professor of mathematics at St. Mary's College in Notre Dame, Indiana.

SHEILA TOBIAS is an advocate of mathematics and science literacy and a pioneer in the diagnosis and treatment of "math anxiety." She is best known for her work in women's studies and her efforts to achieve educational and occupational equity for women and minorities. She is the author of *Overcoming Math Anxiety* (Norton, 1978) and *Succeed with Math: Every Student's Guide to Conquering Math Anxiety* (College Board, 1987) and visiting scholar in political science at the University of Arizona.

TERESA VILARDI is associate director of the Institute for Writing and Thinking at Bard College and a faculty member in the Bard Freshman Workshop in Language and Thinking.

DAVID WHITE is instructor in English, Walters State Community College, and administrative coordinator for the MATHCAPS Project, East Tennessee State University.

The late HASSLER WHITNEY was professor of mathematics at the Institute for Advanced Study, Princeton, from 1952 to 1977, when he became professor emeritus. He was a member of the Harvard University faculty, 1933–52. Author of numerous research articles in mathematics and of two books on graduate-level mathematics, he was the recipient of the National Medal of Science (1975) and of many other honors. From 1979 to 1982 he was president of the International Commission on Mathematical Instruction. He was a great mathematician — one of the creators of modern topology. In his second career, a calling that he followed for the love of children, his aim was to prevent school mathematics from robbing children of the chance to develop their mental powers. He set an inspiring example in synthesizing research and teaching, or, in his words, "exploring" and promoting "responsible learning." His impact on education will grow gradually as those who were transformed by his gentle guidance become bolder and more self-assured explorers, not letting "rules of the day" get in the way of the meaning of their efforts. Hass died on May 10, 1989, as this volume goes to press. He will be greatly missed.

DALE WORSLEY has written fiction and scripts for performance in several media. His first novel, *Focus Changes of August Pervico* (Vanguard, 1980), received a Creative Artists Public Service Grant. *Cold Harbor*, a play by Mr. Worsley, was produced by Mabou Mines and Joseph Papp at the New York Shakespeare Festival in New York in 1983. His essay "Writing at the Races: Science Essays in a Public School" won the 1988 Merit Award for excellence in Educational Journalism from the Educational Press Association of America. He currently works with Teachers and Writers Collaborative on a General Electric Science Writing Project at a Manhattan high school.

Index

Abel, J. P., 19–20
Ackerman, A., 18
Activities. *See also* Projects
  in expressive writing, 22–27, 160, 173–174, 176n
  in mathematics education case study, 162–175
  in transactional writing, 17–22, 159–160, 174, 176n
Adaptive Control of Thought (ACT) model, 75
Admit slips, writing of, 24
Agency, lack of, 220–221
Akron, University of, 25–26
Albergo, Catherine, 246–248
Algebra, 111
  elementary, 130–131
  math anxiety vs. powerful reasoning in, 272–274
  remedial. *See* Remedial algebra experiment
Algorithms, writing of, 140, 145
Anderson, J. R., 75, 78
Antenoff, Myron, 235–237
Anti-intellectualism, xvi
Applebee, A. N., 99
Aristotle, 127–129
"Aristotle was right" (Donoghue & Holstein), 200
Arithmetic, 129–131
Articles, writing reports on, 89
Atomic structure, microthemes on, 117
Austin, J. L., 4
Autobiographical writing, 24
Azzolino, A., 34, 159

Bahns, Mary, 13, 112, 178–189
Banking method, 157

Bard College, Institute for Writing and Thinking, 56, 113, 277–278
Bartle, R. G., 196
Belenky, M. F., 12
Bell, E. S., 160
Bell, F., 75
Bell, R. N., 160
Benezet, L. P., 275
Bergson, Henri, 132
Berkeley, George, 128
Berlinghoff, William P., 12, 88–94
Bernoulli equation, 202–203
Bertoff, A., 106
Biology, 123, 279
  course announcements and assignments in, 115
  determining grades in, 116
  sample syllabuses for, 115–121
  topic outlines and microtheme assignments in, 116–121
  writing microthemes in learning of, 111, 113–121
Birken, Marcia, 12, 31, 33–47, 80, 279, 291
Bloom, B., 74, 148
Bolyai, Janos, 126
Books, writing of, 20–21
Borasi, R., 19–21, 160
Botstein, Leon, xi–xviii, 12
Brannon, L., 5
Britton, James B., 15–16, 22, 36, 159–160, 175n
Broder, L., 74
Brooklyn public schools, preserving union of numbers and words in, 231–240, 246–248
Bruner, Jerome S., 4, 159–160, 283, 285–286